TABLE OF CONTENTS

EDITOR
LEON WIESELTIER

MANAGING EDITOR
CELESTE MARCUS

———

PUBLISHER
BILL REICHBLUM

———

JOURNAL DESIGN
WILLIAM VAN RODEN

WEB DESIGN
HOT BRAIN

Liberties is a publication of the Liberties Journal Foundation, a nonpartisan 501(c)(3) organization based in Washington, D.C. devoted to educating the general public about the history, current trends, and possibilities of culture and politics. The Foundation seeks to inform today's cultural and political leaders, deepen the understanding of citizens, and inspire the next generation to participate in the democratic process and public service.

Engage
To learn more please go to libertiesjournal.com

Subscribe
To subscribe or with any questions about your subscription, please go to libertiesjournal.com

ISBN 978-1-7357187-1-2
ISSN 2692-3904

———

EDITORIAL OFFICES
1604 New Hampshire Avenue NW
Washington, DC 20009

———

DIGITAL
@READLIBERTIES
LIBERTIESJOURNAL.COM

Liberties

ANTHONY JULIUS

Art's Troubles

I

Duly acknowledging that the plural of anecdote is not data, I begin with some stories drawn from the recent history of liberal democracy.

• In November 2010, the Secretary of the Smithsonian Institution removed an edited version of footage used in David Wojnarowicz's short silent film *A Fire in My Belly* from "Hide/Seek: Difference and Desire in American Portraiture" at the Smithsonian's National Portrait Gallery after complaints from the Catholic League, and in response to threats of reduced federal funding. The video contains a scene with a crucifix covered in ants. William Donohue of the Catholic League claimed the work was "hate speech" against Catholics. The affair was initiated by an article contributed to the Christian News Service, a division of the Media Research Center, whose mission is to "prove — through sound scientific research — that liberal bias in the media does exist and undermines traditional American values."

• In October 2015, Dareen Tatour, an Israeli Arab from a village in the Galilee, was arrested. She had written a poem: "I will not succumb to the 'peaceful solution' / Never lower my flags / Until I evict them from my land." A video clip uploaded by Tatour shows her reading the poem, "Resist, my people, resist them," against the backdrop of masked people throwing rocks and firebombs at Israeli security forces. The day after the uploading, she posted: "The Islamic Jihad movement hereby declares the continuation of the intifada throughout the West Bank.... Continuation means expansion... which means all of Palestine. And we must begin within the Green Line... for the victory of Al-Aqsa, and we shall declare a general intifada. #Resist." In 2018, Tatour was given a five months' jail sentence. In May 2019, her conviction for the poem was overturned by the Nazareth District Court, but not the conviction for her other social media posts. The poem, said the court, did not "involve unequivocal remarks that would provide the basis for a direct call to carry out acts." And the court acknowledged that Tatour was known as a poet: "freedom of expression is [to be] accorded added weight when it also involves freedom of artistic and creative [expression]." The Israeli Supreme Court rejected the state's motion for appeal.

• In 2017, the artist Sam Durant made a public sculpture, "Scaffold," for location in the open grounds of the Walker Art Center in Minneapolis. It was an unpainted wood-and-metal structure, more than fifty feet tall, with a stairway that

7

led to a platform with a scaffold. The work referred to seven executions between 1859 and 2006, including the execution in 1862 of thirty-eight Dakota-Sioux men. Protesters demanded the work's destruction: "Not your story," "Respect Dakota People!" "$200.00 reward for scalp of artist!!" Following mediation, the work was surrendered to the activists, who reportedly dismantled it, ceremonially burning the wood. Art critics endorsed the protest: "In general it's time for all of us to shut up and listen." "White Americans bear a responsibility to dismantle white supremacy. Let it burn." The artist himself denied that he had been censored. "Censorship is when a more powerful group or individual removes speech or images from a less powerful party. That wasn't the case. I chose to do what I did freely."

• In April 2019, three Catholic priests in the Polish city of Koszalin burned books that they said promote sorcery, including one of J.K. Rowling's *Harry Potter* novels, in a ceremony that they photographed and posted on Facebook. The books were ignited as prayers were said and a small group of people watched on. They cited in justification of the ceremony passages from *Deuteronomy* ("The graven images of their gods shall ye burn with fire") and *Acts* ("Many of them also which used curious arts brought their books together and burned them before all men"). In August of the same year, a Roman Catholic pastor at a school in Nashville, Tennessee banned the Rowling novels: "These books present magic as both good and evil, which is not true, but in fact a clever deception. The curses and spells used in the books are actual curses and spells; which when read by a human being risk conjuring evil spirits into the presence of the person reading the text."

• In August 2019, the release of the film *The Hunt*, in which "red state" Americans are stalked for sport by "elite liberals," was cancelled. Donald Trump had tweeted: "Liberal Hollywood is Racist at the highest level, and with great Anger and Hate! They like to call themselves 'Elite,' but they are not Elite. In fact, it is often the people that they so strongly oppose that are actually the Elite. The movie coming out is made in order to inflame and cause chaos. They create their own violence, and then try to blame others. They are the true Racists, and are very bad for our Country!" The studio explained: "We stand by our film-makers and will continue to distribute films in partnership with bold and visionary creators, like those associated with this satirical social thriller, but we understand that now is not the right time to release this film." Nine months later, with a new marketing campaign, the film duly appeared. The director explained: "The film was supposed to be an absurd satire and was not supposed to be serious and boring....... It's been a long road."

• In Germany, a Jewish activist has been litigating to have removed a thirteenth-century church carving of the *Judensau*, or "Jewish pig," an infamous trope of medieval anti-Semitism, from the outer wall of the main church in Wittenberg. A memorial plaque installed in November 1988, containing in Hebrew words from Psalm 130, "Out of the depths, I cry to you," does not satisfy the litigant. The district court ruled that the continued presence of the carving did not constitute evidence of "disregard for Jews living in Germany." The judgement was upheld this year by the Higher Regional Court: the presence at the church of both a memorial to the Holocaust and an information board that explains the *Judensau* as part of the history of antisemitism justified retaining the carving. The campaign to remove the carving has Christian clerical support: "The *Judensau* grieves people because our Lord is blasphemed. And also the Jews and Israel are blasphemed by showing such

9

a sculpture." A local Jewish leader took a different position: "It should be seen within the context of the time period in which it was made," he argued. "It should be kept on the church to remind people of antisemitism."

• Two years ago the artist Tomaz Schlegl built a wooden statue of Trump in Moravce, Slovenia. It was a twenty-six-foot tall wooden structure that had a mechanism to open Trump's red painted mouth full of pointy teeth. The artist explained that the figure has two faces, like populism. "One is humane and nice, the other is that of a vampire." He explained that he had designed the statue "because people have forgotten what the Statue of Liberty stands for." The Trump-resembling statue wasn't actually Trump, but "I want to alert people to the rise of populism and it would be difficult to find a bigger populist in this world than Donald Trump." It was burned down in January 2020. The mayor of the town, deploring the arson, commented: "This is an attack against art and tolerance.... against Europe's fundamental values."

There is something arbitrary about this group of stories — others could have been chosen, without any loss of coherence in the picture of contemporary artistic freedom. There was the campaign against Dana Schutz's painting of Emmett Till at the Whitney Museum, against Jeanine Cummins' novel *American Dirt*, against Woody Allen's film deal with Amazon, which was cancelled, and against his memoir, which was cancelled by one publisher but published by another one. There was the decision by the National Gallery of Art and three other major museums to delay until at least 2024 the Philip Guston retrospective planned for 2020, so that "additional perspectives and voices [can] shape how we present Guston's work" (museum-speak for "we will submit our proposals to a panel of censors"). And though they are all recent stories, the larger narrative is not altogether new. In 1999, Mayor Rudolph Giuliani took exception to certain works in an exhibition at the Brooklyn Museum, notably Chris Ofili's painting *The Holy Virgin Mary*. The mayor relied on a newspaper report: the Virgin was "splattered" with elephant dung, the painting was offensive to Catholics, the museum must cancel the show. (The museum offered to segregate some pictures and withdraw Ofili's, but the mayor responded by withholding funds and terminating the museum's lease. The museum injuncted him; the city appealed; it then dropped the appeal. The Jewish Orthodox Agudath Israel intervened on the mayor's side.) In 2004, in Holland, the Dutch filmmaker Theo van Gogh was shot dead in Amsterdam by Mohammed Bouyeri, a 26 year-old Dutch-born Muslim who objected to the film *Submission* that Van Gogh had made earlier that year, with Ayaan Hirsi Ali, about violence against women in Islamic societies; the assassin left a note to Hirsi Ali pinned by a knife to the dead man's chest. And in 2005, in Denmark, there occurred the cartoons affair. In response to an article about a writer's difficulty in finding an illustrator to work on a book about Mohammed, the newspaper *Jyllands-Posten* published twelve editorial cartoons, most of them depicting him. There was no immediate reaction. The Egyptian newspaper *Al Fagr* republished them, with no objection. Five days later, and thereafter, there were protests by fax, email, and phone; cyber-attacks, death threats, demonstrations, boycotts and calls to boycott, a summons to a "day of rage," the withdrawal of ambassadors, the burning of the Danish flag and of effigies of Danish politicians, the exploding of car bombs, appeals to the United Nations, and deaths — about 250 dead in total and more than 800 injured. A decade later, when similar cartoons were published in the French satirical magazine *Charlie Hebdo*, its staff was massacred in its offices in Paris.

There is more. Behind each story, there stand others — behind the Allen stories, for example, there is the Polanski story and the Matzneff story. And behind those, some more foundational stories. In 1989, the Ayatollah Khomeini issued his fatwa against Salman Rushdie and his novel *The Satanic Verses*, which had already been burned in Muslim protests; there followed riots and murders, and the writer went into hiding for years. (The threat to his life subsists.) Also, in 1989, the Indian playwright and theater director Safdar Hashmi was murdered in a town near Delhi by supporters of the Indian National Congress Party; the mob beat him with iron rods and police batons, taking their time, unimpeded. In the United States in those years, there occurred, among other depredations against literature and the visual arts, the cancelling of the radio broadcast of Allen Ginsberg's poem *Howl*; the campaign against Martin Scorsese's film *The Last Temptation of Christ*; the political, legal, and legislative battles over Robert Mapplethorpe's *The Perfect Moment* and Andres Serrano's *Piss Christ*, and over Dread Scott's *What is the Proper Way to Display the United States Flag?*; the dismantling of Richard Serra's site-specific *Tilted Arc*; and the campaign against Bret Easton Ellis' novel *American Psycho*. There were bombings, boycotts, legislation, administrative action, the ripping up on the Senate floor of a copy of *Piss Christ* by a senator protesting the work on behalf of "the religious community."

Not all these stories have the same weight, of course. But taken together these episodes suggest that new terms of engagement have been established, across political and ideological lines, in the reception of works of art. The risks associated with the literary and artistic vocation have risen. New fears, sometimes mortal fears, now deform the creative decisions of writers and artists. Literature and the visual arts

12

have become subject to a terrible and deeply illiberal cautiousness. (As a Danish imam warned the publisher of the cartoons, "When you see what happened in Holland and then still print the cartoons, that's quite stupid.") The interferences with what Joseph Brodsky called literature's natural existence have grown brutal, overt, proud. We have witnessed the emergence of something akin to a new censorship conjuncture.

There are ironies and complications. This new era of intolerance of, and inhibition upon, literature and the visual arts has occurred in the very era when the major ideological competitor to liberalism collapsed, and with it a censorship model against which liberal democracies measured their own expressive freedom. Or more precisely and ironically, in the era when the Berlin Wall and Tiananmen Square occurred within months of each other — the former exemplifying the fall of tyranny, the latter signifying the reassertion of it. When China conceived the ambition to become the major economic competitor of the capitalist liberal democracies, it also initiated a censorship model to which over time the greatest private corporations of these same liberal democracies would defer. Since artworks are also products that sell in markets — since filmmakers need producers and distributors, and writers need publishers and booksellers, and artists need galleries and agents — they are implicated in, and thus both enabled and constrained by, relations of trade and the capitalist relations of production. Corporations will both accommodate censoring forces and be their own censors. As their respective histories with the Chinese market show, the technology corporations tend to put commercial interests before expressive freedoms. And that is another irony: this assault on art took place even as the World Wide Web, and then the Internet, was invented, with its exhilarating promises of unconfined liberty. But the

13

new technology was soon discovered to have many uses. As Rushdie remarked in *Joseph Anton*, his memoir of his persecution, if Google had existed in 1989 the attack on him would have spread so swiftly and so widely that he would not have stood a chance.

And all the while a new era of illiberalism in Western politics was coming into being, for many reasons with which we are now wrestling. 1989 marked the moment when liberalism's agon ceased to be with communism and reverted instead to versions of its former rivals: communitarianism, nationalism, xenophobia, and religious politics. New illiberal actors and newly invigorated illiberal communities, asserted themselves in Western societies, as civil society groups came to an understanding of a new kind of political activity. So if one were to ask, when did art's new troubles begin, one could answer that they began in and around that single complex historical moment known as 1989. And these contemporary art censorship stories differ from older arts censorship stories in significant ways.

II

All these stories are taken from the everyday life of liberal democracies, or more or less liberal democracies. In not one of these stories does an official successfully interdict an artwork. There are no obscenity suits among them. With just one exception, there are no philistine judges, grandstanding prosecutors, or meek publishers in the dock. Customs officials are not active here, policing borders to keep out seditious material. There are no regulators, reviewing texts in advance of publication or performance. So how indeed are they censorship stories at all? We must reformulate our understanding of censorship, if we are to understand the censorship of our times.

"Censorship" today does not operate as a veto. It operates as a cost. The question for the writer or the artist is not, Can I get this past the censor? It is instead, Am I prepared to meet the burden, the consequences, of publication and exhibition — the abuse, the personal and professional danger, the ostracism, the fusillades of digital contempt? These costs, heterogeneous in everything but their uniform ugliness, contribute to the creation of an atmosphere. It is the atmosphere in which we now live. The scandalizing work of art may survive, but few dare follow.

Censorship today, in its specificity, must be grasped by reference to these profiles: the censoring actors, the censoring actions, and the censored. With respect to the censoring actors, we note, with pre-1989 times available as a contrast, that there has taken place a transfer of censoring energy from the state to civil society. In the West, certainly, we do not see arrests, raids, municipal and central government actions such as the defunding or closure of galleries, prosecutions and lawsuits, or legislation. Insofar as the state plays a part, it tends to be a neutral spectator (in its executive function) or as a positive restraint on censorship (in its judicial function). In respect of civil society, however, there has occurred a corresponding empowerment of associations, activists, confessional groups, self-identified minority communities, and private corporations. The censors among the activists are driven by the conviction that justice will be advanced by the suppression of the artwork. Their interventions have a self-dramatizing, vigilante quality. Artworks are wished out of existence as an exercise of virtue. The groups are very diverse: "stay-at-home moms" and "military veterans" (disparaged by "liberal Hollywood"), policemen (disparaged by rapper record labels), social justice warriors, and so on. Their censorings do not comprise acts of a sovereign authority; they have a random, unpredictable, qualified character, reflecting fundamental social and confessional divisions. As for the corporations, when they are not the instrument of activists (Christian fundamentalists, say), their responses to activists, foreign governments, and so on tends towards the placatory.

Correspondingly, with respect to censoring actions, we find a comparable miscellany of public and private (when not criminal) initiatives in place of administrative and judicial acts of the state. The activists, right and left, have available an extensive repertory of tactics: demonstrations, boycotts, public statements, digital denunciations, petitions, lethal violence, serious violence, and threats of violence, property destruction, disruptions and intimidations, mass meetings, marches, protester-confrontations, pickets, newspaper campaigns. As for corporations, the tactics, again, have become familiar: refusals to contract, and terminations of employment, publishing, and broadcasting contracts already concluded; editing books and films in accordance with the requirements of state authorities in overseas markets.

In all these instances, the wrong kind of attention is paid to an artwork — hostile, disparaging, dismissive. There is no respect for the claims of art; there is no respect for art's integrity; there is no respect for artmaking. Art is regarded as nothing more than a commodity, a political statement, an insult or a defamation, a tendentious misrepresentation. If it is acknowledged as art, it is *mere* art — someone's self-indulgence, wrongly secured against the superior interests of the censoring actors. All these actions are intended to frighten and burden the artist. And so artists and writers increasingly, and in subtle ways, become self-censoring — and thereupon burden other artists and writers with their own

16

silent example. Self-censorship is now the dominant form of censorship. It is a complex phenomenon and hard to assess — how does one measure an absence? But recall the *Jewel of Medina* affair of 2008, the novel about one of the Prophet Mohammed's wives that was withdrawn by Random House because it was "inflammatory." Who now would risk such an enterprise? Instead we are, with rare exceptions, living in an age of safe art — most conforming to popular understandings of the inoffensive (or of "protest"), a few naughtily transgressive, but either way without bite.

As for the censored: what we have described as the given problem of censorship — the heterogeneity of civil society censoring actors; the retreat of the state from censoring activity; the collapse of the Soviet Union as the primary adversary of a liberal order; the emergence of China as a powerful, invasive, artworld-deforming censor; the absence of any rule-governed censorship — has meant, among other things, that the pre-1989 defenses against censorship, such as they were, no longer work. They were deployed in earlier, more forensic times, when the state, the then principal censoring actor, was open to limited reasoned challenge, and when civil society actors were subject to counter-pressure, and were embarrassable. Essential values were shared; appeals could be made to common interests; facts were still agreed upon.

Art now attracts considerable censoring energy. There is no other discourse which figures in so many distinct censorship contexts. It attracts the greatest number of justifications for censorship. We may identify them: the national justification — art, tied up with the prestige of a nation, cannot be allowed

17

to damage that prestige; the governing-class justification — artworks must not be allowed to generate inter-group conflict; the religious justification — artworks must not blaspheme, or cause offense to believers; the capitalist justification — artworks must not alienate consumers, or otherwise damage the corporation's commercial interests.

Yet the properties of art that trouble censors are precisely the properties that define art. An attack on a work of art is thus always an attack on art itself. What is it about art works that gets them into so much trouble? We begin with the powerful effect that works of art have on us. We value the works that have these effects — but they also disturb us, and the trouble that art gets into derives from the trouble that art causes. The arts operate out of a radical openness. Everything is a subject for art and literature; everything can be shown; whatever can be imagined can be described. As the literary critic Terence Cave observed, fiction demands the right to go anywhere, to do anything that is humanly imaginable.

Art works are playful, mischievous; they perplex, and are elusive, constitutively slippery, and therefore by their nature provocative. Art serves no one's agenda. It is its own project; it has its own ends. This has an erotic aspect: playfulness has its own force, its own drive. Art preys upon the vulnerabilities of intellectual systems, especially those that demand uniformity and regimentation. Art is disrespectful and artists are antinomian. The artist responds to demands of fidelity, *Non serviam*. He or she is consecrated to a resolute secularity and an instinct to transgress boundaries: the writer makes the sacred merely legendary, the painter turns icons into portraits. (The religious artist does not altogether escape this effect.) It makes sense to say, "I am a Millian" or "I am a Marxist," but it does not make sense (or not the same sense) to say, "I am a Flauber-

18

tian" or "I am a Joycean." The opinions that may be mined are typically amenable to contradictory interpretations — they *invite* contradictory interpretations. And let us not overlook the obvious: parody and satire, comedy and farce, are aesthetic modes. Laughter lives inside literature.

Identity politics tends to be fought out on the field of culture because identity is among art's subjects. Art confers weight and depth upon identity; and so it is no wonder that identity groups now constitute themselves in part through their capacity for censoriousness. Race politics, gender politics: art has a salient place in them, as do art controversies, in which the various communities pursue cultural grievances by denying legitimacy to certain symbolic expressions. Identity warfare is attracted to art in much the same way that class warfare is attracted to factories. Politics in our day has taken a notably cultural turn, and so art has become a special focus of controversy. Of course, low politics also plays a role in these outrages against art — the Ayatollah's fatwa was a power-play against Saudi hegemony, and Giuliani's protest against a sacrilegious painting was a means of distracting Catholics from his pro-choice record. But the problem cannot be reduced to such politics alone.

Unlike artists, art cannot be manipulated. Specifically, works of art are immunized against fake news, because they are all openly fabricated. Novels are openly fictional: that is their integrity. The artist is the last truth-teller. As already fictional accounts, artworks cannot be subverted by "alternative facts," and as forms of existence with a distinctively long reach, and a distinctive endurability, they are more difficult to "scream into silence" (Ben Nimmo's phrase for the phenomenon described by Tim Wu as "reverse censorship," a pathology of internet inundation). But this is hardly to

19

say that works of art — and their makers — are not vulnerable. Artworks are accessible: books can be burned, canvases can be ripped, sculptures can be pulled down. They are also susceptible to supervision — by, among others, pre-publication "sensitivity readers." One measure of censorship's recent advance is the phenomenon of "publishable then, but not publishable now," and "teachable then, but not teachable now," and "screenable then, but not screenable now." The essayist Meghan Daum relates that when she asked a professor of modern literature whether he still taught *Lolita*, he replied, "It's just not worth the risk." This widespread attitude is of course an attack on an essential aspect of art's existence — its life beyond the moment of its creation.

III

To whom should we look for the defense of art?

Not the state. Of course, the state should provide effective protection for its citizens who are writers and artists. But the state cannot be art's ally, in part because of its neutrality and in part because of its partisan tendencies. Even in those states which have a tradition of government patronage of the arts, the state must not take sides on aesthetic or cultural questions. Art criticism is not one of the functions of government, and the history of art under tyrannies, secular and religious, amply shows why not. Moreover, the state, or more specifically government, has its own interests that will most certainly interfere in the free and self-determined development of art and literature: its desire for civil peace, which may cause it to intervene in cultural controversy; its privileging of religious freedom, as defined by the confessional communities themselves; its desire for the soft power that art of a certain kind gives; its majoritarian prejudices; and so on.

What is more, the arguments for state involvement in the arts usually exclude too much art, preferring instead national projects with social and economic benefits, which are usually inimical to art's spirit. Whatever the individual artist's debts and responsibilities to her society, as an artist she works as an individual, not a member, not a citizen. It has often, and correctly, been said that the social responsibility of the writer is to write well. When the conditions of artistic freedom are present, the artist represents only her own imagination and intellect. John Frohnmayer, the chairman of the National Endowment of the Arts during the culture wars of the late 1980s and early 1990s, mis-stepped when he wrote: "We must reaffirm our desire as a country to be a leader in the realm of ideas and of the spirit." That is not an ambition that any writer or artist should endorse.

Not the right. Simply stated, there is no decent theory of free speech (let alone free art speech) that has come from the illiberal right in any of its various, and often contradictory, reactionary and conservative versions. We will not find a defense of free intellectual and artistic speech in the counter-Enlightenment, or in the illiberal reaction to the French Revolution, or in the conservative or reactionary movements of the late-nineteenth century and early mid-twentieth century. The very notion of free speech is problematic to those traditions. They promote authority's speech over dissenting speech. They reject the Kantian injunction, *sapere aude,* dare to know; they reject its associated politics, the freedom to make public use of one's reason. They esteem reason's estrangement — prejudice — in all its social forms: superstition, hierarchy, deference, custom.

In the United States, to be sure, the situation is different. There is, after all, the First Amendment. Conservative articulations of freedom of speech are frequent and well-established. But if one subtracts from their positions what has been borrowed from the liberal order and what is merely self-interested (it is *my* speech I want heard), is there anything that remains upon which the arts may rely for protection? Let us disaggregate. There are the increasingly noisy and prominent activists of the alt-right, the Trumpists, the neo-Confederates, the militia groups at the Charlottesville "Unite the Right Free Speech March," and the like. In the matter of free speech they are the merest and most discreditable of opportunists: we should not look to the champions of statues of Confederate generals to protect free speech. Then there are the publicists and the pundits, the Fox commentators, the Breitbart journalists, and the like. They are part borrowers, part opportunists. We should not look for a renewal of free speech thinking to the authors of *The New Thought Police: Inside the Left's Assault on Free Speech and Free Minds; Bullies: How the Left's Culture of Fear and Intimidation Silences Americans; The Silencing: How the Left is Killing Free Speech; End of Discussion: How the Left's Outrage Industry Shuts Down Debate, Manipulates Voters, and Makes America Less Free (and Fun); Triggered: How the Left Thrives on Hate and Wants to Silence Us*, and so on. Their defenses of free speech altogether lack integrity; they are merely ideological (and often paranoid) in their polemics.

And then there are the lawyers, the right-wing academics, think tanks, and lobby groups, the administrators, legislators and judges, and the corporations. The widely noticed "turn" of the political right towards the First Amendment had led only to its redefinition in the interests of conservative grievances and objectives: to the disadvantage of liberal causes (anti-discrimination measures, exercise of abortion rights free of harassment, university "speech codes," and so on); to the disadvantage of trade unions (compulsory deduction of fees enlists employees in causes they may not support); to the benefit of for-profit corporations (conferring on "commercial speech" the high level of protection enjoyed by "political speech"); to the general benefit of right-wing political campaigns (disproportionately benefited by the striking down of campaign finance law in the name of corporate — or "associational" — free speech); and to the benefit of gun-rights activists (advancing Second Amendment interests with First Amendment arguments). So, again: part borrowers, part opportunists. These three prominent currents of American conservatism, united by their self-pity and their pseudo-constitutionalism, have nothing to contribute to a climate of cultural and artistic freedom. In the matter of a principled free speech doctrine, we can expect nothing from the right.

Not the left. There is no decent theory of free speech, let alone free art speech, that has come from the left. (Rosa Luxemburg is an exception.) There are only leftist critiques of liberal doctrine, external and immanent, respectively. In the external critique, liberal rights are mere bourgeois rights; they are a fraud, of instrumental value to one class, worthless to the other class. This criticism was pioneered by Marx, and successive generations of leftists have regularly rediscovered it in their own writing. A recent example is P.E. Moskowitz's book *The Case Against Free Speech*, in which we read that "the First Amendment is nearly irrelevant, except as a propaganda tool ... free speech has never really existed." In the immanent critique, liberal rights are recognized but must be dramatically enlarged, even if they put the greater liberal undertaking in jeopardy; certainly, received liberal thinking about free speech is too tender to commercial interests, while weakening

23

the interests of non-hegemonic groups (including artists and creative writers). Free speech requires campaign finance laws (to enable effective diversity of expressed opinion), restrictions on speech that inhibits speech, and so on.

While liberals may safely dismiss the external critique, they are obliged to engage conscientiously with the immanent critique. The elements of greatest relevance to art free speech relate to two discourses deprecated by the immanent critique. One is "hate speech," the other is "appropriation speech." It is frequently argued that minority groups characterized or addressed in a "hateful" way should not have their objections defeated by any free speech "trump." Jeremy Waldron has given the most compelling (not least because it is also the most tentative) liberal critique of hate speech. He understands hate speech in terms of "expression scrawled on the walls, smeared on a leaflet, festooned on a banner, spat out onto the Internet or illuminated by the glare of a burning cross." What then of literature and the visual arts? Here he is somewhat casual, writing in passing of "an offensive image of Jesus, like Andres Serrano's *Piss Christ*." Regarding "appropriation speech," in this case the censor arrives on the scene as a territorialist, and addresses the over-bold artist: "This art, this subject, this style, etc. is *mine*. Stay in your lane. You cannot know my situation; you lack epistemic authority. You strain for authenticity, but it will always elude you." This cultural nativism owes an unacknowledged debt to Herderian values and counter-Enlightenment ideas: the spiritual harmony of the group, the irreducible individuality of cultures, the risks of contamination and theft, and so on — in many ways a rather unfortunate provenance.

Sometimes hate speech and appropriation speech combine: "In *your* mouth, *this* is hate speech." Sometimes, the one is treated as an instance of the other: "Appropriation speech *is* hate speech." Though this hybrid is at least as old as *Lamentations* ("*ani manginatam*," "I am their song," the author writes of his vanquishers), it is largely a post-1989 phenomenon. Against it, the literary artist, the visual artist, is likely to respond with Goethe: "Only by making the riches of others our own do we bring anything great into the world." Notwithstanding all this, however, and the broader switching of sides with the right on free speech (which is often overstated), the left remains an occasional ally.

Not the confessional communities. Religions are constitutively, even if not centrally, coercive systems. Within those systems of conformity, there are censorship sub-systems, protective of divinity and its claims, of institutions and clergy, of practices and dogmas. The master prohibition of these sub-systems relates to blasphemy. Religions are coercive of their own members, and in many cases also of non-members. Whether or not they hold political power, and no religion has been averse to it, they hold communal and social and cultural power. They certainly do not respect artistic autonomy, though they have permitted great artists to flourish in the doctrinal spaces in which they were commissioned to work. There is no decent theory of free speech that has come from any of the major religions. Certainly not from the monotheisms: they take ownership of speech. It is sacred both in its origins ("In the beginning was the Word") and in its most elevated uses (Scripture, worship). Its lesser and other uses are denigrated or proscribed. Historically speaking, freedom of speech developed as a revolt against ecclesiastical authority.

Religions are invested in art, and they control it when they can — both their own art and the art of non-members. They subordinate the artist to confessional and institutional purposes. Christianity does so the most — its aesthetics are

. 25

theological: just as God the Father is incarnated in God the Son, so God the Son is incarnated in the Icon, writes the art historian and philosopher Thierry de Duve. The Christian work of art, though it may be breathtakingly beautiful, affirms the theological and historical truth of the Christian story. The model religious artist is the Biblical artisan Bezalel, and the model religious artwork is his sumptuous construction of the Tabernacle in the desert. "Bezalel" means, in Hebrew, "in God's shadow." The general stance of the church towards art may be termed Bezalelian. "Artists avoid idolizing the arts," writes a contemporary Bezalelian, "by resisting any temptation to isolation and instead living in the Christian community, where worship is given to God alone."

Religion has too many red lines; it is too used to being in charge; it cleaves to the non-negotiable ("the Bible is our guide"); it must have the last word. And when the drive to subordinate art is denied, when the desired orthodoxy is frustrated or broken, a strong sense of grievance is generated, and this in turn leads repeatedly to scandalized protests — to the burning of books and the destruction of artworks. In a word, to iconoclasm, in its old and strict sense, as the doctrinally justified destruction of art with heterodox meanings, or the use of force in the name of religious intolerance.

To be sure, confessional communities are ardent in defense of Bezalelian artists — of wedding photographers who refuse to photograph, and bakers who refuse to make cakes for same-sex marriages. And there is some truth in the argument that religion and art have common adversaries in the everyday materialism of consumerist societies, and could make common cause against everyday philistinism and banality. The history of the association of religion with beauty is long and marvelous. But in the matter of securing artistic freedoms, the confessional communities are simply not reliable. Certainly they have not been allies in recent times.

Not writers and artists. Though they are anti-censorship by vocation; though they *named* censorship ("Podsnappery," "Mrs. Grundy"); though much of the best anti-censorship writing in modern times came from them (Wilde, Orwell, Kundera, Sinyavsky), advocacy is for writers and artists an unfair distraction and burden. It takes them away from artmaking. In 1884, the novelist George Moore, in *Literature at Nurse*, wrote: "My only regret is that a higher name than mine has not undertaken to wave the flag of liberalism." Called upon to defend their work, artists get understandably irritated: "I don't feel as though I have to defend it," answered Ofili regarding *The Holy Virgin Mary*. "The people who are attacking this painting are attacking their own interpretation, not mine." Moreover, their work is often opaque to them. It always holds more meanings than they know, than they designed. Byron cheerfully admitted as much: "Some have accused me of a strange design / Against the creed and morals of the land, / And trace it in this poem every line: / I don't pretend that I quite understand / My own meaning when I would be very fine... " And artists are often poor advocates in their own cause. They too readily concede the principle of censorship; they pursue vendettas, and they grandstand; they turn political; they contradict themselves; they advance bad arguments, which sometimes they mix up with better ones; they misrepresent their own work. What is more, they frequently undermine in their art the defenses that are commonly deployed on their behalf.

"But every artist has his faults," Maupassant once said to Turgenev. "*It is enough to be an artist.*" In this censoring moment, that should be the beginning of wisdom.

Art's Troubles

IV

This leaves the liberals. Will *they* rise to the defense of literature and the visual arts? Freedom of speech, after all, is integral to a liberal society. As a historical matter, free speech is liberalism's signature doctrine. It is embraced by all the major liberal thinkers; it is incorporated into all the international legal instruments that comprise the liberal order. Execrations of censorship are to be found everywhere in canonical liberal discourse — in Milton, in Jefferson, in Mill, in Hobhouse, in William James. Censorship stultifies the mind, they all affirm. It discourages learning, lowers self-respect, weakens our grasp on the truth and hinders the discovery of truth. Liberals typically figure prominently among the champions of oppressed authors and banned books; they tend to recoil, with a certain reflex of contempt, when in the presence of affronted readers or minatory censors.

But there is a problem. Liberalism has traditionally cast a cold eye on literature and the visual arts, and has been peculiarly unmoved by their vulnerability. Literary and artistic questions have not been pressing for liberals, in the matter of free speech. We may even speak of a failure within liberalism to value literature and the visual arts, or to value them in a way that translates into a defense of them within a broader defense of free speech.

To begin with, there is an historical circumstance that contributes to the explanation for this peculiar neglect. The defense of free speech in the liberal tradition is significantly tied up with the political virtue of toleration of religious dissent. This is reflected, for example, in the First Amendment to the American Constitution: "Congress shall make no law respecting an establishment of religion, or prohibiting the free exercise thereof; or abridging the freedom of speech, or of the press ..." The free exercise of religion requires the free exercise of speech. Liberalism was tied at its inception to the defense of confessional dissent. Starting from a position in which loyalty to the state requires loyalty to its ecclesiastical institutions (in Protestant states) or to the ecclesiastical institutions favored by it (in the case of Roman Catholic states), liberals asked: Can the state accommodate citizens who wish to give their loyalty to it, but not to its ecclesiastical institutions? They gave several reasons for their affirmative answer. Tolerance is itself a theological matter. It derives from a respect for the individual conscience. It is not just a defense of theological dissent; it is itself an act of theological dissent. But none of this, of course, has anything to do with the welcoming of art, of artists, of artmaking. What was applied to religious works, practices, beliefs, and collectives was not applied to literary works, practices, or collectives. No question of tolerance in respect of the creative writer or artist arose for liberalism, within its own historical trajectory. (Indeed, when illiberal elements sought to exercise a censoring influence over art, they were often accommodated by liberals).

This is not to say that liberal arguments for free speech are limited to religion. But if we look at its arguments, we search in vain for literature and the visual arts. Instead we are instructed, quite correctly, that the validity of a proposition cannot be determined without exposing it to challenge, and that a silenced opinion may be true, and that a false opinion may yet contain a portion of the truth, and that true opinions may become mere prejudices if we are forced to defend them — and so all opinions must be permitted. We are also told, again correctly, that free speech is the precondition for controlling abuses and corruptions of state power, since it empowers citizens to act upon the government, and impedes the freedom of governments to act on citizens. It reverses the flow of power, governments do not limit citizens; citizens limit governments. And also that free speech is the precondition of deliberative democracy: autonomous citizens cannot act autonomously, that is, weigh the arguments for various courses of action, if they are denied access to relevant facts and arguments. The promoting of public discussion requires a vigorous, generous free speech regime. The liberal tradition also includes, particularly in Humboldt and Mill, the ideal of self-realization, which broaches the large realm of free communication and free culture.

But where does art figure in all this? Almost nowhere. Alexander Meiklejohn, the American philosopher and educator who wrote authoritatively about freedom of speech, did observe that "the people need novels and dramas and paintings and poems, because they will be called upon to vote" — a defense of the arts, but not in their integrity, a utilitarian defense. (He denied that the people needed movies, which are engaged in the "enslavement of our minds and wills.") We can instead trace a liberal indifference, and in some cases even a liberal hostility, toward literature and the visual arts. How many liberals would have endorsed Schiller's declaration that "if man is ever to solve the problem of politics, he will have to approach it through the problem of the aesthetic, because it is only through Beauty that Man makes his way to Freedom"? The great liberal thinkers have not found artworks to be useful texts to think with. Indeed, the liberal complaint that the literary sensibility has a reactionary character dates back to the French Revolution, its adversaries and its partisans. Writers such as Paine and Cobbett directed some of their most venomous attacks against a literary imagination whose origin they saw in a morally bankrupt, libertine, aristocratic culture.

The confrontation thus framed, the decades that followed merely deepened it, with creative writers fully returning fire. Poets and novelists made nineteenth-century liberalism their declared enemy (Baudelaire, Dostoyevsky); twentieth-century liberalism is modernism's declared enemy (Joyce is the honored exception); reactionary politics and avant-garde art are taken to be, in M.H. Abrams' phrase, mutually implicative. This ignores, of course, the enlistment of the arts in the modern revolutions; but liberals are not revolutionaries.

It is therefore little wonder that when one surveys the modern intellectual history of liberalism, there are very few liberal thinkers for whom, in the elaboration of a theory of free speech, literature and art figured. I count two, both of them outside the Anglo-American tradition: Benjamin Constant and Alexis de Tocqueville. Here is Constant, in a direct affirmation of inclusiveness: "For forty years I have defended the same principle — freedom in all things: In religion, in philosophy, in literature, in industry, and in politics." Constant defended this freedom against "the majority," which in his view had the right to compel respect for public order and to prohibit expression of opinion which harmed others (by provoking physical violence or obstructing contrary opinions) but not to otherwise restrict expression. Constant was himself a man of letters, a novelist of the poignancies of love — a Romantic, who brings to mind Victor Hugo's description of Romanticism as "liberalism in literature."

As for Tocqueville: in *Democracy in America* he wrote about democracy's inhibiting effects on fresh and vigorous thought. "There is a general distaste for accepting any man's word as proof of anything. So each man is narrowly shut in himself, and from there, judges the world." This does not lead to debate. Each man mistrusts all others, but he is also no better than others. Who then to trust? "General sentiment," by which Tocqueville means the tyrant he most fears in an open society: "public opinion." He famously observed that "I know of no country where there is less independence of mind and true freedom of discussion than in America." But then he went on to offer a brief account of the significance of literature in the growth of democratic sentiment, and a longer account of the type of literature that a democratic society might foster. Literature, he believed, is a counter to despotic tendencies. This is not literature passing as political theory; this is literature in its aesthetic integrity.

Constant and Tocqueville — but not Mill. This is surprising, since it was literature — the French writer Marmontel in particular — that saved Mill from his nervous breakdown and alerted him to the emotional limitations of utilitarianism. And yet it is Mill's name that we must give to liberalism's defeat in its first major test in respect of arts censorship. It was in 1858 that he completed *On Liberty*, one of the very scriptures of modern liberalism — but which, in this context, must be remembered as the great work on freedom of expression in which the philosopher failed to address three major setbacks to artistic freedom that happened even as he was writing it: the trial for obscenity ("an outrage to public morality and religion") of Flaubert's *Madame Bovary*, the trial for obscenity ("an insult to public decency") of Baudelaire's *Les Fleurs du Mal,* and the passage in Parliament of the Obscene Publications Act, which allowed the British state to seize and destroy works of art and literature without even giving their makers a right to be heard. It must also be added that in this failing Mill had successors in the weak response of liberals to the attack on Rushdie: not only were they few in number, but their defenses of the novelist rarely included defenses of the novel, of the dignity of his aesthetic project, of the autonomy of art and its right to blaspheme. The same blindness to art and its rights disfigured many liberal interventions in the American controversies of the late 1980s and early 1990s. They attacked Jesse Helms and company for many good reasons; just not this one.

~~~

We have discovered a problem. Even liberals are not good on literature and the arts, and this matters now more than ever before. How might things improve? We could attempt to give liberals reasons why they should take literature and the visual arts seriously. We might make the case for a liberal literature — the case advanced finely by Martha Nussbaum in her discussion of *The Princess Casamassima,* which she reads as contending for "liberalism as the guiding principle in politics," taken by her to include "a demand for artist's freedom of expression." But what about works of art that contend for a conservative politics? No, the case for artistic freedom must be made *only on the grounds of art as such.* Writers and artists will not find relief from their troubles unless art itself, aesthetic expression as such, is explicitly inducted into the class of protected free speech.

There are many reasons to do so. I will give only some. Art is a human good. An attack on literature and art is an attack on capacities and practices that constitute human beings as human and allow us to flourish. When we attack writers and artists, we attack ourselves. We are species-constituted by our artmaking and art-experiencing capacities; we realize ourselves by our artmaking and art-experiencing practices. The arts aid mental development and social harmony; they offer representations of a transfigured world. Art contributes to our understanding of ourselves and of the world; art makes it easier for us to live peaceably together. That is to say, it makes us more transparent to ourselves, and it makes the world more transparent, as well as less threatening and more beautiful. Artworks are goods whose desirability cannot adequately be expressed in individual terms — that is to say, they are "public" or "communal" goods.

We must recognize (and value) the form of existence of the writer and the artist. People who pursue the literary and artistic life are pursuing an estimable life, and the fruits of their pursuit, their literary and art works, should be secure. They have a "plan," in the liberal sense of the word; in more heroic and Tocquevillian terms, they seek to forge their own destiny. They certainly pursue a conception of the good life. That is, to make use of a distinction drawn by Jeremy Waldron, they are to be held to account not by reference to what they have done, but rather by reference to what in general they are doing. Free speech occupies a special place in this "plan." It is the precondition to the artistic vocation. None of this has anything to do with the seeking of privileges. That some will pursue this plan in a degraded manner is not to any point. The pornographer stands to the art world as the fundamentalist stands to the religious world. Each is reductive, blinkered, unthinking — but it would be an inconsistency to grant toleration to the one and deny it to the other.

The makers of art (and the audiences for art) merit recognition as a distinct group. Artists are not best imagined as individuals under contract; they should be recognized as members of their own communities, with their own practices and institutions. Artmaking is the characteristic activity of art-communities. And if art-makers are in their own way a group, then they, and their art, merit the protective attention that identity- and religious-groups and their products typically receive in liberal societies. Indeed, the liberal state should take positive steps to ensure that art-making flourishes when threatened by confessional or other "identity" groups. In certain respects, the art community is the ideal community, and a model for all given communities; the free speech that it needs is the free speech that we would all need for our ideal existence.

The art community is many communities. None is coercive. All are time-bound: specific formations do not last. They have no transcendental quality. They are fully secular. They are self-constituting: they do not require myths of origin. They are non-exclusive. They are unboundaried; there are no impassable barriers to entry. They are open to the world; they address the world; their solicitations are gentle and may always be refused. Literary and art communities are communities for anti-communitarians. They can *never* be a menace to society, in the sense that fanatical communities, or fanatical members of other communities, are a menace.

Art is a liberal good: to defend literature today is to defend liberalism, not as an ideology or a political doctrine but by modelling the benefits of its freedoms. How do we name the members of a liberal society? One way is to call them citizen-readers. Among art's forms and kinds, it is the novel — with its many standpoints, its diversity of human types, its provisionality, its interest in ambiguity and complexity — that comprises the distinctive art form of a liberal democratic society. To make war on the novel really is to make war on liberal democracy.

Literature and the visual arts have so many things in common with liberal societies. They are both committed to a certain process of making explicit. "The liberal insistence," writes Waldron, "[is] that all social arrangements are subject to critical scrutiny by individuals, and that men and women reveal and exercise their highest powers as free agents when they engage in this sort of scrutiny of the arrangements under which they are to live." He goes on, "society should be a transparent order, in the sense that its workings and principles should be well-known and available for public apprehension and scrutiny." Does this not describe the work of the writer? And they are both reflexive: for the liberal, identities should be treated as a matter for continuous exploration, receiving at best only conditional and contingent statement. And they both tend to the agonistic. By the agonistic, I mean interests or goods in irresolvable conflict — one that cannot be settled and cannot be won. There can be no resolved triumph of one over the other. The understanding by each of the other is bound up with each's self-understanding; neither recognizes itself in the account given of it by the other. Liberal societies exist to accommodate agonistic conflicts, and art exists to explore them. It also has its own agons — with religion, with philosophy, with science, with history. The work of art, said Calvino, is a battleground.

Both liberal societies and the arts are committed to a flourishing civil society. Precisely because literature, in its difference from other writing, solves no problems and saves no souls, it represents a commitment to the structural openness of a wholly secular space, one which is not programmatic, not driving towards any final, settled state in which uniformity rules. The artwork, like the open society, is promiscuous in the invitation that it extends. It is available to all; all may enjoy it; all may interpret it; all may judge it. Both liberal societies and the arts, in sum, have the same necessary condition. That condition is *freedom*. Illiberal societies prescribe a literature and visual arts that is both a diversion ("bread and circuses") and an instrument of legitimation ("soft power"). But liberal societies need the existence of a *free* literature and art. Works of art are liberal public goods.

From time to time, and in our time almost daily, events occur that prompt the question: Is liberalism equal to the challenge? I do not believe that the censorship of literature and the visual arts is the worst evil in our world, but it is a bad thing, and there is too much of it around. In these censoring times, liberals should strive to give to aesthetic expression an honored place in their theory of free speech.

37

NICHOLAS LEMANN

A New Politics, A New Economics

The major political phenomenon of the past decade has been a popular revolt against the economic arrangements that took form at the end of the twentieth century. The revolt is global. It takes both left- and right-wing forms, and often presents itself as overtly anti-immigrant or otherwise ethnonationalist, but the undercurrent of deep economic dissatisfaction is always there. Inequality in the developed world has been rising steadily for forty years now. The aftermath of the financial crisis of 2008 activated the politics of economic populism: in the United States, the rise of Bernie Sanders, Elizabeth Warren, and other politicians on the economic left, plus the Tea Party movement and to some extent Donald Trump and his acolytes who rail against globalization, Wall Street, and the big technology companies. In Europe, there is Brexit, new nativist parties (even in Scandinavia), and the Five Star movement in Italy, among other examples. What all of these have in common is that they took the political establishment utterly by surprise. And all of them regard the establishment, and any consensus that it claims to represent, with contempt.

The dynamic of this moment brings to mind the politics of the early twentieth century. During the nineteenth century, succeeding waves of the industrial revolution created (along with enormous and highly visible wealth) a great deal of displacement, exploitation, and want, which at first manifested itself in radical rebellions — in the United States they took the forms of agricultural populism and labor unrest. This was followed by a series of experiments in translating economic discontent into corrective government policy. Then as now, popular sentiment and electoral politics came first, and the details of governance came later. Most of the leading intellectuals of the Progressive Era were deeply uncomfortable with populism and socialism. The young Walter Lippman, in *Drift and Mastery*, called William Jennings Bryan, three-time presidential nominee of the Democratic Party, "the true Don Quixote of our politics." But Lippmann and his colleagues shared the view that private and institutional wealth had become more powerful than the state and that the imbalance had to be righted, so they set about devising alternate solutions. We are now in the early stages of a similar period of forging a new political economy for this still young century. It is going to be a large, long-running, and not very orderly task, but those who don't take it seriously are going to find themselves swept away.

It shouldn't be necessary, but it probably is, to stipulate that economies are organized by governments, not produced naturally through the operations of market forces. National economies do not fall into a simple binary of capitalist or not; each one is set up distinctively. Government rules determine how banks and financial markets are regulated, how powerful labor unions are, how international trade works, how corporations are governed, and how battles for advantage between industries are adjudicated. These arrangements have a profound effect on people's lives. The current economic discontent is a revolt against a designed system that took shape with the general assent of elite liberal and conservative intellectuals, many of whom thought it sounded like a good idea but were more closely focused on other issues to pay close attention to the details. To begin the discussion about a new system requires first developing a clearer understanding of the origins of the current one.

In an essay in 1964 called "What Happened to the Antitrust Movement?," Richard Hofstadter noted that for half a century, roughly from 1890 to 1940, the organization of the economy was the primary preoccupation of liberal politics. Hofstadter meant antitrust to be understood as a synecdoche for a broader concern with the response to industrialism in general and the rise of the big corporation in particular. He was not mourning liberalism's shift in focus; instead, he was typical of midcentury liberal intellectuals in thinking that the economic problems that had preoccupied the previous generation or two had been solved. And that view of the postwar decades still resonates even all these years later, in the economically dissatisfied political present. During last year's presidential campaign, Donald Trump's "Make American Great Again" and Joe Biden's "Build Back Better," both backward-looking slogans, share the embedded assumption that at some time in the past, roughly when Hofstadter was writing, the American economy worked for most people in a way that it doesn't now. But was that really true? And if it was, what went wrong?

~ぐ≈

Most people would probably say that the economy really was better back in the mid-1960s — that it had earned, through its stellar performance, the conventional view that it was working well — and that what changed was globalization: in particular the rise of the United States' defeated opponents in the Second World War, Japan and Germany, and previously unimaginable advances in communications and data-processing technology, and the empowerment of Saudi Arabia and other oil-producing Arab countries. But if that is what most people think, it highlights a problem we have now in addressing political economy, which is a belief that economic changes are produced by vast, irresistible, and inevitable historic forces, rather than by changes in political arrangements. That is a momentous mistake. A more specific account of the political origins of the mid-century economy, and of what blew it apart, is a necessary precondition for deciding what to do now.

41

In the presidential election of 1912, Theodore Roosevelt ran on a program he called "The New Nationalism," and Woodrow Wilson on "The New Freedom," with the third major candidate, William Howard Taft, having a less defined position. This was the heart of the period when economic arrangements were the major topic of presidential politics. (The perennial Socialist candidate, Eugene Debs, got his highest-ever total, 6 per cent of the vote, in 1912.) Advised by Lippmann and other Progressive intellectuals, Roosevelt proposed a much bigger and more powerful federal government that would be able to tame the new corporations that seemed to have taken over the country. Wilson, advised by Louis Brandeis, called for a restoration of the economic primacy of smaller businesses, in part by breaking up big ones. It is clear that Hofstadter's sympathies, as he looked back on this great debate, were on Roosevelt's side; he considered Wilson's position to be sentimental, impractical, and backward-looking, in much the way that Lippmann had thought of Bryan's economic inclinations as quixotic. Wilson won the election, but Roosevelt probably won the argument, at least among intellectuals. (Politicians, because they represent geographical districts, have a build-in incentive to be suspicious of economic and political centralization.) The years immediately after the election of 1912 saw the advent of the Federal Reserve, the income tax, and the Federal Trade Commission — early manifestations of the idea that the national government should take responsibility for the conduct of the American economy.

The argument between Roosevelt and Wilson never entirely went away. During the New Deal, when the economic role of the federal government grew beyond Theodore Roosevelt's wildest dreams, there were constant intramural debates within economic liberalism, between centralizers such as Adolf Berle, the highly influential Brain Truster-without-portfolio, and de-centralizers such as Thurman Arnold, the head of the antitrust division of the Justice Department. Despite major defeats, notably the Supreme Court's striking down of the National Industrial Recovery Act in 1935, the centralizers generally had the better of it, especially after the American entry into the Second World War, when the federal government essentially took over industrial production and also set wages and prices, with an evidently happy result.

After the war, Berle and his younger allies, John Kenneth Galbraith among them, celebrated the taming of the once menacing industrial corporation, thanks to the forceful and long-running intervention of government. Big corporations remained economically dominant, but because they were now answerable to a higher authority, they no longer ran roughshod. It is important to note that these were not the benign, socially responsible corporations one hears touted today — they were *forced* to be socially responsible, by government legal and regulatory decree. The liberal debate about corporations in the postwar years was primarily sociological and cultural, over whether they had eroded the American character by engendering a pervasive "conformity" — not over whether they exploited workers or dominated government. The economy was growing in ways that — in sharp contrast to today's economy — conferred benefits at all income levels. As Hofstadter put it, "The existence and the workings of the corporations are largely accepted, and in the main they are assumed to be fundamentally benign." Only conservatives, he asserted, with their resistance to modernity, failed to accept the reality of corporate dominance.

Partly because the main economic problems seemed at that point to have been solved, and partly because mainstream midcentury liberal thought was almost unimaginably unaware of national problems such as race, women's rights, and the environment that demanded urgent attention, most liberals turned their energies toward those neglected non-economic topics. Hofstadter wrote that antitrust "has ceased to be an ideology and has become a technique, interesting chiefly to a small elite of lawyers and economists." But that glosses over a crucial element in the development of economic liberalism.

43

Keynesian economics, which was in its infancy during the heyday of the New Deal, had become so prestigious by the 1960s as to have become the conventional way of thinking about government's role in addressing economic problems — not just among economists, but by anybody who had ever taken an undergraduate economics course. For Keynesians, the most potent economic tools at government's disposal were adjusting the money supply, tax rates, and overall government spending — not directly controlling the economic activities of corporations, through antitrust, regulation, and other means. (Adolf Berle used to boast that half the industries in America were regulated by federal agencies, and it was inevitable that the other half would be soon.) So the kind of government economic role advocated by a long line of liberal intellectuals, even as they squabbled over the details, fell out of the conversation.

It is always easy to see the vulnerabilities of a regime in retrospect. The mid-twentieth-century economic order depended on the corporation to provide a range of social benefits — good wages and salaries, employment security, pensions, health care, social services, and a measure of personal identity — that in most other developed nations would likely have come from government, or the church, or a stable local community. The American political system didn't seem willing to expand the New Deal into a full-dress social democracy, and corporations were available to perform these quasi-state functions — but that meant they were bearing a lot of weight. They did not command the loyalty of those whom they did not enfold in their warm embrace, so they had a limited number of political allies.

Even more important, the corporation-based social order rested on the assumption of their economic invulnerability.

Corporations had to be able to afford the social burdens being imposed on them by government. What could cut into the economic resources that would require? Three possibilities come to mind: a demand by shareholders that they get a higher return; a weakening of customer loyalty; or competition from other businesses. Adolf Berle's classic work (with Gardiner Means) *The Modern Corporation and Private Property,* which appeared in 1932, declared that corporations' shareholders, their supposed owners, had no power because they were so widely scattered: how could the hundreds of thousands of individual owners of stock in AT&T force management to do anything? After the Second World War, Berle only increased his estimate of the power and stability of the largest corporations, and of the irrelevance of their shareholders. So that was one potential threat assumed away. Galbraith agreed, and made the claim of corporate immortality even more capacious by observing that corporations were also invulnerable to fluctuations in consumer taste, because advertising had become so effective. There went another threat. And much of the rest of the world was still flat on its back after the Second World War, which took away the threat of competition, at least from abroad. Berle and others regular predicted the demise of Wall Street — heavily constrained by regulation since the advent of the New Deal — as a force in the American economy, because big corporations, ever larger and more powerful, would have so much capital of their own that they would no longer need access to the financial markets. Another common claim in that era was that innovation would, and could only, come from large corporations, because only they had the resources to operate substantial research divisions.

The corporate social order, taken for granted by many millions of people who lived within it, and not particularly appreciated by political thinkers on the left or the right, began to come apart spectacularly in the 1980s — which was also, not coincidentally, when the rise in inequality began. The forcing mechanism for this was the "shareholder revolution" — a great reorienting of the corporation's priorities toward increasing its asset value in the financial markets (and therefore its shareholders' wealth), and away from the welfare of its employees or of society. Most people credit Milton Friedman with launching the shareholder revolution, specifically with an article in the *New York Times* in 1970 called "The Social Responsibility of Business Is to Increase Its Profits." This suggested an ideal for corporations that was almost precisely opposite to Adolf Berle's, but it didn't propose specific techniques for achieving it. The true chief theoretician of the shareholder revolution was Michael C. Jensen, a University of Chicago-trained conservative economist, who neatly reversed Berle's life's work by making the re-empowerment of the shareholder his own life's work.

Jensen proposed such mechanisms as putting a corporation under the control of a single purchaser, at least temporarily, instead of a widely dispersed body of small stockholders (that's the private equity business), and paying chief executives primarily in stock options rather than salary, so that they would do whatever it took to increase their companies' share prices. Such measures would permit the corporation to attend to its new sole purpose. Jensen ceaselessly promoted these and related ideas through the 1970s, 1980s, and 1990s, with highly influential publications (he is the co-author of one of the most cited academic papers of all time), his popular teaching at Harvard Business School (whose graduates shifted from being corporate employees to corporate dismantlers), and public

46

appearances before Congressional committees and elsewhere. This coincided with a great wave of mergers, acquisitions, and buyouts that remade corporate America in ways that stripped out the social and political functions that had been imposed on it since the New Deal.

Since his work had large political as well as economic implications, Jensen may stand as the most under-recognized public intellectual of the late twentieth century. But his influence, like that of anyone whose ideas have consequences, was substantially a matter of context. He arrived on the scene at a time when the kinds of institutional arrangements on which the midcentury political economy rested had fallen deeply out of fashion. The large economic disruptions of the final quarter of the twentieth century, when they are not attributed to inevitable market forces, are often laid at the feet of an organized corporate-conservative effort to remake the political economy, beginning, perhaps, with the future Supreme Court Justice Lewis Powell's famous memo to the U.S. Chamber of Commerce in 1971 suggesting the building of a new conservative infrastructure of think tanks, publications, and campus leadership training institutes. But this misses a couple of important elements. One is the tension between corporations and finance — that is, between Main Street and Wall Street. When a company like IBM or General Electric dropped its de facto guarantee of lifetime employment and its company-paid defined benefit pensions, this was "corporate" only in the sense of corporations were now being run for Wall Street investors, not in the sense of benefiting Organization Man-style corporate employees.

Also liberalism was changing, and many of these economic rearrangements happened with liberal (or at least elite liberal) assent. For one of many possible examples, consider that the

47

crusade against the airline-regulating Civil Aeronautics Board, now of blessed memory, which had to approve every route and every fare (and one of whose creators was Adolf Berle), was led by Senator Ted Kennedy, with another future Supreme Court Justice, Stephen Breyer, as his chief advisor. It had the enthusiastic support of Alfred Kahn, the liberal economist who was Jimmy Carter's appointee as the euthanasiast chairman of the CAB. (Ralph Nader, then probably the leading liberal activist in Washington, was another participant in this crusade.) There was little or no liberal opposition to the supersizing of Wall Street, which mirrored the downsizing of the industrial corporation; the shareholder revolution would not have been possible without dozens of regulatory changes that enabled it, which didn't attract much notice because at that moment economic deregulation was seen as an uncontroversial good cause. Much of the newly emerging economic Brahmin class was populated by elite liberals: graduates of Ivy League universities who worked at McKinsey or Goldman Sachs or Google, proudly and profitably "disrupting" the old economy for a living. People at such companies became an important part of the funding base of the Democratic Party, playing the role that political machines and unions had previously played. The old instinct that the way to solve problems is by making corporatist bargains among government, labor, and business had faded away. A fluid, fast, transaction-oriented society, which proposed instead to solve problems by dismantling institutional arrangements and putting more innovative, efficient ones in their place, was now the ideal.

I don't want to sound facilely dismissive of these ideas. I was entranced by them when I was young. In those days one still saw people who had served in the New Deal strolling through downtown Washington — Tommy Corcoran, Ben

Cohen, Joe Rauh. They appeared to me not as honored participants in a supremely successful political and economic order, but as ghosts, men who had outlived their times. "Neoliberal" had not yet become a dirty word. Books proposing to save liberalism by jettisoning its traditional formations, such as Theodore Lowi's *The End of Liberalism* and Mancur Olson's *The Rise and Decline of Nations,* were mesmerizing. Liberal heterodoxy was in the air. Why couldn't liberalism off-load all those clunky appurtenances of its past, the labor unions and the interest groups and the government agencies, and just solve problems? Why did we have to defend to the death vast, wasteful, expensive programs such as Social Security and Medicare? Why couldn't we be less political, more efficient, smarter, more attuned to real needs and less to powerful constituencies? Didn't the sluggish economy need the kind of jump-start that deregulation and a general embrace of markets could provide?

Maybe the Civil Aeronautics Board had indeed outlived its usefulness. The problem was that this broad antinomian logic was applied everywhere. With hardly a peep except from self-interested industry groups, the United States ended broadcast regulation, ushering in the age of hot-blooded talk radio and cable news. It set up the Internet to be an unregulated information platform that enriched a handful of immensely wealthy and powerful companies and made no effort to distinguish between truth and falsity. It declined to regulate the derivatives markets that brought down the global economy in 2008. In all those cases, policies that sounded good by the standards of the newly dominant form of economic liberalism wound up having old-fashioned libertarian effects that should have been predictable: more inequality, greater concentration of wealth and power, more disruption of social and economic arrangements that had been comfortable and familiar for many millions of people. The flaws in the new system were not immediately evident to its designers, because they were prospering. But many of the less well educated, more provincially located, and less securely employed eventually made their vehement dissent known through their voting behavior. That is where we are now.

People get to choose how to involve themselves in politics, as participants and as voters. It would be wildly unrealistic to demand that everyone's politics be "about" some topic that seems preeminent to you, or that their politics align with an outsider's balance-sheet determination of their interests. If you are reading this, it's likely that Donald Trump cut your taxes. Did you vote for him? Or did you vote because of longstanding party loyalty, or your values, or the way the candidates struck you, or what you think the American government should stand for at home and abroad? It is especially foolhardy to imagine that politics can be about economics rather than, say, race, or gender, or religion, or culture — or that it can be rigorously empirical, based on meticulous scientific determinations of the truth. Still, because democratic politics is meant to determine the activities of the state, and much of what the state does is allocate resources, in the end economics runs through just about everything in politics, including matters that do not present themselves as economic.

Racism would not command the public attention it does if blacks and whites were economically indistinguishable, and most of the proposed remedies for racism entail big changes in how governments get and spend their money. Nativism may express itself as hatred of the other, but it takes root among people who see immigrants as competitors for jobs and government benefits. The bitter controversies over the pandemic have been powered by the highly different ways it has affected people's health and employment depending on where they stand in the class system. So, even when politics is not obviously about economics, it is still about economics. To address the deep unfairness of the current economic order requires political solutions, but they have to be political solutions that meet people where they are — that do not seem distanced and abstract. That will be the only way to build popular support strong enough to enact them.

The fundamental test of the American political economy ought to be whether it can offer ordinary people the plausible promise of a decent life, with a realistic hope of economic progress and their basic needs met: health care, a good education, protection from want, security in old age. The country has failed that test for a generation. Until it succeeds economically and socially, it will not function well politically. And to function well politically requires addressing an enormous economic problem, which can come across as dry and statistical, in ways that feel immediate and palpable enough to inspire passionate engagement.

I am proposing a great remaking of the political economy as a primary task over the next generation. At this moment the most useful next step in that project is not to produce a specific policy agenda, but instead to outline an approach to politics that could create widespread popular support for the larger project. In recent years the gap between voters and technically oriented policymakers who are genuinely concerned about inequality has been very wide — wide enough for pure grievance to take up the political space that ought to be devoted to fixing the problem. I will suggest three guiding principles for how to proceed.

Work through institutions. Consequential human activity takes place through institutions. It has been an especially self-destructive element of recent thought to exaggerate the disadvantages of "bureaucracy" and other aspects of institutional life and to overestimate how much can be accomplished without them. This turn has coincided with the severe deterioration of the traditional bulwark institutions of American liberalism, such as labor unions and churches. Media and messaging meant to influence public opinion, organizing campaigns conducted only on social media — these are the snack foods of politics, far less effective over the long term than building institutions that have more conventional functions like structured meetings, ongoing rituals, and planned campaigns aimed at specific government policy outcomes.

It is a familiar irony that the opponents of an inclusive economy have often used anti-institutional rhetoric while building up powerful institutions of their own. During the twenty-first century, we have seen a great consolidation of one economic sector after another, always made possible by favorable political arrangements, which only become more favorable as the sector gains more economic, and therefore political, power. To curb the power of big tech, big finance, big pharma, and big agriculture will require countervailing institutions. Institutions (which are not the same thing as communities) are necessary to achieve change, and also to instantiate change. Awakening consciences and changing minds is noble and necessary, but such advances lack staying power unless they lead to the creation of consequential new laws and institutions.

Address inequality upstream, not downstream. It is deeply ingrained in our economic thinking that the solution to inequality is redistribution. That way, in theory, a society can have the best of both worlds: the efficiency, flexibility, and growth associated with unimpeded markets, plus the corrections to markets' inequities that only the state can provide. The master tool for redistribution is a progressive income tax system, but there are plenty of more specific tools that address economic injustice in the same spirit: unemployment benefits for people who lost their jobs, food stamps for the hungry, retraining for people whose workplace moved abroad. All of these instruments have in common that they offer a remedy after something bad has happened to people, rather than trying to prevent something bad from happening to them in the first place.

A decade ago the political scientist Jacob Hacker suggested "pre-distribution" instead of redistribution as a model. In this way of thinking, the aim is to throw some sand in the gears of pure market function, so that it cannot so easily disrupt people's lives. Strong labor laws are a good example: they boost workers' pay and benefits and make it more difficult to fire them, which is far more dignity-promoting than the Silicon Valley model of economic justice, with no unions, a gig economy, and the cold solace of a universal basic income for those who experience misfortune. Another is restrictions on absolute free trade and outsourcing of employment. Another is making it more difficult for private equity companies to load expenses onto the companies they acquire, which puts them under irresistible pressure to break whatever compact they had with their employees.

Most working people are focused on the particular place where they live and the particular company where they

53

work. A politician's signal that she understands this and will try her best to keep those arrangements in place will be far more meaningful than a promise to pursue abatements after people's lives have been pulled apart. Economic policymakers for years have regarded policies with this goal as the province of petty rent-seeking politicians, the kind who created the Smoot-Hawley tariff back in the 1920s: all they can accomplish is to create a static, declining society; real economic policy has to be redistributionist and Keynesian. It is a longstanding part of conservative lore that liberals scored a landmark and unfair victory when they torpedoed the Supreme Court nomination of Robert Bork in 1987 — but during the borking of Bork, his liberal opponents barely mentioned what was by far his most influential belief, which was that economic efficiency and consumer benefit were the only proper concerns for government as it regulated companies' economic activities. They barely mentioned it because they had accepted it. That same year, the *New York Times* published a lead editorial titled "The Right Minimum Wage: $0.00." (On the day this essay is going to press, the *Times'* lead editorial is titled "Let's Talk About Higher Wages.") The economic program on which Joe Biden successfully ran for President, heavily emphasizing saving jobs and keeping small businesses open, was by far the most pre-distributionist by a Democratic candidate in decades. The tide is only just beginning to turn, and the Democrats' relatively new economic constituencies are not going to be pushing the Biden administration to reinvent the party's notion of an ideal political economy.

Decentralize power. In 1909, in *The Promise of American Life,* which is still as good a framing device for twentieth-century American liberalism as one can find, Herbert Croly proposed that the country tack away from the political tradition of

Thomas Jefferson and toward the tradition of Alexander Hamilton. In the present, it is necessary to be reminded of what Croly meant by that: to his mind, Jefferson was not primarily a plantation slaveholder, but an advocate for farmers, artisans, and other smallholders, and for localized government, and Hamilton was not primarily an immigrant who took his shot, but an advocate for centralized and nationalized government, and the father of the American financial system. For Progressives such as Croly, it was axiomatic that the world had become far too complex for a Jeffersonian approach to work. Like Theodore Roosevelt a few years later, Croly believed that the national government had to become bigger and more powerful — and also to employ technical, depoliticized expertise that would be beyond the capabilities of local governments. This way of thinking about government has an irresistibly powerful face validity for members of the category of people who would staff its upper ranks. Think about the coronavirus: wouldn't you want trained public health professionals to have been in charge nationally, rather than governors of highly variable quality?

Yet Croly's position is a temptation to be avoided, for a number of reasons. Expertise is not, *pace* the insistence of the social-media mob and Fox News, merely a pretext for the exercise of power. Experts have both knowledge in their domains, and an obligation to set aside their pure, unruly human instincts and attempt to approach the world more dispassionately. They marshal evidence. They answer, rather than insult or stereotype, people who do not agree with them. That they operate with some degree of honor doesn't make them infallible or supra-human, of course. Like everybody else, experts live in their own enclosed worlds, and they often operate on distinctive, non-universal, and not fully conscious assumptions that nobody they encounter ever challenges. Technocracy is not a guarantee of truth or wisdom. No matter how smart and epistemologically sophisticated they are, experts miss things. Over the past few decades, the list has been long: the collapse of the Soviet Union; the 2008 financial crisis; the dramatic rise and political empowerment of evangelical religion; the rise of populism. The problem with centralized, elite expert rule is not only that it creates an inviting target, but that it also requires a check on its power, a system built to incorporate alternative views. To paraphrase James Madison, expertise must be made to counteract expertise; and, in a democracy, experts must be prepared to respect and honor what the great majority of citizens who aren't experts think.

It is impossible to separate economic and political power in the way that the Progressives envisioned, and their present-day heirs still do. Great economic power, of the kind that the major technology and financial companies have today, requires favorable political arrangements; in return, it uses its economic power to enhance its political power. The gentle treatment that big finance and big tech have gotten from government, including from Democratic administrations, is closely related to their role as major political funders and employers of past and future high government officials. The federal government is no longer capable of functioning as a countervailing force to all elements of economic plutocracy at all times: a Democratic administration may be able to stand up to Koch Industries, but not to Google or Goldman Sachs.

A far better vision for liberals should be of a pluralistic society that does not assume that one major element will be so automatically good that it should be super-empowered. Super-empowerment may be the ill that ails us the most.

Over the past few decades, inequality has increased substantially not just for individuals, but for institutions. The top five banks control a higher percentage of assets than they ever have in American history. The gap between the richest universities and the struggling mass is greater. The great metropolitan newspapers of the late twentieth century — the *Los Angeles Times* and the *Philadelphia Inquirer* and the *Chicago Tribune* and so on — aren't great anymore. Book publishing is in the hands of the "big four" houses. Five big companies dominate the technology business. If all these arrangements are working nicely for you personally, you should not take too much comfort from that. Think about what it would feel like if people you find abhorrent had control of these institutions — it is a much better guide than thinking about the system you would want when the good guys, by your lights, are in charge.

Politics is the arena that allowed these inequalities to flourish, and politics will be how they can get corrected. You should think in particular about what kind of political system you would want, if the bad guys were winning. You would want checks on the power of the President and on the more politically insulated parts of the federal government, such as the Supreme Court and the Federal Reserve. You would want good state and local governments to have room to do what the national government can't do or won't do. You would want to prevent economic royalty, individual or corporate, from being able to control political outcomes. You would want Congress to have more power than the President, and the House of Representatives to have more power than the Senate. You would want minority groups to be organized enough to be able to impress their distinctive point of view on a majority that ignores it. In other words, squabbling, bargaining, self-interest,

57

partisanship, and "gridlock" would be signs of political health, not dysfunction. Influence would come from the sustained effort it takes to be effective through democratic means, not from finding workarounds to open, participatory politics.

That these are ways of structuring politics, not of assuring the victory of one side or of arriving at a policy, ought not detract from their urgency. Politics should make people feel heard and attended to. It should address pressing problems successfully. Politics manifestly is not doing those things now. If the way it is framed and conducted does not change fundamentally, democratic politics, which is to say, democratic society, will not be able to function properly. Tasks that are essential to powerful interests will get accomplished, but not tasks to which they are indifferent, even if they affect the welfare of vast numbers of people. Building a new politics will take a long time, because there is a lot to undo.

ALFRED BRENDEL

On Playing Beethoven: Marginalia

Interpretation? Some musicians have little patience for this word, while on the other side there is a recent surge of musicologists who strive to do it justice by elucidating its essence, its development, and its historical peculiarities. After a lengthy period of purely structural reasoning about musical works, topics such as psychology, character, and atmosphere are being considered again. Every tiny *portamento* or *cercar la nota* throughout the history of bel canto is being unearthed. Recapitulations are scrutinized with the help of the stopwatch in order to find out whether, why, and by how much they may exceed the scope of the exposition.

The anti-interpreters consider all this to be a waste of time. All they ask for is a reliable edition of the score. The rest will be provided by their own genius. Here I would like to interpose and remind the reader of the fact that to decipher a score precisely and sympathetically is a much more demanding task than most musicians realize, and a more important one as well. Among the composers who had the skill to put on paper distinctly what they imagined, Beethoven is an outstanding example. Do not register his markings with one eye only: it will not provide you with the full picture. I am thinking of his dynamic indications in particular — Beethoven was well aware of where his crescendi and diminuendi should start or end. The metronome markings are another matter. The unhesitating adherence to Beethoven's metronome figures even in the most dubious cases (Op. 106, Ninth Symphony) has resulted in performances that hardly leave any space for warmth, *dolce*, *cantabile*, for — in the words of the prescription in his Missa Solemnis — "from the heart — may it reach out to the heart" (*von Herzen — möge es wieder zu Herzen gehen*). They also leave no room for Beethoven's humor.

While, in the past, it was the cliché of Beethoven the hero and the titan that was harmful to an appreciation of the variety of his music, the danger now comes from the predilection for breakneck speeds and virtuoso feats. Tempi are forced on the music instead of derived from it. My own experience has taught me to trust Beethoven's markings — if not the metronome indications — almost completely, and to consider them important hints about tempo and atmosphere.

The terms from *largo* to *prestissimo* that Beethoven uses to indicate tempo and character seem to me frequently more suggestive than metronome prescriptions. Listening to some contemporary performances, the majority of allegros sound to me like *presto possibile*. The diversity of the tempi gets lost. The third movement of the Hammerklavier Sonata, called *Adagio sostenuto*, turns into an *andante con moto*. While the speed of the fugue (crotchet = 144) is technically feasible, it prevents the listener from taking in the harmonic proceedings. (For many pianists, playing too fast may come easier than slightly reining in the tempo.)

Another bone of contention is the metronome's unshakeable steadiness. There are musicians who do not permit themselves or their pupils to use a metronome because it purportedly contradicts the natural flexibility of feeling. Obviously music should breathe, and it presupposes, not unlike our spine and pulse, a certain amount of elasticity. Yet this does not hold true for all music: not only jazz and pop, but also a considerable part of twentieth century music, would, without a rigorous tempo, be senseless. And there is another beneficial function of the metronome: it prevents progressive speeding up. Many young musicians are unaware of what they are doing to the tempo while practicing, and there are virtuosi who consider it their privilege to accelerate the pace while playing fast notes — a habit no orchestra or chamber ensemble could get away with.

I cannot acquiesce in the widespread assumption that a soloist may indulge in all conceivable liberties, even the most outlandish ones, because he or she is neither a member of an ensemble nor the helpless prisoner of an orchestra. Quite a few soloists seem to adhere to the belief that only soloistic independence will issue in true music-making that emanates from their innermost interior, unfettered by the straitjacket of ensemble playing. Any pianist who is about to play a Beethoven sonata should listen to a good performance of a Beethoven quartet — by, say, the Busch Quartet — in advance.

On Playing Beethoven: Marginalia

And there is more to learn from the best conductors, singers, and orchestras than from all-too-soloistic soloists.

Do you know the story of the eminent pianist who early on in his career was accused by a critic of playing semiquavers as if counting peas — with the result that, from then on, rhythmic steadfastness evaporated from his playing? Many years of appearing with orchestras and dealing with string quartets have confirmed my ideal of a rhythmic control that, in solo music, should never stray too far from ensemble playing. After all, the greatest piano composers — excepting Chopin and, in their young years, Schumann and Liszt — have all been ensemble composers as well, if not primarily. It seems highly unlikely that a composer should harbor two distinctly different concepts of rhythm and tempo, one for soloists, another for ensemble players. "Freedom" of playing should be confined to cadenzas, recitatives, and sections of an improvisatory nature. It goes without saying that Beethoven's scores are neither entirely complete nor apt to be put into practice by a computer. To prepare the onset of a new idea, to give sufficient time to a transition, to underline the weight of an ending: these were self-evident matters that the performance of tonal music implied.

62

Compared to the younger and short-lived Schubert, Beethoven had more time and opportunity to hear his own works performed, and to react to the performances. His hearing trouble was probably not so severe that it would have prevented him from perceiving certain tones and nuances. The Schuppanzigh Quartet, an institution that had already been associated with Haydn, accompanied his string quartet production to its very end. This was the first professional quartet in performance history, and it seems to have been available to Beethoven consistently. When Schuppanzigh stayed away from Vienna for a number of years, Beethoven halted his composition of string quartets, only to take it up again when Schuppanzigh returned. His quartet in E-flat Op. 127 was premiered within the series of "classical" chamber music concerts that Schuppanzigh inaugurated. This performance, however, turned out to be inadequate, and in due course several other performances with different players were organized to give connoisseurs the chance of getting better acquainted with such novel music. (The fact that this was feasible may have been due to the unparalleled triumph of Beethoven's patriotic creations *Wellington's Victory* and "*Der glorreiche Augenblick,*" or "The Glorious Moment," which marked the peak of his popularity as well as the low point of his compositional output.)

The profusion and the distinctiveness of Beethoven's markings in the late string quartets did not result entirely from imagining them — it was connected to performance practice as well. Only in his fugues do we find a lack of detailed instructions. In these passages the players have to intervene and provide additional dynamic information, unless they are intent on drowning the listener of Beethoven's "Grosse Fuge" in long stretches of *fortissimo*.

Schuppanzigh's concert series were mainly geared towards string quartets (regularly those of Haydn, Mozart and Beethoven), but they also included quintets, nonets and ("to divert the ladies") piano trios. Solo piano works were hardly performed in public until Liszt invented the piano recital in London in 1840. Like Beethoven's late quartets, his late piano sonatas became too difficult to be executed by domestic players. In order to tackle works such as the Sonata Op. 101

On Playing Beethoven: Marginalia

you had to be as proficient as Dorothea Ertmann, Beethoven's much-admired pupil and friend to whom the sonata is dedicated. Works such as Op. 106 and Op.111 were deemed unplayable. Only in the second half of the nineteenth century did they start to seep into musical consciousness, thanks mainly to the advocacy of Hans von Bülow.

In spite of the commitment of performers such as Bülow, Arthur Schnabel, Edwin Fischer, and Peter Serkin, the appreciation of the Diabelli Variations took considerably longer. Only recently has this magnum opus turned into a parade horse of many pianists as well as an endurance test for audiences that have now learned to sit through, and even relish, a work that is fifty-five minutes long and almost entirely in the key of C major. Among the reasons for this delay was the mythological misconception of the late Beethoven as "a loner with his God," when in fact the profane was no less available to him than the sublime, the musical past no less than the musical present and future. In the Diabelli Variations, virtuosity and introspection, humor and gracefulness, cohabit under one roof.

According to his assistant Schindler, Beethoven conceived these variations while "in a rosy mood," and humor ("the sublime in reverse," according to Jean Paul) reigns over wide stretches of the work. Wilhelm von Lenz, who took piano lessons from Liszt and became the author of the first detailed appreciation of all of Beethoven's works, calls him "the most thoroughly initiated high priest of humor." Conveying humor in music had been one of Haydn's great achievements, and Beethoven linked up with it. Of course, the performer of humorous music should never appear to be forcing the comical. In the Diabelli Variations, the wit ought to become apparent, as it were, by itself, while the enraptured and enigmatic pieces provide the depth of perspective.

Beethoven had a predilection for placing the ridiculous next to the sublime. The bottomless introspection of Variation XX is followed by a piece in which a maniac and a moaner alternate. After concluding his work on the Sonata Op. 111, his last piano sonata, Beethoven turned to finishing his Diabelli Variations, the theme of which is motivically related to the Sonata's Arietta. Once more, the sublime and the "sublime in reverse" face one another.

It has been claimed that Beethoven's late style narrows down into the subjective and esoteric. What I find in it, however, is expansion and synthesis. Opposites are forced together, refinement meets bluntness, the public is paired with the private, roughness stands next to childlike lyricism. Does the inclusion of the Diabelli Variations into the wider repertory suggest that, these days, we have learned to listen to Beethoven's late music with open ears? What we can take for granted is that no amount of familiarity with these pieces is going to erase their tinge of mystery.

65

PAUL BERMAN

The George Floyd Uprising

I

Overnight mass conversions to the cause of African American rights are a rare phenomenon in America, and, even so, a recurrent phenomenon, and ultimately a world-changing phenomenon. The classic instance took place in 1854 in Boston. An escaped slave from Virginia named Anthony Burns was arrested and held by United States marshals, who prepared to send him back into bondage in Virginia, in accordance with the Fugitive Slave Act and the policies of the Franklin Pierce administration. And a good many white people in Boston and environs were surprised to discover themselves erupting in violent rage, as if in mass reversion to the hot-headed instincts

of their ancestors at the glorious Tea Party of 1773. Respect-
able worthies with three names found themselves storming
the courthouse. Amos Adams Lawrence, America's wealthiest
mill owner, famously remarked, "We went to bed one night
old-fashioned, conservative, Compromise Whigs & waked up
stark mad Abolitionists." John Greenleaf Whittier experienced
a physical revulsion:

> I felt a sense of bitter loss, —
> Shame, tearless grief, and stifling wrath,
> And loathing fear, as if my path
> A serpent stretched across.

Henry David Thoreau delivered a lecture a few weeks later
under the scathing title, "Slavery in Massachusetts," in support
of blowing up the law: "The law will never make men free; it is
men who have got to make the law free." And in upstate New
York, the businessman John Brown, taking the fateful next
step, declared that "Anthony Burns must be released, or I will
die in the attempt," which sounded the note of death. Burns
was not released. John Brown went to Bleeding Kansas, where
the note of death produced the Pottawatomie Massacre in 1856,
and thence to Harper's Ferry and everything that followed.

    A second instance took place in March 1965, this time
in response to a police attack on John Lewis and a voting-
rights march in Alabama. The event was televised. Everyone
saw it. And the furor it aroused was sufficiently intense to
ensure that, in our own day, the photo image of young Lewis
getting beaten, though it is somewhat blurry, has emerged
as a representative image of the civil-rights revolution. It
was Lyndon Johnson, and not any of the business moguls or
the poets, who articulated the response. Johnson delivered a

speech to Congress a few days later in which, apart from calling for the Voting Rights Act to be passed, he made it clear that he himself was not entirely the same man as before. "We shall overcome," said the president, as if, having gone to bed a mere supporter of the civil rights cause, he had waked up marching in the street and singing the anthem. He went further yet. In a speech at Howard University, he defined the goal, too: "not just equality as a right and a theory, but equality as a fact, and equality as a result," which inched his toe further into social democratic terrain than any American presidential toe has ever ventured.

And, a week after the Voting Rights Act duly passed, the violent note of the 1960s, already audible, began to resound a little more loudly in the Watts district of Los Angeles, prefiguring still more to come over the next years — violence in the ghettos, and among the police, and among the white supremacists, and eventually on the radical left as well. All of which ought to suggest that, in the late spring of 2020, we saw and perhaps participated in yet another version of the same rare and powerful phenomenon: an overnight conversion to the cause of African American rights, sparked by a single, shocking, and visible instance of dreadful oppression, with massive, complicated, and, on a smaller scale, sometimes violent consequences.

During the several months that followed the killing of George Floyd, which occurred on May 25, 2020, close to eight thousand Black Lives Matter demonstrations are reported to have taken place in the United States, in more than two thousand locales in every part of the country. Many of those demonstrations must have drawn just a handful of people. Then again, a protest parading under my own windows in Brooklyn in early June filled eight lanes and took half an hour to pass by, and, far from being unusual, was followed by similar marches from time to time, week after week, eventually dwindling in size, then swelling up again, and never disappearing, not for several months. It is reasonable to assume that, nationwide in America, several million people took part in those demonstrations. These were the largest anti-racist demonstrations in the history of the United States, and they were echoed by still other Black Lives Matter demonstrations in a variety of other countries, which made them the largest such event in the history of the world. The scale of the phenomenon makes clear that, whatever the precise size of the crowds, enormous numbers of participants had to be people who, like Amos Adams Lawrence, went to bed as quiet citizens and waked up transformed into militants of the cause, ready to paint their own placards (a disdain for printed placards or anything else bespeaking the dead hand of top-down obedience was a style of the movement) and carry them through the streets, chanting "Black lives matter!" and other, scrappier slogans ("Why are you in riot gear? / I don't see no riot here!") that, until yesterday, would never have been theirs.

This has been, in short, a major event not just globally, but intimately and individually, one marcher at a time. The intimate and individual aspect has made itself visible, too, in the wave of professional groups and institutions of many sorts that have announced campaigns of their own to break up the segregated aspect (or worse) of institutional life in America — protests and campaigns in any number of business organizations and academic and cultural institutions, unto Kappa Alpha, the Robert E. Lee-revering college fraternity. And, in conformity with the historical pattern, the undertow of violence and destruction has likewise made itself visible, some of it a low-level political violence on the radical left, some of

The George Floyd Uprising

it in prolonged versions too (which is a fairly novel development); some of it a violence on the radical right, the ominous posturing with guns in public, the wave of right-wing car-rammings, the terrorist plots in Michigan, and some murders; and some of it outbreaks of looting, not on the urbicidal scale of the 1960s, but epidemically spread across the country, hotspot to hotspot.

The furors of 1854, 1965, and 2020 arose in response to particular circumstances, and a glance at the circumstances makes it possible to identify more precisely the intimate and even invisible nature of the mass conversions. The circumstances in 1854 amounted to a political betrayal. The mainstream of the political class had managed for a quarter of a century to persuade the antislavery public in large parts of the North that it was possible to be antislavery and conciliatory to the slave states at the same time, in the expectation that somehow things were going to work out. Instead, the Kansas-Nebraska Act of 1854, by enabling further triumphs of the slave system, demonstrated that nothing was working out. People who thought of themselves as patient and moderate reformers concluded that they had been played. And, with the arrest of a fugitive slave in antislavery's principal city, the patient and moderate reformers felt personally implicated, too. They erupted in wrath on behalf of Anthony Burns, who was in front of them, and on behalf of the American slaves as a whole, who were mostly far away. They erupted on behalf of America and the principles of the American Revolution, which they understood to be identical to the antislavery cause (as expressed by Walt Whitman, still another *enragé*, in his poem on the Burns affair, "A Boston

Ballad"). But they erupted also on their own behalf, one person at a time. They were earnest Christians who discovered, to their horror, that they had allowed themselves to be duped by smooth-talking politicians into acceding for a quarter of a century, through association with the abomination of slavery, to their own moral degradation or damnation.

The "stifling wrath" (Whittier's phrase) was different in 1965, but not entirely so. Opinion in large parts of the country had come around in favor of civil rights, timidly perhaps, but with a feeling of moral righteousness. The philosophical battle against segregation and invidious discrimination seemed to have been won, as shown by Johnson's success, a year earlier, in pushing through the Civil Rights Act. Under those circumstances, to see on television the state troopers of the rejected Old South descend upon the demonstrators in Selma, quite as if the country had not, in fact, already made a national decision — to see the troopers assault young John Lewis and other people well-known and respected for their noble agitations — to see, in short, the unreconstructed bigots display yet again, unfazed, the same stupid, brutal arrogance that had just gone down to defeat — to see this was — well, it did not feel like a betrayal exactly, but neither did it feel like a simple political setback. It felt like a national insult. It was an outrage to everyone who had waked up singing "We Shall Overcome." It was an outrage to the murdered President Kennedy. Then again, to some people the spectacle signified the futility of political action and self-restraint and, in that fashion, it opened the gates of limitless rage.

The political origins of the mass response to the killing of George Floyd are likewise identifiable, though I will confess that, if you had asked me a day before it started to predict the future of radical reform in America, I would have identified a different set of origins, and I would have extrapolated a different outcome. The origins that did lead to the uprising had everything to do with Black Lives Matter as an organization, and not just as a vague movement. Everyone will recall that, in 2013, a Florida vigilante named George Zimmerman was acquitted of the murder of a black teenager named Trayvon Martin, and the acquittal led to furious demonstrations in Florida, California, and New York. A politically savvy young black woman in San Francisco named Alicia Garza posted stirring responses to the incident on Facebook which included the phrase "black lives matter," simply as a heartbroken thought and not as a slogan, and which was reposted by others using #blacklivesmatter. Garza and a couple of her Californian friends, Patrisse Cullors and Opal Tometi, converted their hashtag into a series of social media pages and thus into a committee of sorts.

Garza was a professional community organizer in San Francisco, and, as she makes plain in her account of these events, *The Purpose of Power: How We Come Together When We Fall Apart,* she and the little committee did know how to respond to unpredicted events. The next year, when the police in Ferguson, Missouri, shot to death Michael Brown, a spontaneous local uprising broke out, which was the unpredicted event. Garza and her group made their way to Ferguson, and, by scientifically applying their time-tested skills, helped convert the spontaneous uprising into an organized protest. Similar protests broke out in other cities. The Black Lives Matter movement was launched — a decentralized movement animated by a sharply defined outrage over state violence against blacks, with encouragement and assistance from Garza and her circle, "fanning the flames of discontent," as the Wobblies used to say, and then from other people, too, who mounted rival and schismatic claims to have founded the movement.

In New York City, the marches, beginning in 2014, were large and feisty — marches of young people, sometimes mostly white, sometimes multihued, with flames fanned by the New York Police Department, whose uniformed members managed to choke to death Eric Garner, guilty of the peaceable crime of selling bootleg cigarettes. I did a little marching myself, whenever an attractive cohort was passing by. Some of these marches were, in fact, attractive. Then again, some of them seemed to be youth adventures, a little daffy in their anti-police fervor. I kept expecting to discover, at the rear of one march or another, a graduate-student delegation wheeling an antique caboose loaded with dogmas of the university left, barely updated from the identity politics of the 1970s and 1980s, or shrewdly refitted for the anti-Zionist cause. And, to be sure, Angela Davis, who spent the 1970s and 1980s trying to attach the black cause in America to the larger cause of the Soviet Union, had come out with a book in 2016 called *Freedom Is a Constant Struggle: Ferguson, Palestine, and the Foundations of a Movement*, trying to merge, on intersectionalist grounds, Black Lives Matter in Missouri to the Palestinian struggle against Israel.

As it happens, the anti-Zionists had some success in commandeering an umbrella group of various organizations, the Movement for Black Lives, that arose in response to the upsurge of Black Lives Matter demonstrations. But the anti-Zionists had no success, or only fleeting successes, in commandeering Black Lives Matter itself. Nor did the partisans of any other cause or organization manage to commandeer the movement. Alicia Garza makes clear in *The Purpose of Power* that, in regard to the maneuverings and ideological extrava-

The George Floyd Uprising

gances of sundry factions of the radical left, she is not a naïf, and she and her friends have known how to preserve the integrity of their cause. Still, she is not without occasional extravagances of her own. In her picture of African American history, she deems the "iconic trio" of freedom fighters to be Martin Luther King, Malcolm X, and, of all people, Huey Newton, the leader of the Black Panther Party in the 1960s and 1970s, "the Supreme Servant of the People" — though Garza's San Francisco Bay Area must be filled with any number of older people who surely remember the Supreme Servant more sourly.

An occasional ideological extravagance need not get in the way, however, of a well-run organizing project. In San Francisco, a black neighborhood found itself suddenly deprived of school busses, and, as Garza describes, she and her colleagues efficiently mobilized the community, even if that involved the followers of Louis Farrakhan, of whom she appears to be not too fond. And lo, bus service resumed. Mobilizing a few neighborhoods around police violence is not any different. Still, the ideological impulses are sometimes hard to repress. From Garza's standpoint, the overriding necessity during the presidential campaign of 2016 was to denounce the Democratic Party for its evident failings. Militants of Black Lives Matter duly made dramatic interventions in the campaign — at one of Bernie Sanders' events, in order to denounce Bernie for failing to give black issues a proper consideration; and at an event of Hillary Clinton's, in order to denounce Hillary for her own related inadequacies. But those were less than useful interventions. They seemed likely only to dampen popular black enthusiasm for the Democratic Party, precisely at a moment when the cause of anti-Trumpism depended on black enthusiasm — which led me to suppose, back in 2016, that Black Lives Matter was bound to remain a marginal movement, brilliantly capable of promoting its single issue, but incapable of maneuvering successfully on the larger landscape.

The leftwing upsurges that, in my too fanciful imagination, seemed better attuned to the age were Occupy Wall Street, which got underway in 2011, and Sanders' 2016 and 2020 presidential campaigns. Occupy mostly evaded the dismal fate that skeptical observers predicted for it (namely, a degeneration into mayhem, Portland-style); and the Sanders campaigns only partly indulged, and mostly evaded, its own most dismal possibility (namely, a degeneration into full-tilt Jeremy Corbynism). Instead, the two movements gathered up large portions of the American radical left and led them out of the political wilderness into the social mainstream — in the case of Occupy, by transforming the anti-Main Street hippie counterculture into a species of hippie populism, 1890s-style, with a Main-Street slogan about "the ninety-nine per cent"; and, in the case of Bernie's campaigns, by convincing large portions of the protest left to lighten up on identity politics, to return to an almost forgotten working-class orientation of long ago, and to go into electoral politics. Those were historic developments, and, in my calculation, they were bound to encourage the more practical Democrats to make their own slide leftward into a renewed appreciation for the equality-of-results idea that Lyndon Johnson had tried to get at. And then, with the pandemic, a leftward slide began to look like common sense, without any need to call itself any kind of slide at all. In the early spring of 2020, *that* was the radical development I expected to see — a dramatic renewal of the unnamed social-democratic cause. Not an insurrection in the streets, but something larger.

The George Floyd Uprising

Instead, there was an insurrection in the streets. The insurrection owed nothing at all to nostalgias for the 1890s or Eugene V. Debs or LBJ. It was an antiracist uprising. What can explain this?

The video of George Floyd explains it. Six or seven years of skillful agitations by the Black Lives Matter movement had made everyone aware of the general problem of police killings of black men, one killing after another, not in massacres, but in a grisly series. The agitations had made everyone aware of the furious resentment this was arousing in black communities everywhere. But Black Lives Matter had also tried to make the argument that police killings represent a larger underlying cruelty in American life, something built into the foundations of society. And, until that moment, the agitations had not been able to overcome a couple of widely shared objections to that last and most radical of contentions.

There was the objection that, however ghastly the series of killings had proved to be, the series did not constitute a unified wave, and nothing in particular was responsible for it. Ijeoma Oluo is a journalist in Seattle, whose book *So You Want to Talk About Race* is one of several new popular tracts on these themes. And she puts it this way:

> In this individualist nation we like to believe that
> systemic racism doesn't exist. We like to believe that if
> there are racist cops, they are individual bad eggs acting
> on their own. And with this belief, we are forced to
> prove that each individual encounter with the police is
> definitively racist or it is tossed out completely as mere

coincidence. And so, instead of a system imbued with the racism and oppression of greater society, instead of a system plagued by unchecked implicit bias, inadequate training, lack of accountability, racist quotas, cultural insensitivity, lack of diversity, and lack of transparency — we are told we have a collection of individuals doing their best to serve and protect outside of a few bad apples acting completely on their own, and there's nothing we can do about it other than address those bad apples once it's been thoroughly proven that the officer in question is indeed a bad apple.

The second objection was the opposite of the first. It conceded Ijeoma Oluo's points about police departments. But it went on to argue that, contrary to her contention, the failings of policework are, in fact, widely understood, and a campaign to address the failings is well underway. Perhaps the campaign has not advanced very far in the retrograde America that still flies the Confederate flag, but in other parts of the country, in the enlightened zones, where cities are liberal, and mayors likewise, and police chiefs are reform-minded, the campaign to modernize the police has been sincere, or mostly, and it has been social-scientifically sophisticated, and it has taken aim at racial biases. And if problems persist, these may amount to a failure of communication — the failure to conduct the kind of face-to-face conversations among reasonable people that President Obama promoted at the White House by having a beer with Professor Henry Louis Gates, Jr., and the police officer who had treated Gates as a burglar on his own doorstep. Minor problems, then — problems calling for articulate presentations of up-to-date civic values from liberal politicians and reform leaders.

The George Floyd Uprising

But the video was devastating to the first objection. And it was devastating to the second. The video shows a peaceful day on the sidewalks of enlightened Minneapolis. George Floyd is on the ground, restrained, surrounded by police officers, and Officer Derek Chauvin plants a confident knee on his neck. The officer looks calm, self-assured, and professional. Three other cops hover behind him, and they, too, seem reasonably calm, the group of them maintaining what appears to be the military discipline of a well-ordered police unit. Apart from Chauvin's knee, nothing alarming appears to be taking place. No gunshots ring in the distance, no commotion rises from the street, no shouts against the police or anyone else — nothing that might panic the cops or enrage them or throw them into confusion. And, in that setting, the video shows the outcome. Floyd moans that he cannot breathe. Someone on the sidewalk tries to tell the oblivious Officer Chauvin that something is wrong. And, for the many millions of people who watched the video, the shocking quality was double or triple.

If even a firecracker had gone off in the distance, the viewers could have concluded that Officer Chauvin was overcome with fear, and his actions might be understandable, though a more skillful cop would have known how to keep his cool. Or, if only Officer Chauvin had looked wild-eyed and upset, the viewers could have concluded that here was a madman. But, no. Chauvin and the other cops, maintaining their unit discipline, plainly show that all was well, from their standpoint. The four of them make no effort to prevent the people on the sidewalk from observing the event. No one seems embarrassed. These are cops who appear to believe themselves to be operating by the book.

And yet, how can they believe such a thing? Everyone who watched that video was obliged to come up with an explana-

78

tion. The obvious one was that, in Minneapolis, the four police officers do not look like rule-breaking rogues because they are not, in fact, breaking rules — not in their own minds, anyway. Yes, they may be going against the advice proffered by their reform-minded department chief and their hapless mayor, the bloodless liberal. But they are conforming to the real-life professional standards of their fellow officers, which are the standards upheld by the police unions everywhere, which are, in turn, the standards upheld by large parts of the country, unto the most national of politicians. "Please don't be too nice," said the president of the United States to the police officers of Long Island, New York, in July 2017, with specific advice to take people under arrest and bang their heads as they are shoved into police vehicles. Why, then, should the four cops in Minneapolis have considered themselves rogues? *That* was the revelation in the video of George Floyd's death.

And a large public drew large conclusions. To draw momentous conclusions from a single video shot on the sidewalks of Minneapolis might seem excessive. Yet that is how it is with the historic moments of overnight political conversion. There were four million slaves in 1854, but the arrest of a single one proved to be the incendiary event. In the case of George Floyd, the single video sufficed for a substantial public to conclude that, over the years, the public had been lied to about the complexities of policing; had been lied to about bad apples in uniform; had been lied to about the need for patience and the slow workings of the law. The public had been lied to by conservatives, who had denied the existence of a systemic racism; and had been lied to by liberals, who had insisted that systemic racism was being systematically addressed. Or worse, a large public concluded that it had been lied to about the state of social progress generally in America, in regard to race — not just in regard to policing relations but in regard to practically everything, one institution after another. Still worse, a great many people concluded, in the American style, or perhaps the Protestant style, that, upon consideration, they themselves had been terribly complicit, and, in allowing themselves to be deceived by the police and the conservatives and the liberals, they had abandoned the black protesters, and they had allowed the police violence and the larger pattern of racial oppression to persist. Those were solemn conclusions, and they were arrived at in the most solemn of fashions, by gazing at a man as he passes from life to death.

So masses of people marched in the streets to rectify the social wrong. But they marched also to rectify the wrong nature of their own relation to society. This of course raises the question of what would be the right nature — which happens to be the topic of the new and extraordinarily popular literature of American antiracism.

II

The literary work that shaped the mass conversion to antiracism in 1854 was *Uncle Tom's Cabin*, by Harriet Beecher Stowe, from 1852 — which was much despised by James Baldwin a century later for its demeaning portrait of the very people it was meant to support. The book that, more than any other, shaped the mass conversion in 1965 was *Dark Ghetto*, a sociological study from that same year, by Kenneth B. Clark — which was much despised at the time by Albert Murray, the author of *The Omni-Americans*, for what he, too, took to be a demeaning portrait of the very people it was meant to support. The book that, more than any other, has shaped the mass conversion of our own moment is *Between the World and Me*, by Ta-Nehisi Coates, from 2015 — which was written in homage to Baldwin, and yet is bound to make us wonder what Murray would have thought, if he had lived another few years.

Between the World and Me has shaped events because, in a stroke of genius, Coates came up with the three main and heartrending tropes of the modern crisis behind the antiracist uprising — to wit, "the talk;" the killing by the police of a young black man; and the young man's inconsolable mother. The form of the book is a frank and emotional letter from Coates to his young son, which amounts to "the talk," advising the son on the realities of black life in a hostile white America. The killing that takes place is of an admirable young black man from Coates' social circle at college. The inconsolable mother is the young man's mother, whom Coates goes to visit. In laying out these elements, Coates has supplied a vocabulary for speaking about the realities of modern police violence against blacks, which is a language of family life: an intimate language, Baldwinesque and not sociological, a language of family grit and grief.

Then again, he speaks insistently and emotionally but also somewhat abstractly about the black body and its vulnerability — not the beauty of the black body, but, instead, its mortifications, considered historically. These are the physical horrors of slavery long ago, conceived as horrors of an ever-present era, as experienced by himself as a young boy growing up in the rough neighborhoods of Baltimore, or as a child subjected to what appear to have been his father's disciplinary beatings. This aspect of the book, the contemplation of the body and its mortifications, amounts, in effect, to a theory of America. Or rather, it amounts to a counter-theory, offered in opposition to the doctrine that he describes as the capital-D "Dream." The Dream, as he lays it out, is the American idea that is celebrated by white people at Memorial Day barbecues. Coates never

81

specifies the fundamentals of the idea, but plainly he means the notion that, in its simple-minded version, regards America as an already perfect expression of the democratic ideal, a few marginal failings aside. Or he means the notion that, in a more sophisticated way, regards 1776 as the American origin, and regards America's history as the never-ending struggle, ever-progressive and ever-victorious, a few setbacks aside, to bring 1776 to full fruition. A theory of history, in short.

His counter-theory, by contrast, postulates that, from the very start, America has been built on the plundering of the black body, and the plundering has never come to an end. This is an expressive idea. It scatters the dark shadow of the past over every terrible thing that happens in the present, which is never wrong to do, if the proportions are guarded. Yet Coates adopts an odd posture toward his own idea, such that, in one way or another, he ends up miniaturizing certain parts of his story. When he conjures the Dream, the precise scene that he brings to life is of little blond boys playing with toy trucks and baseball cards at the Memorial Day barbecue, as if *this* were the spectacle that arouses his resentment. When he conjures his own adult experience with the historic mortifications, he describes a disagreeable altercation on an escalator on the Upper West Side of Manhattan, where a white lady treats him and his toddler son in a tone of haughty disdain, and is seconded by a white man, and the temperature rises — as if *this* were the legacy of the horrors of long ago.

The incident on the escalator comprises a climax of sorts in *Between the World and Me* — the moment when Coates himself, together with his toddler, has to confront the reality of American racism. And yet the incident is inherently ambiguous. He gives us no precise reason to share his assumption that the woman and the man are angry at him on a racist basis — an observation made by Thomas Chatterton Williams in his discussion of the scene in his own book, *Self-Portrait in Black and White*. Williams wonders even if Coates' anger at the lady's haughtiness might not have alarmed the lady and the man, with misunderstandings of every kind likely to have resulted — an easy thing to imagine in a town like New York, where sidewalk incidents happen all the time, and whites presume their own liberal innocence, and blacks do not, and correct interpretations are not always obvious. The ambiguity of the scene amounts to yet another miniaturization. The miniaturized portraits are, of course, deliberate. They allow Coates to express the contained anger of a man who, in other circumstances, would be reliably sweet-tempered.

He does present himself as a loving man — as a father, of course (which confers a genuine tenderness on the book), but also in regard to African American life as a whole. And yet something about this, too, his love for black America, ends up miniaturized. His principal narrative of African America is a portrait of Howard University from his own school-days, presented as an idyllic place, intellectually stimulating, pleasant, socially marvelous, affection-inspiring and filled with family meaning, too, given that his father, the Black Panther, had worked there as a research librarian — an ideal school, in sum, designed to generate graduates such as himself, therefore a splendid achievement of black America. But the argument that he makes about the ever-present universe of American slavery and the eternal vulnerability of the black body makes it seem as if, over the centuries, black America has achieved nothing at all, outside of music, perhaps, to which he devotes a handful of words. It is a picture of the black helplessness that racist whites like to imagine, supine and eternally defeated. This was Albert Murray's objection to the black

83

protest literature of the 1960s, with its emphasis on victim-hood — the literature that was unable to see or acknowledge that, in the face of everything, black America has contributed from the very start to what Coates disparages as the Dream, or what Murray extolls as the Omni-America, which is the mulatto civilization that, in spite of every racial mythology, has always been white, black, and American Indian all at once.

I do not mean to suggest that Coates' bitterness is inauthentic. Frank B. Wilderson III is twenty years older than Coates and, with his degrees from Dartmouth, Columbia, and Berkeley, is today the chair of the African-American Studies department at the University of California Irvine. His recent book, *Afropessimism*, conjures a similar landscape of anger and bitterness, as if in confirmation of Coates, except in a version that is far more volcanic, or perhaps hysterical. Coates during his college years in the 1990s was, as he explains, an adept of Malcolm X, but then outgrew the exotic trappings of Malcolm's doctrine, without rejecting the influence entirely. Wilderson, during his own youth in the 1970s, was a "revolutionary communist," in an acutely intellectual, Third Worldist fashion. He was an admirer of the Black Liberation Army, which was the guerrilla tendency that emerged from Eldridge Cleaver's faction of the Black Panthers on the West Coast (and from City College in New York). The great inspiring global example of revolutionary resistance, in Wilderson's eyes, was the Popular Front for the Liberation of Palestine, given its uncompromising struggle against the Zionist state — which, being a man of ideologies, he imagined (and evidently still imagines) to be a white European settler colony. And the Black Liberation Army, in his view, was the PFLP's American counterpart.

Revolutionary communism left him feeling betrayed,

however, or perhaps singed — damaged and enraged not by his black comrades in the United States, but by everyone else: by the whites of the revolutionary communist movement (namely, the Weather Underground, who gave up the struggle and returned to their lives of white privilege), and even more so by the non-blacks "of color." He felt especially betrayed by the Palestinians. He was horrified to discover that a Palestinian friend in his hometown of Minneapolis, who despised Israelis, reserved a particular contempt for Israel's Ethiopian Jews. And, in despair at the notion that even Palestinians, the vanguard of the worldwide vanguard, might be racist against blacks, Wilderson turned away from revolutionary Marxism, and he distilled his objections and complaints into a doctrine of his own — it *is* a doctrine, though a very peculiar one — which he calls Afropessimism.

The doctrine is a racialized species of post-Marxism. Wilderson thinks that, instead of the world being riven by Marx's economic class conflict, or by the imperialist versus anti-imperialist conflict of Marxism in its Third Worldist version, it is riven by the conflict between the non-blacks and the blacks. The non-blacks regard themselves as the capital-H Human race, and they do so by seeing in the blacks a sub-human race of slaves. And the non-blacks cannot give up this belief because, if they did so, they would lose their concept of themselves as the Human race. Nor is there any solution to this problem, apart from the "end of the world," or an apocalypse. The idea is fundamentally a variant of certain twentieth-century theories about the Jews — e.g., Freud's notion that hatred of the Jews supplies the necessary, though unstated, foundation for the Christian concept of universal love. Freud's theory is not especially expressive, though. Wilderson's theory expresses. It vents. But the venting is not

The George Floyd Uprising

meant to serve a constructive purpose. Wilderson tells us that he studied under Edward Said at Columbia University, and he was greatly influenced. He admired Said's resolute refusal to accept the existence of a Jewish state in any form. But Said's revolutionary aspiration, in conformity with the Popular Front for the Liberation of Palestine, was to replace the Jewish state with something else. Wilderson's Afropessimism entertains no such aspirations. It is "a looter's creed," in his candid phrase — meaning, a lashing out, intellectually violent, without any sort of positive application. Positive applications are inconceivable because the non-black hatred of blacks is unreformable.

Still, he does intend Afropessimism to be a demystifier, and in this regard his doctrine seems to me distinctly useful. The doctrine beams a clarifying light on the reigning dogma on the American left just now, which is intersectionalism — a dogma that is invoked by one author after another in the antiracist literature, with expressions of gratitude for how illuminating it is, and how comforting it is. Intersectionalism is a version of the belief, rooted in Marx, that a single all-encompassing oppression underlies the sufferings of the world. Marx considered the all-encompassing oppression to be capitalism. But intersectionalism considers the all-encompassing oppression to be bigotry and its consequences — the bigotry that takes a hundred forms, which are racism, misogyny, homophobia, and so forth, splintering into ever smaller subsets. Intersectionalism considers that various subsets of the all-encompassing oppression, being aspects of the larger thing, can be usefully measured and weighed in relation to one another. And the measuring and weighing should allow the victims of the many different oppressions to recognize one another, to identify with one another, and to establish the universal solidarity of the oppressed that can bring about a better world.

But Wilderson's Afropessismism argues that, on the contrary, the oppression of blacks is not, in fact, a variation of some larger terrible thing. And it is not comparable to other oppressions. The oppression of blacks has special qualities of its own, different from all other oppressions. He puts this hyperbolically, as is his wont, by describing the bigotry against blacks as the *"essential"* oppression, not just in the United States — though it ought to be obvious that, whether it is put hyperbolically or not, the oppression of blacks throughout American history does have, in fact, special qualities. On this point he is right. He is committed to his hyperbole, however, and it leads to an added turn in his argument. He contemplates, as an exercise in abstract analysis, the situation of a black man who rapes a white woman. In his view, the black man ought to be regarded as more oppressed than his own victim. The man may have more force, but he has less power. He is the victim of the "essential" oppression, and she is not, which makes his victimhood deeper. Wilderson's purpose in laying out this argument is to shock us into recognizing how profound black oppression is.

Only, the argument leads me to a different recognition. I would think that, if black oppression cannot be likened to other oppressions — if a special quality renders the black oppression unique — the whole logic of intersectionalism collapses. For if the black oppression is sui generis, why shouldn't other oppressions likewise be regarded as sui generis? The oppression experienced by the victims of rape, for instance — why shouldn't that, too, be regarded as sui generis? Why not say that many kinds of oppressions are genuinely terrible, and there is no point in trying to establish a system for comparing and ranking the horrible things that people undergo? There might even be a virtue in declining to compare and rank one oppression with another. A main result of comparing and ranking the various oppressions is, after all, to flatten the individual experience of each, which softens the terribleness of the oppression — an especially misguided thing to do in regard to the racial history of the United States.

It may be a mistake to argue with Frank Wilderson III too much. He is a brilliant man with a literary gift that is only somewhat undone by a graduate-school enthusiasm for critical theory. But, at the same time, a cloud of mental instability or imbalance drifts across his book. He explains in his opening pages that his shock at discovering a casual anti-black racism among Palestinians induced in him a serious nervous breakdown, and he appears never to have fully recovered. He describes the sinister persecution that he believes he and his lover underwent at the hands of the FBI, and his account hints of paranoia. Then, too, it is striking how insistently he goes about miniaturizing his own picture of the anti-black racism against blacks that he believes to be inherent in the whole of civilization. The great traumatic experience of Wilderson's childhood appears to have been the moment when the mother of a white friend persisted in asking him, "How does it feel to be a Negro?"

He is traumatized by the poor reception of his incendiary ideas at an academic conference in Berlin, not just among the straight white males whose essence it is to be oppressive, but among the women and non-whites whose intersectional essences ought to have impelled in them a solidarity with his oppressed-of-the-oppressed outlook. Especially traumatic for him is a Chinese woman at the scholarly conference, who, in spite of being multi-intersectionally oppressed, fails to see the persuasive force of his ideas. Then, too, a fight that turns

88

nasty with a white woman in the upstairs apartment back in Minneapolis seems to him a recursion to the social relations of slavery times. The man has no skin. Every slight is a return to the Middle Passage. His book resembles Ta-Nehisi Coates' in this respect yet again, except with a pop-eyed excess. The shadow of slavery times darkens even his private domestic satisfactions. He appears to regard his white wife as, in some manner, his slave master, though he seems not to hold this against her. It is positively a relief to learn from his book that, during his career as communist revolutionary, he went to South Africa to participate in the revolution (by smuggling weapons, while working as a human-rights activist for Amnesty International and Human Rights Watch), but had to flee the country because he was put on a list of "ultra left ists" to be "neutralized" by the circle around Nelson Mandela himself — a level-headed person, at last!

But it is dismaying also to notice that, for all his efforts to identify anti-black racism and to rail against it, the whole effect of Wilderson's Afropessimism is to achieve something disagreeably paradoxical. He means to make a forward leap beyond Marx, and he ends up making a backward leap to the era, a generation before Marx, when Hegel felt entitled to write the black race out of capital-H History. Hegel believed that black Africa, where slavery was practiced, existed outside of the workings of historical development that functioned everywhere else — outside of the human struggles that make for civilization and progress. Hegel was, of course, hopelessly ignorant of black life. Wilderson is not, and, even so, he has talked himself into reproducing the error. Wilderson, too, believes that blacks live outside of History. It is because blacks have never ceased to be the slaves that Hegel imagined them permanently to be. Wilderson explains: "for the Slave, historical 'time' is not possible." Here is the meaning of the bitterness that Wilderson expresses wildly, and that Coates expresses not wildly. It is more than a denial of the black achievement in America, along the lines that exasperated Murray half a century ago. It is a denial, in effect, of tragedy, which exists only where there is choice, which is to say, where there is history. It is an embrace of the merely pitiful, where there is no choice, but only suffering — an embrace of the pitiful in, at least, the realm of rhetoric, where it is poignant (these are literary men), but lifeless.

Ibram X. Kendi appears, at first glance, to offer a more satisfactory way of thinking in his two books on American racism, *Stamped from the Beginning: The Definitive History of Racist Ideas in America*, which runs almost six hundred pages, as befits its topic, and the much shorter *How To Be an Antiracist,* which distills his argument (and does so in the autobiographical vein that characterizes all of the current books on American racism). Kendi does believe in history. He thinks of the history of racism as a dialectical development instead of a single despairing story of non-progress, as in Wilderson's despairing rejection of historical time, or a single story of ever-victorious progress, as in the naive celebration of the sunny American "Dream." He observes that racist ideas have a history, and so do antiracist ideas, and the two sets of ideas have been in complicated conflict for centuries. He also observes that black people can be racist and white people can be antiracist. He cites the example of the antislavery American white Quakers of the eighteenth century. He is the anti-Wilderson: he knows that the history of ideas about race and the history of races are not the same.

His fundamental approach is, in short, admirably subtle. Still, he feels the allure of simplifying definitions. Thus: "A racist idea is any idea that suggests one racial group is inferior or superior to another racial group in any way." And, with this formula established, he sets up a structure of possible ideas about blacks in America, which turn out to be three. These are: (a) the "segregationist" idea, which holds that blacks are hopelessly inferior; (b) the "assimilationist" idea, which holds that blacks do exhibit an inferiority in some regard, but, by assimilating to white culture, can overcome it; and (c) the "antiracist" idea, which holds that no racial group is either superior or inferior to any other "in any way." His definitions establish what he calls the "duality of racist and antiracist." And with his definitions, three-part divisions, and dualities in hand, he goes roaming across the American centuries, seeking to label each new person or doctrine either as a species of racist, whether "segregationist" or "assimilationist," or else as a forthright "antiracist."

In *How to Be an Antiracist*, he recalls a high school speech-contest oration that he delivered to a mostly black audience in Virginia twenty years ago, criticizing in a spirit of uplift various aspects of African-American life — which, at the time, seemed to him a great triumph of his young life. In retrospect, though, sharpened by his analytic duality of racist and antiracist, he reflects that, in criticizing African Americans, his high-school self had fallen into the "assimilationist" trap. He had ended up fortifying the white belief in black inferiority — which is to say he had therefore delivered a racist speech! Is he fair to himself in arriving at such a harsh and humiliating judgment? In those days he attended Stonewall Jackson High School in Manassas, and, though he does not dwell over how horrible is such a name, it is easy to

91

concede that, under the shadow of the old Confederacy, a speech criticizing any aspect whatsoever of black life might, in fact, seem humiliating to recall. On the other hand, if every commentary on racial themes is going to be summoned to a high-school tribunal of racist-versus-antiracist, the spirit of nuance, which is inseparable from the spirit of truth, might have a hard time surviving.

Kendi turns from his own mortifying student oration to the writings of W.E.B. Du Bois. He recalls Du Bois' famous "double consciousness" in *The Souls of Black Folk*, which reflected a desire "to be both a Negro and an American." In Kendi's reasoning, an "American" must be white. But this can only mean, as per his definitions, that W.E. B. Du Bois was — the conclusion is unavoidable — a racist, in the "assimila-tionist" version. Du Bois was a black man who wished no longer to be entirely black. Or worse, Du Bois wanted to rescue the African Americans as a whole from their "relic of barbarism" — a racist phrase, in Kendi's estimation — by having the African-Americans assimilate into the white majority culture. Du Bois' intention, in short, was to inflict his own racism on everyone else. Such is the ruling of the high-school tribunal.

It is an analytical disaster. The real Du Bois was, to the contrary, a master of complexity, who understood that complexity was the black fate in America. Du Bois did not want to become white, nor did he want to make the black popula-tion as a whole into whiteness. He wanted black Americans to claim what was theirs, which was the reality of being black and, at the same time, the reality of being American, a very great thing, which was likewise theirs. He knew that personal identity is not a stable or biological fact: it is a fluidity, created by struggle and amalgamation, which is the meaning, rooted in Hegel's *Phenomenology of Mind*, of "double consciousness." A man compromised by "assimilationist" impulses? No, one of the most eloquent and profound enemies of racism that America has ever produced.

Kendi is confident of his dualities and definitions. He is profligate with them, in dialectical pairings: "Cultural racist: one who is creating a cultural standard and imposing a cultural hierarchy among racial groups." Versus: "Cultural antiracist: One who is rejecting cultural standards and equalizing cultural differences among racial groups." And, with his motor running, one distinguished head after another falls beneath his blade. He recalls Jesse Jackson's condemnation, back in the 1990s, of the campaign to teach what was called Ebonics, or black dialect, to black students. "It's teaching down to our children," said Jackson, which strikes Kendi as another example of "assimilationist" error. But Kendi does not seem to recognize who Jesse Jackson is. In his prime, Jesse Jackson was arguably the greatest political orator in America, after the assassination of King — the greatest not necessarily in what he said, which ran the gamut over the years, but in the magnificent way he said it. And the grandeurs of Jackson's oratorical technique rested on the grandeurs of the black church ministry, which rest on, in turn, the heritage of the English language at its most majestic, which means the seventeenth century and the King James Bible. In condemning the promotion of Ebonics, Jackson was not attacking black culture. He was seeking to protect black culture at its loftiest, as represented by his own virtuosity at the pulpit and the podium — or so it seems to me.

But then, Kendi does not like the hierarchical implications of a word like "lofty." Naturally he disapproves of the critics of hip hop. He singles out John McWhorter, who has seen in hip

93

hop "the stereotypes that long hindered blacks," but he must also have in mind critics like the late Stanley Crouch, who condemned hip hop on a larger basis, in order to defend the musical apotheosis that Crouch identified with Duke Ellington — condemned hip hop, that is, in order to defend the loftiness of black culture in yet another realm. In this fashion, Kendi's dualities of racist and antiracist turn full circle, and Ibram X. Kendi, the scourge of racism, ends up, on one page or another, the scourge of entire zones — philosophy, oratory, jazz — of black America's greatest achievements.

His ostensible purpose is to help good-hearted people rectify their thinking. It is a self-improvement project, addressed to earnest readers who wish to purge their imaginations of racist thoughts, in favor of antiracist thoughts. This sort of self-improvement is, of course, a fad of the moment. An early example was *Race Talk and the Conspiracy of Silence: Understanding and Facilitating Difficult Dialogues on Race,* by the psychologist Derald Wing Sue, from 2015, a serious book with its share of genuine insights into microaggressions and other features of the awkward conversations that Americans do have on topics of race. *White Fragility: Why It's So Hard for White People to Talk About Racism*, by Robin DiAngelo, a diversity coach, is perhaps the best-known of these books — a slightly alarming book because its reliance on identity-politics analyses has the look of the right-wing race theoreticians of a century ago, except in a well-intentioned version. Ijeoma Oluo's *So You Want to Talk About Race*, with its breezy air, is the most charming of the new books, though perhaps not on every page. But Kendi's version is the most ambitious, and the most curious.

He does not actually believe in the possibilities of personal rectification — not, at least, as a product of education or moral suasion. In *Stamped from the Beginning,* he observes that "sacrifice, uplift, persuasion and education have not eradicated and will not eradicate racist ideas, let alone racist policies." The battle of ideas does not mean a thing, and racists will not give up their racism. The people in power in the United States have an interest in maintaining racism, and they will not give it up. "Power will never self-sacrifice away from its self-interest. Power cannot be persuaded away from its self-interest. Power cannot be educated away from its self-interest." Instead, the antiracists must force the people in power to take the right steps. But mostly the antiracists must find their own way, in his phrase, of "seizing power." The phrase pleases Kendi. "Protesting against racist power and succeeding can never be mistaken for seizing power," he says. "Any effective solution to eradicating American racism" — he means any effective method for eradicating it — "must involve Americans committed to antiracist policies seizing and maintaining power over institutions, neighborhoods, countries, states, nations — the world." And then, having seized power, the antiracists will be able to impose their ideas on the powerless.

This attitude toward the seizure of power is known, in the old-fashioned leftwing vocabulary, as putschism. But as everyone has lately been able to see, there is nothing old-fashioned about it. The manifesto that was signed not long ago by hundreds of scholars at Princeton University, calling for the university administration to ferret out racist ideas among the professors, was accepted, and the university announced its intention to set up an official mechanism for investigating and suppressing professorial error. Can this really be so? It is so, and not just at Princeton. The controversies over "cancel culture" are controversies, ultimately, over the putschist instinct of crowds who regard themselves as antiracist (or as progressive in some other way) and wish to dispense with

The George Floyd Uprising

the inconveniences of argument and persuasion, in favor of getting some disfavored person fired or otherwise shut up. And the controversies have spread from the universities to the arts organizations and the press. I would think that anyone who admires Kendi's argument for seizing power could only be delighted by the successful staffers' campaign at the *New York Times* to fire its eminently liberal op-ed editor, whose error was to adhere to the *Times* tradition of publishing contrarian right-wing op-eds from time to time — though other people may suppose that putsches in the newsroom and in the universities amount to one more destructive undertow in the larger constructive antiracist wave.

A difficulty with putschism, in any case, has always been that putsch begets putsch, and the hard-liners will eventually set out to overthrow their wimpier comrades, and the reactionaries will set out to overthrow the lot of them; and truth will not be advanced. But apart from the disagreeable impracticality of the putschist proposal, what strikes me is the inadequacy of Kendi's rhetoric to express the immensity and the depth of the American racial situation. It is a dialectical rhetoric, but not an expressive one. It amounts to a college Bolshevism, when what is required is — well, I don't know what is required, except to remark that, when you read Du Bois, you do get a sense of the immensity and the tragedy, and the inner nature of the struggle, and the depth of the yearnings.

Isabel Wilkerson's alternative to this kind of thinking, presented in *Caste: The Origins of Our Discontents*, manages to be lucid and poetic at the same time, perhaps not in every passage, but often enough over the course of her few hundred pages. She wishes to speak principally about social structures, and not as much about ideas. Only, instead of looking at economic classes, which is what people typically think of when they think about social structures, she speaks about social castes, as in India. The caste system in traditional Indian society is a rigid and ancient social structure, which divided and still divides the population into inherited classes, whose members work at certain occupations and not others, and perhaps dress in certain ways, or are physically distinct, or have distinctive names, and are forever stuck in the eternity of their caste status.

There was a vogue in the 1930s and 1940s for social scientists to venture into the scary old American Deep South and, by applying surreptitiously the techniques of anthropology, to look for social structures of that kind in Jim Crow America. Isabel Wilkerson is fascinated by those people — by the anthropologist Allison Davis especially, a pioneering black scholar, to whom she devotes a few enthusiastic pages in her book. She is taken with Davis' insights and those of his colleagues. She sets out to update the insights to our own era. And, in doing so, she comes up with a marvelous insight, though it takes her until her fourth chapter to lay it out. A caste system, as she describes it, is defined by its antiquity. "It resembles a theater play that has been running for a long time, with actors who have inherited roles," she explains, "the people in these roles are not the characters they play, but they have played the roles long enough to incorporate the roles into their very being." They have grown accustomed to the distribution of parts in their play — accustomed to seeing who plays the lead, who plays the hero, who are the supporting actors, who plays the comic sidekick, and who constitute the "undifferentiated chorus." The play and the roles are matters of habit, but they take them to be matters of reality.

She glances at India in search of perspective into caste structures and customs, and, although Indian civilization differs in every possible way from American civilization, she is struck by the American parallels — by the visible similarities between the African-American caste status in the United States, the disdained or reviled bottom of American society, and the status of the lowest caste in India, the Dalits, or untouchables, the disdained or reviled bottom of Indian society. She does seem to be onto something, too. She tells us that, in India, Dalit leaders and intellectuals have been struck by the same parallels, and have recognized the far-away African-Americans as their own counterparts, and have felt an instinctive and sympathetic curiosity. And then, seeking to deepen her perspective, Wilkerson examined a third instance of what she believed to be a caste structure, which was the situation of the Jews under Nazis in Germany.

This seems to me only partly a good idea. There is no question that, in traditional Christian Europe, as well as in the traditional Muslim world, the Jews occupied the position of a marginalized or subordinate caste, with mandated clothing, sundry restrictions, humiliations, and worse. Traditionalism, however, was not the Nazi idea. Still, it is true that, on their way to achieving their non-traditional goal, the Nazis did establish a caste system of sorts, if only as a transitional state, with the Jews subjected to the old ghetto oppressions in an exaggerated form. And some of those measures drew overtly on the Jim Crow precedent in America. Wilkerson reminds us that, in preparation for establishing the Nuremburg Laws for Jews in Germany in 1935, the Nazi leaders undertook a study of American racial laws, the laws against miscegenation, the laws on blood purity, and so forth. And with the American example before them, the Nazis established their Law for the

Protection of German Blood and German Honor and their larger code. She tells us that, in regard to blood purity, the Nazis even felt that America, with its "one drop" mania, had gone too far! — which is not news, but is bound to horrify us, even so.

But she also draws another benefit from making the Nazi comparison, which has to do with the tenor and the intensity of her exposition. The Nazi comparison introduces a note from abroad, and the foreign note allows her to speak a little more freely than do some of the other commentators on the American scene. The foreign note, in this instance, is an uncontested symbol of political evil, and, having invoked it, she feels no need to miniaturize her American conclusions, and no need to introduce into them an aspect of childhood traumas. She does not draw a veil of critical theory over her presentation. Michel Foucault's focus on the body appears to enter into her thinking not at all. Nor does she feel it necessary to toy with mental imbalances and nihilist gestures. Nor does she look for ways to shock anyone, beyond what is inherent to her topic.

She points at the Nazis, and at the American champions of Jim Crow, points at the medical doctors in Germany, and at their medical counterparts in America, who, in the grip of their respective doctrines, felt free to conduct monstrous scientific experiments on victims from the designated inferior race. And any impulse that she may have felt to inhibit her expression or resort to euphemism or indirection disappears at once. In short chapters, one after another, she paints scenes — American scenes, not German ones — of mobs murdering and disfiguring their victims, of policemen coolly executing men accused of hardly anything, of a young boy murdered because of a love-note sent to a girl from the higher caste. She paints tiny quotidian scenes of minor cruelty as well — the black Little Leaguer who is prevented from joining his white teammates in a joyous festivity, or, then again, the Negro League career of Satchel Paige, perhaps baseball's greatest pitcher, who watched his prime years go by without being able to display his skill in the Major Leagues. She does not twist her anger at these things into something understated, or into something crazy. Nor does she redirect her anger at secondary targets — at the white American resistance to discussing these things, or the lack of communication, or the lack of sympathy. Silence and the unspoken are not her principal themes.

Her theme is horror, the thing itself — the murdered victims dangling from the trees. Still, she does get around to addressing the phenomenon of denial and complacency and complicity, and, when she does so, her analytical framework allows her to be quietly ferocious. She reminds us that, apart from leading the Confederate troops in their war against the American republic, Robert E. Lee was a man who personally ordered the torture of his own slaves. He was grotesque. She tells us that, even so, there were, as of 2017, some two hundred thirty memorials to Robert E. Lee in the United States. To underscore her point, she describes in a flat reportorial tone a public hearing in New Orleans on the matter of what to do about a statue of Lee, at which a retired Marine Corps officer spoke: "He stood up and said that Erwin Rommel was a great general, but there are no statues of Rommel in Germany. 'They are ashamed,' he said. 'The question is, why aren't we?'" — which is Isabel Wilkerson's manner of staring her readers in the eye.

It would be possible to go through *Caste* and pick it apart, from the standpoint of social theory. But social theory is not really its theme, even if the anthropologists of the 1930s are

Wilkerson's heroes and their concept of social caste drives her book forward. Mostly the work is an artful scrapbook of various perspectives on the black oppression in America, divided into short sections — on the idea of caste, on the Indian social system, on Indian scholars she has met, on her visits to Germany, on Nazi legal codes, on the horrors of lynching, and still more horrors of lynching, on the severity of Jim Crow laws, on the pattern of police murders of blacks, and, then again, on her own experiences. She recounts any number of vexing or infuriating encounters that she has undergone with people at airports or restaurants, the DEA agents who decide that she is suspicious, the waiter who manages not to serve her table, together with vexing experiences that other black people have had — a distinguished black man mistaken for a bicycle messenger in his own apartment building, a student from Nigeria, whose language is English, praised for being able to speak it.

Certain of these incidents may seem ambiguous, and yet they do add up, such that, even if one or two of the incidents might be viewed in a kinder light by someone else, the pattern is hard to deny. The meaning of the pattern becomes identifiable, too, given the historical scenes that she has described. And yet, although she has every desire to register and express her own fury, and no desire to tamp it down, she has also no desire to drown in it. She looks for reassuring signs of a liberating potential, and she finds them here and there — in the moral progress of the Germans and their reckoning with civic monuments. Barack Obama's presidency strikes her as a not insignificant step forward. As for what came after Obama — well, she concludes the main text of her book with a sentimental anecdote about a surly MAGA-hatted white plumber, unhappy at having to work for a black lady in her leaky basement, who softens up after a while, which suggests the possibility of progress, in spite of everything.

I suppose that hard-bitten readers will figure that Wilkerson goes too far in clinging to some kind of optimism for poor old America. But then, I figure that I have some acquaintance with the potential readership for her book and the several other books that I have just discussed, if only because the readership spent several months in the spring and summer of 2020 marching around my own neighborhood. I can imagine that each of those books is bound to appeal to some of those militant readers, and to disappoint the others. Ta-Nehisi Coates will always be a popular favorite, if only because of his intimate voice, which has an attractive tone regardless of what he happens to be saying. Then again, in the course of the uprising, a carload of gangsters profited from the mayhem to break into a liquor store around the corner from my building and to carry away what they could. And those particular people, if they happen to be book readers, which is entirely possible, may look on Coates with a cold eye, given how lachrymose and virtuous he insists on being. They also won't care for Alicia Garza's California life-story and organizers' tips in *The Purpose of Power*, and they are certainly not going to see anything of interest in the cheerful suggestions to white people in Ijeoma Oluo's *So You Want to Talk About Race*. The gangsters might like Frank Wilderson III's *Afropessimism*, though. Heartily I recommend it to them. Still other people, large numbers of them, will prefer the scholarly dialectics and historical research of Ibram X. Kendi.

And yet, I suspect that among the book-reading protesters, the largest number will prefer, as I do, Isabel Wilkerson and her *Caste* — prefer it because of her emotional honesty and directness, and because of her anger, which somehow ends up angrier than everyone else's among the writers, and, then again, because it is refreshing to find someone with a greater interest in the shape of society than in the marks of interior belief, and still again, because of her streak of optimism. I cannot prove it, but, in my own perception, directness, anger, and a streak of optimism were main qualities that marched in the streets during those months — even if some people were adrift in academic leftism, and other people were looters, and still others rejoiced in singing, "Jesus is the answer / for all the world today." The protesters chanted only a handful of slogans, which testified to the discipline that mostly dominated those enormous marches. Sometimes — not often — they chanted "George! Floyd!" — which was the most moving chant of all: the note of death, which underlay the vast national event. But mostly the protesters chanted "black lives matter" — which was and is a formidable slogan: an angry slogan, plaintive, unanswerable. And somehow "black lives matter" is a slogan flecked with a reform spirit of democratic hopefulness, not *exactly* as in 1854, and not *exactly* as in 1965, and yet, given the different circumstances, *pretty much* as in those other eras, in conformity with the invisible geological structures of the American civilization.

JORIE GRAHAM

Without

It is a warm winter mid-afternoon.
We must understand what happened is
happening. The colossus stands before us with its signature
pre-emptivity. It glints. It illustrates.
At my feet the shadow of the winter-dead bushes wave
their windburnt stalks. Their leaves
cast gem-cut ex-
foliations on the patio-stone—bushfulls of shadow
blossoming—& different-sized
heads—& in them leaves, flowers, shoots, burgeonings—
though when I look up again from their grey chop & slip
what is this winterdead bush
to me. This is how something happens but what.
Inside, the toddlers bend over and tap. They cannot yet
walk or talk. They sit on the floor one in the high chair. They
wait. They tap but make no sound. The screen they peer
down into waiting is
too slow. The trick
won't ever happen
fast enough. They are waiting for their faces to
dissolve, to be replaced by the
quick game.
If you speak to them, they don't look up.
The story doesn't happen fast enough.

The winterdead heads move in a sudden breeze.
The wilderness grows almost giddy with alternatives
on the cold patio. I stand barefoot in it.
I always do this as it
always does this.
It lies on me. Scribbles a summer-scrawl. I watch my
naked feet take on the shadow-blossoming without a trace
of feeling. It feels
good. As long as I see it it feels
like years, invasions, legends—a thing with something at its heart—
it moves the way the living move absent of will—
the wind will define what is happening here—I call
a name out—just to check—
at the one wearing the purple jumpsuit
with the small blue elephant
stitched into
it. The young
of the elephant starve because the matriarch
is killed before it can be passed on—where water is, where safe passage,
how
to forage, how remember, how mourn. But I
was talking about the logo.
If you try to rebuild the world you will go crazy.
Come outside,
come out take off your shoes.
What did you do when the world was ending.
Before the collapse.

In the lull.
They look down into the screen. I can hear
a towee make two notes then stop. Can hear, further off,
a woodpecker search the hollow. *Tap tap.* A silence
which goes in way too deep
filling this valley
I think.
I had not heard it till
a minute ago.
Tap tap. Seeking the emptiness. What breeds in it. The festering.
The nourishment.
The whole valley echoes. *Tap.*
And a single-engine plane now, like a blender.
When it goes by the sky is much smoother.
And the brook running through when wind dies down.
There it is.

We Refused

amputation. Above the
knee. You
r so cold. Winter
light moves up

your neck to yr
lips. For the duration of
this song to u
mother the cold

light moves from yr
lips to yr new
permanently
shut eyes. You

can't rave any
more, slapping
fury over the countdown of
minutes, u can't force yr

quip in. The hills
where the sun's heading
maintain their dead
rest. No wind. No rain. The new

wrong temps in-
filtrate the too-dry
grove, each stiffly curling silvery
leaf—all up

the slopes. All gleams
momentarily.
Each weed at
the foot adds its

quick rill of
shimmering. Then off
it goes. The in-
candescent touches it, then

off it goes.
All afternoon day will do
this. Touching,
taking each thing up—no

acceleration.
Dry. Cold. Here
mother is when it reaches
yr eyes, the instant when it

covers yr
lids, curved to catch all
brilliance, nothing
wasted, carved, firm,

while whatever

is behind them,

mind-light, goes.

Maybe it will
rain again
the glittering says,
but until then I

will imitate the
sheen of
nourishment, of plenty, it says, I
will be yr water,

yr rivulet of

likewater—while I, I, out here,

bless you with
this gorgeous
uselessness
mother, this turning

of the planet onto
yr eyes that refuse
the visible now & ever
again....

We kept u
as long as we
cld whole.
I have no idea

what this realm is

but it is ours,

and as long as u
are stuck in
appearance I
wish for the

wind-glitter
to come each day once
to where you lie
and wash you

clean. Losing
information yr gleaming
shut lids light
the end of the whole

of this day

again. Let it

happen again.

FOUAD AJAMI

The Story of Dalal

When the mighty men came back from faraway places, they were strangers in their own homes. They were catered to and kept in the dark. At some point the fathers had to be brought in, implicated if you will, in the deeds of their sons and their daughters, but until that day dawned, until a daughter's transgressions became too public a matter to be ignored, or a son's ways could no longer be indulged, the men were pampered and left ignorant. In the dark hours, when a reckoning could no longer be avoided, when the code of the place had been stretched to the breaking point, the women had to do things of great cruelty. It was their burden, their task.

"She is the sister of men" was the highest compliment paid a woman who had to keep the world intact. To the women fell the task of smuggling diamonds from Sierra Leone because the skilled man of affairs who insisted that the high officials of the customs office were in his back pocket had gotten himself deported out of the country. The women were the ones who kept the constituents of a member of Parliament from finally having it out with him. They were the ones who prepared their sons for the duel and who stiffened their backs, reminded them of the hidden defects and capricious ways of their fathers. And it was their responsibility, of course, to keep the daughters in line. It was but a short distance from the daughter's conduct, after all, to the mother herself. Better grieve for a daughter than play havoc with the order of things. This is the way things were understood here.

It happened among us that a woman of radiant strength had to "do something" about one of our daughters. The daughter's indiscretions had become too much to bear. The pompous and dangerous head of the household had signaled that his patience was running out. The sturdy woman would do the task that was hers to do. Dalal was taken to her father's village for burial. The young woman, it was announced, had committed suicide. But it was commonly known that her mother had struck. It had about it an air of inevitability. Dalal had rejected all offers of help and punctured all the pretenses of her people's code. She had taken a step into a world she could not understand, and she had not known where to draw the line. The evasions and the consolations of the old world, the world of her mother and her aunts, were denied her, but the new ways were not yet internalized by the young woman, who had just begun to see the world on the other side of the prohibitions.

Dalal had been given the best of what a generation on the make thought their children should be given. Parents who toiled in Africa made possible boarding schools, a new prosperity, a new freedom, less encumbered and burdened by inherited ways of seeing and encountering things. The fears of the old world, the need to "walk by the wall" and to "kiss the hand that you cannot confront," the fear of the unknown and of the alien, the need to placate and to conceal — from all this the young woman seemed released. The limits that had defined the world of her mother and her aunts had irretrievably collapsed, and with their collapse it was hard to distinguish the permissible from the impermissible.

Dalal had ventured into the world on the other side of the divide; she was the first of her kin to venture beyond the line of the familiar sounds and customs. She developed a sudden and total disdain for the ways of her elders, for their tales, for their dire warnings. They, in turn, were unable to explain how the young woman should juggle the two worlds on the margins of which she had been placed. There came a time when she began to complain about the women from the village, the grandmothers and great-aunts who came visiting and who stayed at her home. She complained about their tattoos, about their wrinkled and toothless faces, about their prayers and the ablutions that preceded them. Above all, she complained of the smell that clung to the old women: she believed that they came with a special smell. And so she recoiled when they approached her and wanted to kiss her and wish her a life of honor and rectitude in the home of a decent God-fearing man. Yes, Dalal, if you go about doing what is asked of you, if you follow the straight path, if you remain untarnished and your reputation remains unblemished, happiness will come your way, and you will go from the home of your father to the home of your husband, an honored woman in whose reputation and whose conduct your father and brothers can take pride. No other man could humble your family by having his way with you. No ill-wisher could point to you whenever men and women sought to devour the reputations of others.

A relative of Dalal prided herself on the fact that she had been the first to detect early signs of trouble. The world here came in very small ways and expressions. The unwashed relatives from the village noted that Dalal did not invite relatives and friends to join a meal in the way that such invitations should be extended. Dalal would only offer a single invitation. And when the guest insisted that he or she had just eaten, she always took them at their word and left them to eye the food. In the protocol of the villagers you had to extent endless invitations and drag the guest to the table. Then you watched the guests who had "just eaten" stuff themselves with abandon. But the sophisticated young woman who had broken with her world would not play the game.

Nor would she willingly join, it was noted in retrospect, her mother and her mother's friends and guests when she was called to do so. In those sessions, young women learned the ways of their elders and the ways of the world. When she was forced to participate, Dalal was never fully there. She would not engage in the sonorous language and its clichés, she would not play along. When a visiting friend of her mother told her that Dalal and her son Shawki would make an ideal couple, Dalal had no qualms about saying that Shawki was a buffoon, that she had no interest in him whatsoever, that she would not be traded over coffee between two women from an obsolete generation.

A strange kind of honesty made Dalal see the hypocrisies of her elders' world. She began to view their deeds with new eyes, and gradually she began to judge. And because she did, she made her elders self-conscious. In her presence, her tough mother and aunts would at times squirm, and animated discussions would often come to an end whenever she walked in.

But Dalal knew many things that they thought had eluded her. She tired of hearing pieties that were betrayed in daily practice. She had seen through the falsities of her elders. A few years before the trouble began, while still a young girl, Dalal had been used as an alibi for many indiscretions by the older women in her life. She recalled the record of each of the virtuous women who later came to lecture her about her own behavior. She laughed at the pretensions of the cuckolded husbands who knew perfectly well what was going on but preferred to look the other way.

Dalal had seen her pretentious paternal uncle Abu Hassan pass himself off as a man of the world, proudly displaying his women, letting the word out that he had finally seduced the voluptuous Leila and beaten out the competition. She then set this alongside what she knew of Abu Hassan's wife. Fair-skinned and vain, sure of her beauty and more sure of the prerogatives of her new money, Abu Hassan's wife exercised her own options as well. Two or three young men were in the wings, and it was rumored that they were being kept and provided for by the lady herself. Abu Hassan, Dalal knew, was both a rooster and a cuckold. In his own code, of course, he was a hunter and victorious. And in the pronouncements of his wife, the lady was queen in her house, a virtuous woman, cleaner than the ways of the cynical city.

Dalal's angle of vision enabled her to see the whole thing. Thus, when the virtuous woman said that she had spotted Dalal coming out of one of the furnished apartments on Hamra Street, Dalal recited what she knew of the other woman's comings and goings. When given a chance to deny what she had been charged with, Dalal refused. She declined to participate in the charade and the theater that was Lebanese honor. Early marriage suggested itself as a remedy. A man, it was believed, could rein in this kind of passion. Dalal would have her own home, shoulder new responsibilities, and the storm would blow over. She could then begin to make her own discreet trips to the tailor and offer the excuses and the evasions of other women of honor and responsibility. A smug official of her father's generation was the man recruited to cap the volcano. Dalal's mother insisted that the man was Dalal's own choice, that it was an affair of the heart.

A respectable dowry was given to the unlikely couple. That was what money made in Africa was supposed to do — schools for the boys, dowries for the girls. All prayed that the young woman's story was over. The determined mother had pulled it off. Dalal had walked from the home of her father to the home of her husband.

But the hopes turned out to be short-lived. As the young woman explained it, surely she deserved something other than what she got. The man in her life was a man of reasonable distinction. He had studied on his own and risen in the bureau-cracy. But like her parents, Ali was a squatter in Beirut. He had about him the kind of clumsiness that Dalal's generation was so fond of deriding and so quick to see in a man's speech, in the kind of tie he wore, in the way he shook hands. Ali was doomed in the young woman's eyes: he spoke the Shia dialect of the south. His French was not refined enough. His pronunciation amused the young woman who had learned French properly. That mighty badge of distinction, the French "r," never tripped off his tongue the way it should have.

This was a world of mimic men. A dominant culture from afar, its acquisition and its display, its word and its jokes, were what set people apart from one another, what gave some of them a claim to power and self-worth. French pronunciation gave away the origin of men and women, the "age" of money in a particular household: new money spoke French in one way, old money in quite another way. Boys who learned it under the husk tree — or was it the oak tree? — as Ali proudly proclaimed to have done, had no chance of passing themselves off as sophisticated men of a very demanding place.

The young Tolstoy, who grew up in a culture that borrowed the trappings and the language of France for its court and its gentry and its salons, divided the social world into two principal categories: *comme il faut* and *comme il ne faut pas.* Tolstoy's *comme il faut* consisted "first and foremost in having an excellent knowledge of the French tongue, especially pronunciation. Anyone who spoke French with a bad accent at once aroused my dislike. 'Why do you try to talk like us when you do not know how?' I mentally inquired with biting ironies."

Dalal's husband was definitely *comme il ne faut pas.* He knew nothing of the ups and downs of the relationship between Jacques Charrier and Brigitte Bardot. He was not familiar with the songs of Charles Aznavour and Sasha Distel. He told what for his wife and her companions were dreadfully boring stories about his triumphs in the bureaucracy, how this or that political boss needed his help and his patronage, how he had clashed with the minister and how the cabinet member had backed down because of his own superior knowledge and judgment. And he endlessly recited the familiar tale of how he had come into Beirut a quarter-century ago, how he had studied by the light of a kerosene lamp, how he had been one of the very first Shia boys from his world to graduate from the Lebanese University, how vain city boys taunted him about his village and his past, about the idiom and the twang of the countryside.

The man of position had achieved all he could have hoped to achieve. But none of it mattered to the irreverent young woman by his side. That kind of tale would have filled the heart of a woman a generation older than Dalal with great pride. A different woman — denied, or spared, the world that Dalal had now seen — would have viewed his triumph as hers, and that of her kin. But this was not the kind of man to cut an acceptable figure in the mind of a young woman who had grown up on a diet of French novels and films, who was courted by young men who had nothing to do other than sharpen their skills for the hunt: those effeminate young men with shirts unbuttoned to their navels, those dandies with their gold chains, with their melodramatic and insinuating puffs on their *Gitanes*, with new cars purchased by fathers who tackled hell in remote places, were surely no match for the sturdy qualities of Ali, with his yellow socks and bad French.

A real man, the sober official insisted, should not be compared to such flimsy material. But this flimsy material was the new world, the world to which his treasured young wife belonged. Ali could not take the chic young woman back to where he and her father had come from, to the village where women still dried and saved cow-dung for fuel, where children used the bones of dead animals for toys. How was he to communicate his world, and its wounds and its limits, to someone who had not known it? How was he to tell Dalal of his cruel and terrifying father, who humiliated him at every turn, and of the schemes of his stepmother, and of the distance he had to cover, forever on the run, unable to take anything for granted or to believe that he had anything to fall back upon? His family had thrown him into a mighty storm, and he had been denied even the possibility of a graceful, quiet failure.

As the young woman picked on the filet mignon that was delivered to her doorstep, he very much wanted to tell her, while knowing full well how much of a bore he would be, of the white bundle that used to come to him while away at school, of the few scrawny potatoes in it, of the endless diet of lentils, of the few thin loaves of peasant bread. Child, Ali wanted to scream, and he often did, where have you been and what have you seen? You were spared such terrors and such needs. Ali's generation had ploughed and had sown, and Dalal was the harvest. Ali's generation, the generation of Dalal's father, had never bothered to inquire as to the ends of such striving and such toil. With a hellish world to their backs, they had kept on the run. And now the journey had culminated in *signé* shirts and blouses, in spoiled daughters and sons, in endless trips to reputable tailors, in dining rooms whose décor was declared obsolete soon after it had been lavishly purchased and proudly displayed.

The net that entangled women older than Dalal failed to entangle her. She was too far gone to submit and to accept. Hard as her husband and her mother would try to keep her within the boundaries, the young woman had become brazenly independent. She put very little if any effort and time into covering her tracks. The furious beatings administered by her mother and her husband were to no avail. On the morning after, she would plunge into it again, and ill-wishers would report her latest escapades. She was seen going into and coming out of this or that building, she had succumbed to the blandishments of yet

The Story of Dalal

another dandy who would proudly report his latest conquest. In the carefree city that outsiders loved so much for its freedom and its *joie de vivre*, the men and the women who lived there were suffocated and hemmed in by so many curious, watchful eyes. Even the trees had eyes here, wrote the sensitive novelist Hanan As-Shaykh.

The gossips had seen it coming. The coroner's and police reports about the terrifying day were met with the usual derision: the verdict of suicide, it was said, was secured by the payment of a large bribe. An ivory tusk, an expensive one of which Dalal's family was proud, had exchanged hands and now adorned the coroner's living room. The officials were men of this society, after all: they knew their world and what it drove men and women to do.

When Dalal's body was taken to her father's village, her father and her husband were on hand to receive the condolences of those willing to treat it as a case of suicide. But the day belonged to her mother, the tower of strength, the victim and the killer, sure in her grief that she had done what she did for the sake of her other daughters, of her sons, of her home. The mother wailed, disheveled her hair, tore at her own clothes. She lined up all of Dalal's shoes, all those elegant shoes that the young woman had bought with the new money, and she spoke to them, it was said, about the young woman who had departed at so tender an age. She wanted Dalal, her Dalal, back. The fancy shoes and the primitive code of honor: this country played them side by side.

A new and intense piety overtook Dalal's mother after the deed was done. A few years younger than my own mother, more exposed to the ways of the modern world, she would from then on accompany my mother to the holy shrine of Zaynab, the daughter of Imam Ali, in Damascus. When unable to do so, she would give my mother money and food to give to the poor who gather around the shrine, and to the keepers of the shrine. The "secret" was shared between the two women on one of those journeys to Damascus. My mother was of two minds. She abhorred the deed, but she respected the mighty woman and she knew what pressures and expectations had led her to do what she had done. Dalal, my mother said in defense of the woman, was a "piece of her mother's liver": nothing could be more precious than one's own child. But for some time Dalal's mother had been walking on eggshells. Dalal's father, now a prosperous man, had become restless, and there was a danger that he would go beyond the common indiscretions, that one day a clever young huntress would lure him away from his family. A fallen daughter would serve as a convincing pretext and the honorable man would be released in his own eyes from a home that had disgraced him. Sadness and grief, my mother believed, were better than disgrace. Dalal's mother had done a terrible duty, but decency required that those quick to judge should hold their tongues. Love, even maternal love, was a luxury here. It was given when it could be afforded, when men and women were not up against the wall, when others were not busy clawing away at their reputations, threatening them with exposure and shame, leading them into ditches where even "pieces of their liver" had to be inexorably removed.

After the deed was done, Dalal's mother was never as commanding as she was before, her face never quite as bright. She no longer sounded sure of herself. The tough woman who had survived hellish years in Africa, who had single-handedly built a fortune after her husband was deported out of Ghana, who had put aside enough money to aid her father and a pretentious brother who could never make ends meet, who was generous to the multitude of relatives and of stray men and women who walked to her door with a hard luck story, was transformed overnight.

The letters that I wrote for her to friends and relatives in Africa, which previously had to be read back to her over and over again and repeatedly corrected before they met with her approval, became perfunctory. She trusted the writing, she said, there was no need to read them back. The tales she told in the letters to relatives and friends were no longer crisp and chatty. They had about them a matter-of-fact quality. One letter that she drafted to the overbearing husband, who was always in and out of the country, reported that all was well in the family, that she would see to it that all was well. This letter, and this section in particular, was read to her over and over again at her request. She wanted some hidden meaning to be transmitted, some knife perhaps to jump out of the pages, some sense of the cataclysmic deed that she had done — a reminder to the honorable man that it was she who had to keep the world intact, that he would never quite understand her sacrifice and her anguish.

But the lines penned by the letter-writer fell short of what she wanted. Arabic, the language of cruel innuendo and hidden meanings and intricate alleyways, failed Dalal's mother on that day. And with uncharacteristic sharpness, she told the attentive scribe that his style had deserted him, that he should be sure to plan a future that excluded a writing career. Yet she wanted the young man drafting the letters to stick around that day. She could bear no solitude. More than that: the drafter of the letters had been a friend of Dalal. The two of them had exchanged jibes and put-downs, they had tested one another about the latest fads, about books and movies. Dalal had insisted that the Arabic letters at which the young man excelled, which had brought him not only spending money but also access to the secrets of so many families here, gave him away as a product of the old culture, that the formal structure of the letters, the frequent invocation of Allah's name and blessing and praise, confirmed the old mentality.

Dalal and her friend who was good at Arabic letters had shared what they had shared. It was enough for Dalal's mother that the young man stuck around that day. They both knew when they were speaking of the dead. They both knew the hidden language of lament and yearning. The mother very much wanted her daughter's friend to know, without uttering a word about the entire matter, that it had all been a tragic act of last resort, that nothing else could have been done, that a mother's grief exceeds the imagination of the closest, the kindest, the most outraged of friends.

My family's home was in the village of Arnoun, in the district of Nabatiyya. I was the son of Ali Ajami of Arnoun and Bahija Abdullah of Khiam whose marriage soon ended in divorce. My mother had come to this ill-starred village when she married my father. She had come from a large clan, the Abdallahs, from Khiam, a town in the valley of Marju'un. Khiam was not far away. The distance could not have been more than fifteen kilometers. But that was far enough to make it seem like a distant land. Khiam was a place where children played next to running streams and women had time to tell exquisite and drawn-out tales. The men working Khiam's fields retired to places in the shade; the exuberant women passing by gave more taunting and playful remarks than they received.

Arnoun, at the foot of Beaufort, the Crusader castle, was a different kind of place, harsh and forbidding, surrounded

123

by granite cliffs. There was to the place the feel of living in a quarry. Here the banter was less kind, and the men more sullen and brittle. The women struggling uphill to the wells, with jars on their heads, had little time or energy for chatter. There was a pond in Arnoun at the entrance of the village, near the grey mausoleum where my grandmother's parents were buried, but the pond that drew in the rain always dried up in no time. It was by its cracked, wrinkled surface that I knew the pond.

Hyenas stalked the place. But as they said in Arnoun, the sons of Adam were more frightening than the hyenas. At the edge of the village, beyond its scattered patches of tobacco, its few fig trees, was the *wa'ar*, the wilderness — rocky, thorny land without vegetation. The *wa'ar* was more than a place beyond the village. It was a point beyond censure. It was from the *wa'ar*, the wild heath beyond the village, that the hyenas turned up. The dreaded creature, it was said, could cast a spell on its victims. Stories were told of infants taken to the *wa'ar* who were never brought back. Daughters who dishonored their families were taken to the *wa'ar*. In the legend of the *wa'ar*, there was a rock where a shepherd had killed his sister who had gone astray. He had taken her there, slit her throat, and left her to die. For many years afterward Arnounis still swore they could identify the rock where the shepherd had done horror's work.

My beloved mother, I know of the hellish years that you spent in my father's village, of the backbreaking toil. It hurts me to know what it was like, to think of how much you endured. I know that you spent a good deal of your life without a man's protection and a man's labor and a man's support. I remember that I am a stepson, that my mother is not there to defend me against a heartless father. I know the tales of hurt you want me to remember. I live amid the tales. But all I want is for the tales to release me from their grip. If this is infidelity, so be it. I want to be your son, I shall always be so. But I do not wish to appropriate your sorrow and your defeat and make them mine. Surely in your galaxy of imams and their sayings, in your endless supply of parables and proverbs, there must exist the possibility of a life lived without man being hunter or prey.

125

JACK GOLDSMITH

The Conservatives and The Court

Earl Warren's retirement in June 1969 ended his run as Chief Justice of the most progressive Supreme Court in American history. Richard Nixon appointed Warren Burger to replace Warren, and Republican presidents selected the next five Justices over the seventeen years that Burger presided as Chief Justice. And yet the Burger Court, while tacking a bit to the right, continued to embrace activist interpretive method-ologies and to issue progressive decisions. The most famous example, but a typical one, was its decision in *Roe v. Wade* in 1973. There the Court discerned in the Fourteenth Amend-ment's due process clause a "right to privacy" — a right that appears nowhere in that clause — that gave a pregnant woman the prerogative to abort a fetus until viability. The opinion was written by Harry Blackmun, a Nixon appointee, and joined by Burger and another Nixon appointee, Lewis Powell. In 1983 the title of a book by Vincent Blasi, a professor at Columbia Law School, summed up the state of affairs at the time: *The Burger Court: The Counter-Revolution That Wasn't.*

When I entered Yale Law School in the fall of 1986, the conservative legal movement born in reaction to the Warren and Burger Courts' makeover of American life was in its infancy. In mid-September, the Senate confirmed William Rehnquist, a hard-conservative voice on the Court since 1972, to replace Burger as Chief Justice. That same day it voted 98-0 for Antonin Scalia to replace Rehnquist as an Associate Justice. Scalia was little known outside conservative circles, but he was famous in them for his attacks on jurists who departed from the text of statutes and the Constitution when interpreting them. The Federalist Society, the now-dominant conservative legal organization, had been founded a few years earlier but was still a fledgling force. Conservative ideas were not taken seriously in law schools or the legal culture at the time. Robert Bork, who had left Yale five years earlier, observed that his colleagues found his conservative text-based approach to constitutional interpretation "so passé that it would be intellectually stultifying to debate it."

After Reagan nominated Scalia, Republican presidents chose seven of the next eleven Justices on the Court that is now headed by a George W. Bush nominee, Chief Justice John Roberts. Three of those Justices, Neil Gorsuch, Brett Kavanaugh, and Amy Coney Barrett, were chosen by Donald Trump. And yet despite the fact that Republican presidents have appointed fifteen of nineteen Justices since Warren, and despite undoubted successes, many conservatives are still waiting for the counterrevolution. *Roe* has not been overruled. The Court has recently recognized new constitutional protections for gay rights, including a right to gay marriage. Affirmative action, another constitutional solecism for conservatives, still lives. And in June 2020, in a case called *Bostock v. Clayton County*, the Court, in an opinion by Gorsuch, ruled that the ban on "sex" discrimination in employment in the Civil Rights Act of 1964 made it unlawful to fire an individual merely for being homosexual or transgender.

Gorsuch reached this conclusion in reliance on "textualism" — the method of statutory interpretation championed by Scalia, and for decades a rallying cry of the legal right alongside originalism. Many conservatives were shocked that a Trump appointee invoked Scalia's method to recognize categories of discrimination that conservatives have long sought to deny legal recognition. It was especially shocking since textualism seemed to serve the very judicial activism in the recognition of novel rights that it was designed to foreclose. *Bostock* represents "the end of the conservative legal movement, or the conservative legal project, as we know it," said Senator Josh Hawley, a Yale-trained lawyer and former Supreme Court litigator for conservative social causes, in a fiery speech on the floor of the Senate.

Hawley was exaggerating for political effect. On issues other than the social conservative ones such as abortion and gay rights that he cares most about, the movement has been hugely successful in changing the legal culture and the composition of the federal judiciary, and in moving public law sharply to the right. And that was before Trump replaced the very liberal Ruth Bader Ginsburg with the youthful and very conservative Barrett, four months after Hawley spoke.

The Court's conservative majority is now larger, younger, and more conservative than it has been in a century, and maybe ever. And yet it remains unclear whether the Court will transform American life as the conservative legal movement hopes, and as progressives dread.

The conservative legal movement developed two methodological responses to the perceived excesses of the Warren and Burger Courts. Both purported to be value-neutral mechanisms that were designed to restrain judges.

The main target of conservative legal jurisprudence was progressive interpretations of the Constitution. The Warren Court (1953-1969) recognized a right to marital privacy, including the right to use contraceptives, in the "penumbras" of the Bill of Rights; up-ended the settled understandings of the Fourth, Fifth, and Sixth Amendments to foster a defendant-friendly revolution in criminal procedure; issued many progressive rulings on race, most notably *Brown v. Board of Education*; practically eliminated prayer in school; and dramatically reorganized redistricting and apportionment rules governing elections under the guise, mainly, of equal protection of the law. The Burger Court (1969-1986) continued the progressive trend. It decided *Roe*, temporarily invalidated the death penalty, blessed affirmative action in education, and practically eliminated structural constitutional limits on congressional power.

Laurence Tribe of Harvard Law School, a progressive icon, captured conventional wisdom in the academy when he justified these and similar decisions on the ground that the Court's job in constitutional interpretation is to discern

129

"the contemporary content of freedom, fairness, and fraternity." As Justice William Brennan, an intellectual leader of the Warren Court, explained, "The genius of the Constitution rests not in any static meaning it might have had in a world that is dead and gone, but in the adaptability of its great principles to cope with current problems and current needs." The problem with these views, conservatives maintained, was that they had "almost nothing to do with the Constitution and [were] simply a cover for the Supreme Court's enactment of the political agenda of the American left," as Lino Graglia of the University of Texas put it.

Originalism was the right's response. It maintained that Justices should aim to discern the original meaning of provisions of the Constitution (including the amendments) at the time they were adopted. Ideas akin to originalism had informed judicial theory and practice since the founding of the nation, but "originalism" became the organizing term and principle of conservative constitutional interpretation in the 1980s — due primarily to a series of speeches by Attorney General Edwin Meese that drew national news coverage and responses from two sitting Supreme Court Justices; to Scalia's powerful writings on and off the Court; and to the left's disparagement of originalism during Bork's failed confirmation for a slot on the Supreme Court in 1987.

The basic argument for originalism was that the Constitution is a form of law that should be interpreted consistent with its fixed meaning when ratified. Any departure from that fixed meaning is an illegitimate and unconstitutional arrogation of power by the unelected judiciary. "The truth is that the judge who looks outside the Constitution always looks inside himself and nowhere else," Bork maintained. Originalism, conservatives argued, promoted democratic decision-making by giving priority to the decisions of the polity that ratified the Constitution rather than the preferences of unelected judges. The theory also purported to ensure decisions "would not be tainted by ideological predilection," as Meese put it, by restraining judges to application of neutral principles traceable to the Constitution itself. Originalism thus rested on two types of argument: a positivist claim about what counted as constitutional law, and a pragmatic institutional claim about securing judicial restraint.

The political and academic left subjected originalism to withering criticism because of its supposedly retrograde implications (which contributed to the sinking of the Bork nomination), and because originalism in its early guise was analytically deficient in a number of ways. Even Scalia acknowledged that originalism is "not without warts," and he justified it partly on pragmatic grounds as a "lesser evil" to progressive constitutional interpretation.

But originalist judges and scholars developed more sophisticated and defensible accounts in response to the critics. And over the succeeding decades, as the number of conservative judges and scholars committed to the method grew, it became influential in constitutional interpretation. The method has many important variations, and it is not universally applied even by conservative judges. Yet there is no doubt that constitutional interpretation across the run of cases now focuses more on constitutional text and original meaning than it did during the Warren and Burger courts. And in political debate, confirmation hearings, and the legal culture generally, originalism has had an even bigger impact.

Originalism rose to legitimacy for many reasons. It appealed to ordinary intuitions about what lawyers are supposed to do. The widespread academic attacks on it gave it

131

an implicit legitimation. Progressive scholars failed to generate an equally compelling and accessible justification for their preferred constitutional method, which is often called "living constitutionalism." Scalia's brilliantly crafted and forceful originalist opinions often won the argument even when he was in dissent. And a massive conservative juggernaut (about which more in a moment) successfully promoted the doctrine.

Perhaps the best evidence of originalism's influence is its imitation by progressive scholars. Akhil Amar of Yale Law School deploys ingenious readings of Constitutional text and structure, deeply informed by history, to reach a range of contrarian progressive conclusions about the Constitution, especially the Bill of Rights. Jack Balkin, also of Yale, is even closer to conservative originalism in relying on the original meaning, but he does so at a much higher level of abstraction that allows him to generate progressive interpretations. More generally, courts and scholars across the board now take constitutional history, and especially the history of the adoption of the Constitution and its subsequent amendments, much more seriously than before originalism's ascendance. Originalism has not won over the courts in all constitutional cases — no legal or interpretative methodology has done that. But today it is a legitimate, widely practiced, and growing form of legal argumentation, a remarkable accomplishment since the 1980s.

The second conservative focus was the Warren and Burger Courts' progressive approach to interpreting statutes. This approach tended to de-emphasize the text of the statutes and to be guided instead by Congress' aims in enacting the statute, as discerned, for example, in legislative reports, hearings or floor statements, and other forms of "legislative history." The departures from statutory text almost always served progressive ends.

A classic instance came in 1979 in a case called *United Steelworkers of America v. Weber,* which ruled that affirmative action to favor black employees did not violate the Civil Rights Act's ban on employment discrimination based on "race." The Court rejected a "literal construction" of the statute because a ban on affirmative action was "not within its spirit, nor within the intention of its makers," which was to promote employment among blacks.

Textualism, a cousin of originalism, was a response to cases such as *Weber.* Conservatives — most notably Scalia — argued that the singular "spirit" of a statute was practically impossible to discern, and that often-tendentious legislative reports written by staffers and speeches by individual members of Congress were not reliable guides to such intention. The role of the judge is to interpret the text of the statute — the only words subject to the constitutionally prescribed lawmaking process of bicameral approval and presentment to the president. Except in rare instances, judges who went beyond the text were usurping legislative authority.

This approach sought to ensure judicial restraint and promote democratic decision-making for reasons akin to originalism: by constricting the legitimate sources of interpretive meaning, it curtailed judges' discretion to import their own values into the statute that Congress enacted, and helped to ensure that the people's representatives, not unelected judges, made the law. And like originalism, this theory purported to be neutral about ends. The stated aim was not for judges to achieve particular conservative outcomes, but rather to follow the dictates of Congress in whatever direction that led.

Textualism, like originalism, has been subject to a fierce academic debate during the past few decades. In courts, it has proven even more consequential than originalism. "Scalia's textualist campaign was tremendously influential," noted Jonathan Siegel of George Washington University Law School. "He changed the way courts interpret statutes," and his influence "is visible in virtually every Supreme Court opinion interpreting statutes today." The *Bostock* decision about sexual orientation and transgender rights was basically a fight over the meaning of Scalia's undoubtedly victorious textualist legacy. Not every jot and tittle of Scalia's textualism governs in every Supreme Court statutory decision, but the Court's approach to statutes now always begins and often ends with statutory text. Few if any methodological victories in the Court have ever been so complete.

As this sketch makes plain, no one is more responsible for the rise of conservative legal thought than Antonin Scalia. His "interpretive theories, communicated in that distinctive, vivid prose, have transformed this country's legal culture, the very ground of our legal debate," as Justice Elena Kagan noted in an introductory essay in a volume about Scalia's legal thought. "They have changed the way all of us (even those who part ways with him at one point or another) think and talk about the law." And yet the Scalia revolution, as the modern conservative legal movement could aptly be called, did not take place in a vacuum. It was the fruit of a larger political movement that began meekly in the Nixon administration and then caught fire in the Reagan administration. The movement and its associated network had many nodes, but at its center was the Federalist Society.

134

The Federalist Society began as a response to the ideologically one-sidedness of American law schools like the one I encountered at Yale in the 1980s. (The University of Chicago Law School was an exception to this one-sidedness; it had numerous prominent conservatives on its faculty in the 1980s, including Scalia, who helped the Federalist Society get off the ground.) In 1982, law students at Yale and Chicago convened a conference at Yale as a one-off counterpoint to "law schools and the legal profession [that] are currently strongly dominated by a form of orthodox liberal ideology."

The conference was a wild success, and demonstrated the appeal of a forum for conservatives to discuss their legal ideas. The students quickly organized, got funding from conservative donors, and began to open chapters in law schools and (for practicing lawyers) in cities around the nation. "Conservative law students alienated in their home institutions, desperate for a collective identity, and eager for collective activity provided a ripe opportunity for organizational entrepreneurship," the political scientist Steven Teles remarks in his important study of the movement. Almost by accident, they tapped into and helped organize a larger conservative political demand for changes to the federal judiciary.

The Federalist Society was and remains, at heart, a debating club. (I was briefly a member in the 1990s, and I informally supervise the local chapter at Harvard Law School.) Its founders believed that the best way to develop and spread conservative ideas was to host intellectual exchanges between conservatives and progressives. The emphasis on argument exemplified the intellectual seriousness of the group, and its confidence that the best way to legitimate its ideas was to see how they stood up to the ones that prevailed in the classroom and the bar. It also, as Teles aptly describes it, "made the organization open and attractive to outsiders, moderated factional conflict and insularity, and had a tendency to prevent the members' ideas from becoming stale from a lack of challenge." The main factional conflict then and now — and one that has flared up in recent years — is between the deregulatory libertarian wing that was most interested in judicial efforts to reduce the size of government and the social conservative wing that abhorred (and sought to stop and to reverse) judicial recognition of progressive rights such as abortion.

Yet the Federalist Society evolved into much more than a debating society. It quickly became a focal point for conservative networking for political appointments in the federal government and for clerkships in the federal judiciary. Conservative students thronged to its popular annual convention in Washington, D.C. to watch marquee debates and rub elbows with icons in the movement that the Federalist Society helped to form — Supreme Court Justices, prominent lower court judges, Attorneys General and other Cabinet Secretaries, Senators, and other famous lawyers. It is hard to think of a more important annual conservative gathering, except perhaps the Conservative Political Action Conference meeting.

Through these and related mechanisms the Federalist Society flourished in its influence — especially as its student members grew up and began to populate the federal bench through appointments in the George W. Bush administration and especially the Trump administration. It also grew in its attractiveness to young conservatives, especially as a mechanism to advance one's career. There is no formal pipeline between membership in the Federalist Society and law clerk jobs or executive branch appointments. But membership signals a commitment to conservative legal principles to

136

potential conservative employers and opens many informal channels to them.

Despite its prodigious impact on conservative networking, the Federalist Society has sought to maintain neutrality on legal issues and judicial politics. It accurately claims that it does "not lobby for legislation, take policy positions, or sponsor or endorse nominees and candidates for public service." Its only formal principles are the ones it announces at the outset of every gathering: "that the state exists to preserve freedom, that the separation of governmental powers is central to our Constitution, and that it is emphatically the province and duty of the judiciary to say what the law is, not what it should be."

And yet its careful efforts at broad-mindedness and political detachment have not stopped the Federalist Society from growing more political over the years. At its annual conventions the organization has increasingly showed off its connections to, and influence over, the legal decisions of Republican administrations. And while it has always had senior Republican officials speak at its conferences, these speeches have grown to be less about judicial politics and more about just politics. In a self-consciously partisan speech at the annual convention in 2019, for example, Attorney General William Barr was interrupted with extended applause after he claimed that "the Left" is "engaged in a systematic shredding of norms and undermining the rule of law." He added that "so-called progressives treat politics as their religion," are on a "holy mission," and are "willing to use any means necessary to gain momentary advantage in achieving their end, regardless of collateral consequences and the systemic implications."

The Federalist Society has also grown intellectually narrower and more homogenous. When I began teaching a quarter of a century ago, many conservative legal theories competed for supremacy among Federalist Society members. But in the last decade especially, originalism and textualism have risen to become the society's (and the larger movement's) orthodoxy. "Tonight I can report, a person can be both a committed originalist and textualist and be confirmed to the Supreme Court of the United States," said Justice Gorsuch, seven months after he joined the Court, at the Federalist Society's annual convention. Gorsuch received wild applause for this statement, which everyone in the room understood to be the core of what the Federalist Society is about. He also mocked the Federalist Society's critics, thanked the crowd for its "support and prayers through that process," and vowed to maintain its principles on the Court. *Politico* described the surprisingly political speech as a "victory lap at the Federalist Society dinner."

Gorsuch's pledge of fealty underscored the Federalist Society's astounding impact on the federal bench during the Trump presidency. "We're going to have great judges, conservative, all picked by the Federalist Society," said Trump in 2016. He followed through on that promise by turning over judicial selection to White House Counsel Donald McGahn, a committed Federalist Society member, and Leonard Leo, who for decades served in senior positions in the Society and who remains on its board. Leo took a leave of absence during the George W. Bush administration to help with judges (and was influential in the selection of John Roberts and Samuel Alito), and then did the same during the Trump administration, where he has had an even bigger impact.

The Federalist Society accurately maintains that Leo did this work in his personal capacity. But he was the public face of the Society even if he was formally disconnected from it when he working for the White House, and he drew on his deep relationship to its members in that process. After Leo introduced Vice President Pence as "one of us" at a Federalist Society event in 2019, Pence at the outset of his speech stated that the Trump administration and the nation owe Leo — whom Pence identified as "the Vice-President of the Federalist Society" — a "debt of gratitude" for his "tireless work," a reference to Leo's judge-picking.

Leo is merely exemplary of the deep and multifarious conduits between the Federalist Society and the Trump White House. The organization is so constitutive of the conservative legal movement, and has such a strenuous grip on its imagination, that it would have been enormously influential in Trump's judicial selection even if Leo had not been there. And its influence has been historic. In one of the defining accomplishments of his presidency, Trump placed Gorsuch, Kavanaugh, and Barrett on the Supreme Court, and over two hundred judges on the lower courts. The vast majority of these judges are proud long-time members of the Federalist Society who had been nurtured by it and absorbed its values over the course of their careers. These judges are on the whole immensely well-credentialed and qualified — a tribute (among other things) to decades of Federalist Society-facilitated clerkships on the increasingly conservative Federalist Society-influenced Supreme Court.

This success has invited controversy and pushback consonant with the high-stakes battle for control of an unelected judiciary that has steadily expanded its policy-making writ for a century. The Federalist Society that then-Harvard Law School Dean Elena Kagan said she "love[d]" in 2005 for its commitment to debate and its contributions to intellectual diversity is now widely despised on law school campuses and on the political left more generally. Federalist

Society members at many law schools are today often shunned or put down in strident personal terms, inside and especially outside the classroom. They have gotten the message and speak up less often in class than a decade ago on issues such as affirmative action, gay and transgender rights, immigration, and criminal justice. With rare exceptions, top law schools have throughout my lifetime lacked intellectual diversity on a left-right axis in public law, but the attacks there on disfavored conservative positions have never been more open or vicious. The main impact of these attacks is to make law schools even less interesting intellectually, and to drive conservative students deeper into the Federalist Society cocoon.

Outside of law school, the Federalist Society is often subject to stinging political reproach. Typical is a report in May 2020 by three Democratic Senators that described the Federalist Society as "the nerve center for a complex and massively funded GOP apparatus designed to rewrite the law to suit the narrow-minded political orthodoxy of the Federalist Society's backers." The Federalist Society is no more narrow-minded or political than the dominant legal establishment institutions it was created to challenge. If anything, it is less so, since it continues to operate more thoroughly in the world of ideas and argumentation than its rivals. But it *is* a political organization, and not just the debating society it holds itself out to be. This is so by default if not by design, since it is the intellectual nerve center of the enormously consequential fight for judicial dominance.

In January 2020, the Judicial Conference of the United States' Codes of Conduct Committee circulated a proposal to ban federal judges from being members of the Federalist Society or the American Constitution Society (ACS), the progressive organization founded in 2000 as "an explicit counterpart, and counterweight" to the Federalist Society. ACS never achieved nearly the influence of the Federalist Society, and the proposal clearly sought to hurt the latter. The ostensible reason for the proposed ban was that membership in these groups raises questions about judges' impartiality. The Committee's true aim was revealed when it declined to propose a ban on membership in the American Bar Association, a group that, unlike the Federalist Society, is heavily involved in legal advocacy — primarily for progressive causes. The proposal was dropped a few months later. But it, as well as the Senators' report, are signs of the Federalist Society's enormous political success.

The conservative legal movement's original aim was to separate legal interpretation from personal values in the hope of quelling judicial activism. The rising influence of originalism and textualism, many on the right believe, accomplishes this. On this view, Gorsuch's deployment of textualism to reach a progressive result in *Bostock* is evidence of success, not failure, since it shows that the methodology is value-neutral enough to produce outcomes contrary to a judge's personal wishes. The same is true, for example, of Justice Scalia's occasional originalist opinions that expand criminal defendant rights, and of Justice Thomas' attacks on qualified immunity — a *bête noire* in progressive circles for shielding bad cops from liability — as lacking any basis in Congress' textual commands. To many conservatives these examples illustrate the integrity of their principles. One rarely sees progressive Justices deploying their favored methodology to reach politically conservative results — especially since most lack constraining methodological commitments.

But despite the packaging, conservative methodologies are not value neutral, and they have not always been deployed consistently or in value-neutral ways. Originalism as understood by most conservatives is oriented toward constitutional meaning in 1789 and the post-Civil War period (when the Reconstruction Amendments passed), and away from the progressive gloss put on constitutional provisions from the 1930s through the 1970s. The politically liberal results produced by originalism are the exception, not the rule. *Bostock* is also an exceptional instance of textualism, which on the whole leads to politically conservative results. One of many examples is the Court's reversal of its prior tolerance of plaintiff's suing for relief under federal law absent explicit congressional authorization — a change that has dramatically curbed the scope of federal rights.

The rise of originalism and textualism is one reason why the recognition of new constitutional and statutory rights has slowed in recent decades (the Court's recognition of a robust Second Amendment right to bear arms is an exception), and why American public law generally has moved sharply to the right. On issues ranging from voting rights to structural federalism to free speech and religion to many issues of court access, the Court has curtailed or reversed Warren and Burger Court precedents, and not always through close adherence to originalism or textualism. The Court has also grown aggressively pro-business across a wide range of issues in ways that are often disconnected from judicial philosophy.

As conservatives' power on the Court has grown, judicial restraint — the original justification for originalism and textualism — has diminished. Many conservatives now abjure the deference to democratic enactments that was once the hallmark of conservative legal philosophy, and argue for a more assertive stance to strike down modern state and federal laws based on distant understandings of constitutional meaning. They are also more inclined to reject progressive precedents that conflict with the originalist Constitution. Justice Thomas is a leading proponent of this view on the Supreme Court. As he explained in 2019 in *Gamble v. United States*: "When faced with a demonstrably erroneous precedent, my rule is simple: We should not follow it."

In many contexts, however, conservative disrespect for precedent is not based on a return to original meaning. A good example is the conservative turn on the First Amendment. In 1971, Bork stated the traditional conservative position in a famous article that argued that the First Amendment should be narrowly construed to protect only political speech. When the Court, in 1976, recognized First Amendment protections for "commercial speech," Rehnquist was the lone dissent. Yet in recent decades conservatives have embraced the view that Bork and Rehnquist rejected. They have repurposed the First Amendment as a libertarian sword to strike down all manner of disfavored laws, ranging from business regulations to campaign finance restrictions.

An extraordinary decision in this vein came in 2018, when the conservative majority overruled a four-decade precedent to rule that the First Amendment prohibited the state from forcing public sector workers to pay for union activity when they did not join the union — a long-standard labor practice. The majority, in an opinion by Justice Samuel Alito, barely glanced at the original understanding of the First Amendment. Justice Kagan in dissent charged it with "weaponizing the First Amendment, in a way that unleashes judges, now and in the future, to intervene in economic and regulatory policy." It was a fair critique.

But the main targets of conservative libertarian activism are the federal agencies that, with little concrete guidance from Congress, control policymaking in the United States. "The greatest threat to the rule of law in our modern society is the ever-expanding regulatory state, and the most effective bulwark against that threat is a strong judiciary," Donald McGahn, the Trump White House judge-picker, told the Federalist Society in 2017. Conservative scholars and judges have in the last decade developed new arguments for achieving this end, including imaginative uses of the First Amendment. But none is more remarkable, or revealing, than their flip on an obscure but consequential doctrine about judicial deference to agency rulemaking.

At the dawn of the movement, in the 1980s, the then-very-progressive District of Columbia Circuit — the federal appellate court charged with reviewing most agency decisions — regularly invalidated Ronald Reagan's deregulatory efforts. As a law professor, Scalia had criticized the D.C. Circuit for imposing its values on agencies in defiance of what Congress had prescribed. During his tenure on the D.C. Circuit from 1982 to 1986, Scalia witnessed this trend up close, viewed it as illegitimate, and deployed several tools to fight it. The main one he settled on was the *Chevron* doctrine, which took its name from a Supreme Court case in 1984 about the scope of the Environmental Protection Agency's regulatory power over air pollution. Scalia was not on the Court when that case was decided, and the case was not a big deal when it was announced. But when Scalia joined the Court in 1986, he became its main intellectual champion and began to develop and deploy the *Chevron* doctrine aggressively.

The *Chevron* doctrine requires courts to accept reasonable agency interpretations of statutes that they are charged with administering. It makes it harder to second-guess agency rules — progressive or conservative — except in cases where they defy clear statutory directives. Scalia argued that this deference comported with Congress' wishes, acknowledged agency expertise, constrained judges, and promoted accountable decision-making, since agencies were part of an executive branch headed by an elected official, the president, while courts were unelected. The doctrine also dovetailed with conservatives' infatuation with executive power in the 1980s. (Before then conservatives for six decades had been skeptics of broad executive power, but that is another story.) During Scalia's time on the Court, the *Chevron* doctrine became "a central pillar of the modern administrative state," as Michael McConnell of Stanford Law School has observed.

But then something unexpected happened. About a decade ago, the conservative legal movement started to flip on *Chevron* and related doctrines of administrative deference. Several factors led to the flip. The conservative view of *Chevron* had, remarkably, discounted a statutory requirement that courts reviewing agency decisions "decide all relevant questions of law [and] interpret constitutional and statutory provisions," which some argued — the point remains contested — rules out deference to agencies on many legal questions. Administrative agencies began to use the cover of *Chevron* deference to make administrative rules that to conservatives seemed to depart more and more from the authorizing statutes for agencies.

It was no accident that the conservative turn picked up steam during the Obama administration, which promulgated legally super-aggressive regulations such as net neutrality, the Clean Power Plan (an ambitious environmental initiative), university sexual assault rules, and the implementation rules

145

for Obamacare and Dodd-Frank. For conservatives encountering such rules that seemed to rest on doubtful congressional premises, agency deference seemed lawless. And so they reversed course. Scalia appeared to be backing away from the doctrine at the end of his life. And most younger conservative jurists — including Gorsuch, Kavanaugh, and many conservative legal scholars — are deeply skeptical of *Chevron*. Court watchers predict that the Supreme Court will overturn or weaken *Chevron* in the next few years.

For many religious conservatives, the conservative legal movement's extraordinary accomplishments are belied by the movement's failure to reverse *Roe*, to prevent the rise of constitutional and statutory gay and transgender rights, and to give sure protection to religious freedom in the face of these judicially developed rights. This was the thrust of Senator Hawley's complaint after *Bostock*. Social conservatives, he argued, had for decades gone along with the Republican Party's neo-liberal agenda on trade and taxes in exchange for the promise of "pro-Constitution, religious liberty judges" — a shorthand for judges who will vote the right way on religious social issues.

And yet since the Reagan administration, religious conservatives have watched as Republican appointees refused to embrace the social conservative agenda. Two Reagan appointees, Sandra Day O'Connor and Anthony Kennedy, and one George H.W. Bush appointee, David Souter, refused to overturn *Roe* when that issue was teed up in 1992, on the grounds of "institutional integrity" and respect for precedent. Kennedy — Reagan's appointee after the Bork nomination failed — was also the architect of the Court's gay rights jurisprudence, which culminated in his opinion in 2015, joined by the Court's four liberals, to recognize a constitutional right to gay marriage. More recent conservative appointees seemed to continue this trend. Gorsuch wrote *Bostock* and Roberts joined it. A few weeks after *Bostock*, Roberts shocked conservatives when he joined the Court's four liberal justices to invalidate a Louisiana abortion restriction. Roberts also voted with the liberal wing in the summer of 2020 to deny churches exemptions from state restrictions on worship during the pandemic.

Religious conservatives are embittered that, despite the other successes in the conservative legal movement, and despite Republicans appointing over 79% of the Justices since Warren retired, they cannot find five Justices to embrace their agenda. Hawley attributed the failure to originalism and textualism which, he claimed, produce results that are "the opposite of what we thought we were fighting for." (In 2014, one of the founders of the Federalist Society, Steven Calabresi, argued that the original meaning of the Fourteenth Amendment guarantees a right to same-sex marriage.) Others, such as Adrian Vermeule of Harvard Law School, argue that ostensibly conservative Justices are "educated urban profes- sionals" whose commitments to liberalism dominate their conservative sentiments. Another argument is that the elite press, controlled by progressives, draws conservative Justices leftward through manipulated news coverage. Ed Whelan, a former Scalia law clerk and the president of the Ethics and Public Policy Center, speculates that the type of judicial candidates who have the best chances of being nominated and confirmed — ones good at "charming senators, trotting out a list of liberal friends and admirers, and neutralizing a leftist media" — are ones that are least likely to overrule *Roe*.

Ruth Marcus' book on the Brett Kavanaugh confirmation hearings, *Supreme Ambition*, contains a different explanation that has infuriated religious conservatives, and that was at the base of Hawley's critique of the bad bargain they made with the Republican Party. At the first White House meeting on who should replace Scalia after he died — a deliberation that ended in the selection of Gorsuch, who wrote *Bostock* — White House Chief of Staff Reince Priebus noted that major Republican donors cared little about abortion and same-sex marriage but a lot about chopping down the regulatory state. White House Counsel McGahn, in Marcus' paraphrase, added that conservatives' "emphasis on social conservatism and its associated hot-button issues ended with Scalia," and that now judge-selection is "all about regulatory relief." McGahn stated that on that criterion, Scalia himself "wouldn't make the cut."

Episodes such as these — which confirm religious conservatives' suspicions about the priorities of the Republican elite — have led to a growing split within the conservative legal movement. One intellectual leader on the social conservative side is Vermeule, who argues that "originalism has now outlived its utility, and has become an obstacle to the development of a robust, substantively conservative approach to constitutional law and interpretation." He believes that reversing the progressive moral agenda in the Court cannot be achieved by faux-value-neutral methodologies, but rather requires an overtly "moral reading" of the Constitution and laws to advance a conservative social vision that he calls "Common Good constitutionalism." Vermeule also points out that originalism is, ironically, untrue to the Founding since it ignores the classical legal tradition (including natural law) that the Founders' embraced in creating the Constitution and understanding its terms. Many of my most conservative students and advisees, at law schools around the country, are increasingly disillusioned with originalism and are energized by Vermeule's critique of it, and his approach to constitutional interpretation. And yet originalism remains dominant.

This brings us, finally, to the confirmation of Amy Coney Barrett to replace Ruth Bader Ginsburg. Senate Republicans pushed Barrett through on a short fuse in an election year just four years after they delayed Barack Obama's election-year selection of Merrick Garland to replace Scalia, and then confirmed Gorsuch after Trump won. These hardball tactics to gain control of the Court enraged Democrats, but they were perfectly legitimate from a constitutional perspective and not terribly surprising. Since the stakes have grown so large, the judicial confirmation process has suffered a three-decade downward spiral of diminishing restraint by both sides: Democrats' unprecedented attacks on Bork, which killed his nomination, followed by their unprecedented filibuster of many of George W. Bush's appellate court nominees and their elimination of the filibuster for Barack Obama's appellate court nominees—actions that Republicans reciprocated by eliminating the filibuster for Supreme Court nominees beginning with Gorsuch, before their maneuvers to put Kavanaugh and Barrett on the Court. Norms have been rendered ineffective in this context because the exercise of hard constitutional power promises huge short-term victories.

It is unclear how Barrett will impact the Court. She is a brilliant jurist who clerked for Justice Scalia and she acknowledges that Scalia's "judicial philosophy is mine, too." Social conservatives are hopeful that regardless of judicial philosophy, Barrett is one of their own and will vote their way. They have had this hope before, of course, and have been disappointed. But Barrett's elevation gives the conservative legal movement a 6-3 majority on the Court for the first time, which means that in every case it can absorb a defection and still win.

This historical conservative dominance on the Supreme Court has led many progressives to propose dramatic reforms to regain control of the judiciary, including stripping the Court of jurisdiction over cases that might lead to conservative rulings, or "packing" the Court with Justices to give liberals a majority. Conservative charges that these lawful tactics would violate norms ring hollow in light of the tit-for-tat pattern of events related to judicial politics since the 1980s. But for the foreseeable future, conservatives need not worry. Joe Biden has held his cards closely on the judicial makeover project. And the project is dead on arrival in the Senate in light of the Republicans' strong performance in the recent Senatorial elections, and of the opposition of Senator Joe Manchin of West Virginia, a moderate Democrat, to court-packing and to the elimination of the Senate's 60-vote threshold to break a filibuster. For at least two years, and almost certainly longer, Democrats lack the votes to diminish conservative judicial power through structural reform.

Still, it would be premature for social conservatives to celebrate revolutionary judicial victories on the issues that they care about most. The recognition of gay and transgender rights is practically complete and—unlike abortion rights— is not really legally contested. The most that social conservatives can hope for is that the Court will recognize religious accommodations to the enforcement of these rights. Affirmative action may be on the chopping block, but the practice is deeply entrenched socially, and colleges and other recipients of public funding have developed imaginative ways to use facially neutral identity proxies to achieve preferred outcomes. And *Roe* will be much harder to kill than many conservatives believe. Roberts has noticeably shied away from overruling the nearly five-decade-old decision. And whatever her first-order views on abortion rights may be, Barrett has staked out what the Princeton political scientist Keith Whittington calls a "moderate" position on overruling decisions and "has urged giving precedents more weight than some originalists would prefer." The likely course on *Roe* is a narrowing of the abortion right but not an elimination of it.

Whatever happens, the Court is destined to become a more politicized and controversial institution. When all is said and done, the Court has only itself to blame. Beginning in the 1960s it reached far beyond its proper jurisdiction to grab enormous control over public policy away from democratic institutions, which sparked a conservative counterrevolution in the 1980s that has now won power and on many issues is doing the same thing in the other direction. It is a sign of advanced constitutional decay that so many important decisions in our democracy are made by five or six unelected Justices, and that confirmation battles have become the most consequential political episodes in the nation after presidential elections.

EDWARD LUTTWAK

The Trouble with China

In the summer of 2020, otherwise a time of maximum disunity in the United States amid intersectional uprisings, rioting, and widespread institutional deliquescence, a rock-like national consensus emerged from the political waves: Americans from Nancy Pelosi and Joe Biden to Donald Trump, who vehemently disagreed on everything else, fully agreed that it was urgent to confront the People's Republic of China, technologically as well as politically, within the United States, in Europe, and strategically across Asia and beyond. Within that consensus there were only stylistic differences, from Pelosi's quiet assertion of the incompatibility of the regime with human rights anywhere on the planet to Trump's truculent trade demands.

The break with the past is very sharp: from Nixon in 1972 to quite late in Obama's presidency, the United States did much that accelerated China's rise to wealth and power from the miserable poverty I saw everywhere in that country in 1976, while doing very little to oppose China, aside from resisting its claim to rule Taiwan. By August 2020, by contrast, the Administration and the Congress were competing in finding new ways of limiting Chinese power, from human rights' legislation specifically related to Tibet, Xinjiang, and Hong Kong, to the compulsory sale of a China-based social media platform excessively popular with the young and exceptionally intrusive in its tracking.

With the Chinese navy engaged in threatening exercises off the coast of Taiwan even as the United States reiterated its promise of defending the island, all is set for rancor to explode in an armed clash. It is therefore urgent to try to understand what has happened, and why.

But to proceed one must first toss out any American-centered explanation of what has happened to US-China relations — of which there are many, from America's hegemonic jealousy complete with ancient parallels (alas, no Thucydides Trust protects the brand) or American-white racial jealousy at the rise of the Han, or an American switch to geo-economics (the logic of conflict in the grammar of commerce) in response to the loss of plain economic primacy. The usual suspects blame the arms merchants and Pentagonal lobbies. The problem with all these accounts is that they monocausally attribute the new cold war, if that is what it is, to us. The reason why all American-centered explanations must be wrong as a matter of elementary logic is that relations between China and every other country remotely in its league (except Russia) have undergone exactly the same inversion, from amity to weary suspicion to increasingly vigorous defensive reactions, and it mostly happened on the same timetable or near enough. What we should be studying is not American behavior, but Chinese behavior.

I will give four cases.

I

I was once engulfed in a Chinese wedding party in a vast Melbourne hotel whose inebriated celebrants noisily spilled out onto the main casino floor, handing out little boxes of assorted delicacies such as chicken feet to all and sundry, along with cute little bottles filled with wolf-head *kaoliang* far more alcoholic than vodka. Suburban housewives turned from their slot machines to grimace comically at the chicken feet and laughingly try the *kaoliang*, and everyone I saw at the hotel was just as indulgent with the invasion of tipsy Chinese that blocked the waiters and interrupted conversations at every table. My local friend, unbidden, explained the bonhomie: "They flew 5000 miles to hold their party in Australia and the least we can do is to be nice about it."

In those days there was a lot of good feeling between Australia and China, as Australian exports to China rose every year to reach 30% of Australia's total — and that 30% was also some 90% of the growth in total Australian exports. Not only were wedding parties warmly welcomed but also Chinese purchases of Australian firms, some in high-tech, as well as of Australian housing and land mostly unwanted by other foreign investors. Chinese tourists were also uniquely valuable, and not only because they accounted for much of the total growth in tourism but also because most other tourists were headed for the Great Barrier Reef, which was already under excessive pressure from tourist vessels, while the Chinese came for harmless sightseeing, lucrative shopping, and gambling. Crucially, the Australian welcome extended to the Hanban, China' premier soft propaganda agency, which operates the "Confucius Institutes" of Chinese language and culture. It opened branches in most Australian universities, operated by Chinese personnel who not only provided Chinese language teaching but also helped university administrators to handle the ever-increasing inflow of students from China. In the meantime Australian travel to China was facilitated by the opening of consular offices in six Australian cities (the United States has four), which also provided services for the increasing number of Chinese immigrants — numerous enough to sustain their own newspaper.

In Australia's ascending curve of advancement as well as prosperity, China and the Chinese played an ever increasing role, and there was substance as well as symbolism in the elevation of Kevin Rudd to the premiership in December 2007, the first and still only head of a Western government who spoke Mandarin easily and well. It was in Mandarin that he used to explain to Chinese interviewers that the "slight" political differences between the two countries — he quantified the differences at 15% — should not impede ever broadening cooperation.

Everything is different now. If Chinese gamblers still travel they will still be welcomed, and China can still import all the Australian raw materials it wants, but government scrutiny of Chinese investments is now much stricter than in the United States. All the Confucius Institute programs in New South Wales, Australia's most populous state, have been closed outright, while others persist under very tight scrutiny, in the wake of ample evidence that they were operated as a coordinated propaganda arm of Chinese diplomacy, while their staff compelled Chinese students to function as their operatives, individually to spy on fellow students and together to harass any speaker critical of China or supportive of Taiwan or Tibet. As for the leaders of the Chinese immigrant community, they too are under close observation after some were exposed as Beijing's agents in lobbying Australian politicians.

Most dramatic is the changed strategic attitude to China, from Kevin Rudd's confidence in its leaders' willingness "to make a strong contribution to strengthening the regional security environment and the global rules-based order" to the rising sense of insecurity that in 2011 persuaded the Australian government to invite American combat troops to train in Australia, not once but on a prolonged basis with increasingly permanent base facilities. Off-duty Marines are now to be seen every day in tropical Darwin, that most movie-typical and of course wildly untypical of Australian cities, with leather-hatted Crocodile Dundee look-alikes in their high-riding jeeps, and seriously dangerous crocodiles lurking just outside town, which do worry the Marines practicing amphibious landings among them.

That is the most visible evidence that Australia now views China as an outright threat, but the least visible is very likely the most important: Australia's "strategic dialogue" with Vietnam, China's favorite bullying target (Vietnamese fishing boats are regularly sunk by Chinese coast guard vessels) but also the most resilient of all its neighbors. Yes, it is true: the Vietnamese are highly confident that they can again defeat the Chinese, just as the French and the Americans were defeated. The most recent of the Chinese invasions — they started some two thousand years ago — occurred in 1979, a full-scale affair intended to force the Vietnamese to withdraw from Cambodia before they could defeat China's ally, the mass-murdering Khmer Rouge. The Chinese failed: they withdrew after taking heavy casualties and the Vietnamese finished off the Khmer Rouge.

So what is the Australia-Vietnam dialogue about? Historical reminiscences of Australia's part in the Vietnam war, with 61,000 troops and advisors serving over ten years? Hardly. The clue is that in this case "strategic" is a euphemism for intelligence. Australia is one of the "Five Eyes" countries, along with Canada, the United Kingdom, New Zealand, and the United States, which share deciphered signals and electronic intelligence — the only part of Winston Churchill's dream of a permanent, all-encompassing Anglo-Saxon alliance that was fully realized. Vietnam's long and porous border with China's Yunnan province and its daily observation of the Chinese navy (including its Hainan submarine base) mean that it needs no ground intelligence or marine surveillance, but insofar as its Five Eyes partners allow it, Australia can supply electronic intelligence, crucial information about Chinese radars, communications and whatever signals can be deciphered.

That is how things now are between the Australians and the Chinese: instead of the optimism exemplified by Kevin Rudd, there are weary preparations to protect Australia by strengthening China's Asian antagonists. In other words, without either Obama or Trump, and regardless of the posture of the United States toward China, Australian relations with China devolved on the same descending path, from hopeful and even enthusiastic amity to intense suspicion and active security measures.

II

In Japan, the reversal was far more abrupt.

On March 20, 2009, Japan's Minister of Defense Hamada Yasukazu was in Beijing at the invitation of his Chinese counterpart Liang Guanglie. Footage shows the relaxed body language of both — of course everything had been agreed beforehand, and there was so much of it, all good, starting with a return visit to Tokyo by Liang within the year. The information-sharing arrangements they set up were remarkably extensive and much beyond anything routine: the two sides agreed to coordinate anti-piracy operations off the Somali coast, while an overall "maritime contact mechanism" was to function between the defense ministries of China and Japan. There were to be mutual naval visits in the respective ports with shore activities to broaden their effect on the public: warships would advance China-Japan amity instead of being symbols of hostility. The uniformed military were to broaden and deepen the dialogue of the two ministers with an annual defense exchange plan that might progress to regular inter-service staff officer dialogues involving all services and the Joint Staff of Japan. In addition, the military area commands of the Chinese People's Liberation Army (PLA) and armies of the Japanese Ground Self-Defense Force were to maintain a dialogue, to add another dimension. And to top it all off, China's National Defense University and its Academy of Military Science would conduct joint programs with Japan's National Institute for Defense Studies, while PLA University of Science and Technology and Dalian Naval Academy would cooperate with Japan's National Defense Academy

I was startled to read all this in the next day's *Japan Times* in the metro. What had happened to the US-Japan alliance? Why were the Japanese suddenly going to share all that military information with the Chinese? I was in Japan for other reasons, but a friend arranged a meeting with the leading opposition politician Ichiro Ozawa of the Democratic Party, who seemed very pleased at the government's convergence with China. "I do not like Americans,' He said. "They are too simple — everything is black and white." The time had come for Japan to disengage from the military alliance, to become more neutral.

At the American embassy the foreign-service officer I talked with said that Japan's Liberal Democratic Party, long the country's "ruling party" and until recently the firm upholder of its alliance with the United States, was declining. This political change had thrown everything into turmoil, he explained, and if Ozawa's Democratic Party came to power anything was possible, including the expulsion of the United States Marines from their favorite base in Okinawa, the closure of the small mainland facilities, and even perhaps the departure of the US Navy from Yokosuka, the home port of the Seventh Fleet. Obama, in their view, was turning to the Chinese to help out in the American financial crisis, and he did not seem much interested in military alliances anyway.

And so it seemed that a neutral Japan might indeed emerge, especially if the American market for Japanese exports declined irremediably because of the financial crisis, forcing the country to increase its reliance on China. In September 2009, as the American diplomat had feared, Ozawa's Democratic Party did come to power, and while Ozawa did not become Prime Minister he was the real power behind the government headed by Yukio Hatoyama, who would be followed by two more Democratic politicians who lasted about a year each, including the unfortunate Naoto Kan, who resigned on September 2, 2011 after a disastrous premiership that spanned the catastrophic March earthquake and tsunami. Ozawa's serious interest in revising Japan's national strategy was not shared by Hatoyama, but still it seemed that the United States was on its way to losing perhaps its most important ally in the world, with China gaining at least an economic partner that might become a strategic auxiliary over time.

This prospect was welcomed by significant Japanese figures, including former Prime Minister Nakasone, once Reagan's happy counterpart. He argued that Japan did well in the past by sending poor presents to Chinese emperors who chose to view them as humble tribute, and who would send much richer presents in return to his imaginary Japanese vassals. With this historical analogy Nakasone was implying that Japan could switch from its American horse to a Chinese horse to keep riding for free. For other Japanese, the shift was simply a matter of business: the United States was plunged in a deep financial crisis that was cutting American demand for Japanese cars and everything else, while Chinese demand for Japanese goods kept increasing. Even in the Gaimusho, Japan's Foreign Ministry, the official keeper of the alliance, there was a growing number of converts to neutrality, with some even leaning towards China, so much so that those who resisted the drift became known as the "the Okazaki boys" (though some were women), a reference to the enlightened semi-hard-liner Hisahiko Okazaki, a charismatic rarity among Japanese diplomats who believed in a more vigorous foreign policy.

That was what the future looked like, but what ensued was the very opposite of the China-Japan convergence that would end the American alliance. And the reversal happened entirely because of a unilateral Chinese decision to revive long dormant maritime claims all around China, which in many cases extended very far from China proper. There can only be theories about why these provocations started, because the Communist Party decides everything in the strictest secrecy. (This opacity has become even thicker now that Xi Jinping decides everything and Politburo meetings are reduced to a formality). But on the question of how it happened, there is no uncertainty: very quickly and very sharply.

Coincidentally, I was in Beijing in September 2009 as the guest of a strategic forum run by China's most elevated military officers at the so-called Academy of Military Science, which is nothing like West Point and more like a military-corporate headquarters (with hotel-sized guest quarters of extraordinary luxury). My hosts were friends of long standing in some cases, including the charming and notoriously hawkish retired Admiral Luo Yuan, but I was also looking forward to the participation of the elegant Vice Foreign Minister Fu Ying. No sooner did she arrive than I noticed that she had changed: her tone had become peremptory and her gestures angular, in the brusque manner of a drill sergeant. America down! China up! It was only later that an explanation occurred to me: since the Obama Administration had urgently asked for China's help earlier in the year — it sought, and obtained, massive public expenditures to help relaunch global demand in the usual Keynesian manner (I saw the road-building myself in Yunnan) — the significance of the financial crisis was grossly over-estimated in Beijing. Some must have viewed it as the start of the long-forecast "general crisis of capitalism" that Soviet leaders had awaited with growing impatience since 1945.

When I was startled by Fu Ying's abrupt change (she is still around, in an even higher if largely honorific position), I did not know that some months earlier, on May 7, 2009, China had sent a map to the United Nations that marked its enormous maritime claims — most of the South China Sea's three and a half million square kilometers — with nine dashes in lieu of an actual perimeter, thereby allowing room to extend the claim. But this completely outlandish map did not make the news, and neither did the joint protest of the Philippines, Indonesia, and Malaysia (Vietnam did not bother) of claims to waters within sight of their coasts and very far away from China. That is how the leaders of the Communist Party of China abandoned Deng Xiaoping's famous injunction to "keep a low profile and bide your time" and suddenly challenged the entire world order, because they mistook the tumble in American finances for the downfall of the United States. As of this writing, the crisis thus opened continues, only it is worse.

But back in 2009 nobody paid much attention when China advanced a maritime claim against Japan as well, in part because everybody ritualistically expected more amity in Beijing, and in part because China had revived an especially feeble claim to an exceptionally trivial territory: the uninhabited Senkaku islets and rocks, whose combined dry surfaces amount to some four square miles. Of course even the smallest islands can bring vast exclusive economic zones with them, but in this case any fishing value was irrelevant because Chinese fishermen were already allowed free access, while vague rumors of oil and gas under the seabed were ridiculed by the industry. The Japanese government did not respond to the sudden turn in Chinese policy. With the new Democratic Party in power for the first time, there was no eagerness to take on a new problem, which moreover seemed at most a minor irritant. As compared to Beijing's claims to the three and a half million square kilometers of the South China Sea, outlined in hand-drawn dashes

162

on a map from 1947 with about as much legal value as a child's drawing, the Senkakus drawn to scale would amount to a dot.

Then, on September 7, 2010, the Chinese trawler *Minjinyu* 5179, one of many fishing vessels in Senkaku's waters, collided with not one but two Japanese Coast Guard patrol vessels. The Japanese boarded the trawler and immediately discovered the cause of the incident: the skipper was drunk. He was detained along with his boat. That same day Japan's ambassador in Beijing was summoned to the Foreign Ministry to be told that Japan should stop operating in the Senkaku archipelago. Two days later, the foreign minister announced that China was asserting its jurisdiction over the area, and Japan's ambassador was again summoned to the Foreign Ministry to be told that Japan had to release the trawler and crew immediately. In Japan a routine investigation was underway, for which the skipper of the Chinese fishing vessel was remanded on September 10. Two days later, Japan's ambassador in Beijing was again summoned, but this time by Dai Bingguo of the Council of State, a figure far above the foreign minister, to urge the Japanese government to be wise, and release the fishermen and the trawler immediately. Concurrently, a slew of China-Japan meetings designed to advance the new era of cooperation were delayed, even though Japan announced that the trawler and its crew members were about to be released, with only the skipper detained for the judicial process already underway. The local court, following normal procedure extended his detention till September 29.

That is when the fishing incident stopped being an incident about fishing. A nation-wide campaign of incitement lead by the Chinese Foreign Ministry itself via its daily press briefings started in a matter of hours after the incident, so that already on the next day there was a major protest outside the Japanese embassy with flag-waving and loudspeaker demands for Japan's withdrawal from the islands. More protests followed on a much larger scale, with many demonstrators wearing brand-new "Oppose Japan" shirts, and this time the mob became so menacing that police arrived in great force to block the entire area. Attacks on individual Japanese were reported in several cities, and after an attack on a Japanese school in Tianjin all Japanese schools in China were closed, as mobs formed in front of any Japanese office — while Foreign Ministry spokesmen continued to add to the incitement as incidents spread through China's cities. For good measure, four Japanese corporate employees were arrested and accused of filming military targets, while a rumor was circulated that China would strangle Japan's high-tech manufacturing by stopping the supply of rare earths — cerium, dysprosium, erbium, europium, gadolinium, holmium, lanthanum, lutetium, neodymium, praseodymium, promethium, samarium, terbium, thulium, ytterbium, and yittrium — both obscure and indispensable for high-tech, and at the time produced only in China.

In Japan, there was no clear response by its prime minister, its foreign minister, or indeed anyone in government, except for the duty official at the very small branch office of the Okinawa prosecutor in the remote island of Ishigaki. Finally, on September 22, Chinese Prime Minister Wen Jiabao issued a formal threat: "If Japan persists willfully and arbitrarily, China will take further actions...with dire consequences."

The threat worked: instead of being tried for the damage he inflicted, the captain of the Japanese fishing vessel was released two days later. But the Foreign Ministry spokesman in Beijing who had led the incitement campaign against Japan (even some Toyota drivers were harassed) did not relent, and gleefully demanded in triumphalist tones an apology from

164

Japan and compensation for holding the skipper, ruling out any compensation for the damage that he had inflicted on the Japanese patrol vessels.

In Japan, most people concluded that the country had been humiliated by a weak government, but the resulting crisis of confidence was still unresolved on March 11, 2011, when a powerful earthquake and a uniquely severe tsunami inflicted enormous damage in the northeast of the country, released radiation from a damaged reactor at Fukushima nearer to Tokyo, and traumatized much of the population. Prime Minister Naoto Kan and his government were conspicuously outmatched by events. A little over a month later, the Prime Minister of Australia, Julia Gillard, came to Japan on a long-scheduled visit that she refused to cancel, at a time when nobody else would travel to Japan because of radiation dangers from the Fukushima reactor, wildly exaggerated as usual. In a joint press conference with Japan's prime minister, she replied to a question about China: "We do have a longstanding defense cooperation between our two countries and a trilateral defense cooperation between our two countries and the United States. We've taken the opportunity of our discussions today to talk about furthering the bilateral defense cooperation between us and of course we will be working on a trilateral basis as the United States works its way through its Global Force Posture Review." That technicality was a nice touch, for it underlined what China meant for Julia Gillard in the wake of the Senkaku boat incident, when the exuberant amity of the defense minister's encounter was suddenly replaced by outright hostility. China had made itself into a defense-planning problem, a potential threat to be confronted, and not just an economic partner, no matter how much coal, gas, iron ore, and beef it was importing from Australia. In retrospect,

Gillard's visit to Tokyo in the aftermath of Fukushima can be recognized as the foundational act of the "maritime alliance" that now connects and cross-connects Australia, Japan, Vietnam, and India with the United States, an alliance in which Singapore is a tacit member, and of which Taiwan is at least a beneficiary.

All was set for change in Japan, but it was not until the following year that the electoral calendar allowed the Japanese public to express its views of the Democratic Party, and of China in effect. In December 2012, Shinzo Abe's Liberal Democratic Party won 294 seats out of 480 in the Lower House of parliament, with additional seats controlled by allied parties much more than enough to become the "ruling party" once again, with the slogan "take back Japan" and clear promises of a strong line on the territorial dispute with China, as well as of monetary easing and even higher public spending. The grandson of one of Japan's most important prime ministers and the son of a top political leader who died before he could follow in his father's footsteps, Abe did not double defense spending or issue strident declarations but nevertheless he changed Japan's entire stance on the world scene. He enacted a sharp attitudinal change in the government, and also a reorganization, both very small in scale and very important. Within the Foreign Ministry, the "Okazaki boys" became decisively stronger without any need to purge the shrinking number of "panda-huggers," and within the armed forces there was an upsurge of morale as the protection of Japan's national territory would no longer be impeded by political timidity.

But it was a seemingly minor reorganization completed

within a year that really set the new course: some diplomats, some military officers, and some intelligence officials were re-assigned to a new National Security Secretariat. That obscure bit of bureaucratic engineering was actually a large break from the past. Until then, Japanese diplomats had coordinated important matters with their American counterparts, and the Japanese military of the different services had coordinated with their uniformed American counterparts, but there was no need for inter-Japanese coordination because it was the Americans who decided strategic matters and managed any crisis. Yet as soon as the new National Security Secretariat started operating, it became clear that Japan had become its own crisis manager and could forge its own foreign policy as an active ally of the United States instead of just a passive follower.

The Chinese had issued a demand for negotiations over the Senkakus but did not even obtain a denial — it was simply ignored, because the islands were Japanese and there was nothing to discuss. And there matters stand until today, as Japan also completed its trajectory from optimistic amity towards China to weary suspicion, accompanied by both self-strengthening and a reaching out for allies. That meant the United States, of course, and Australia, whose government had taken the initiative, but it also meant India, with which Shinzo Abe had an unexpectedly strong connection. It had started as an inheritance from his grandfather Kishi's visit to India in 1957, which achieved almost nothing but was nonetheless important because no Japanese political leader had shown his face outside Japan since 1945, and none would have been welcomed in a long list of countries, especially those that had suffered from Japan's wartime conduct. India, too, was invaded by Japan, but it was then British India, and Prime Minister Jawaharlal Nehru told Kishi that Japan had been the great inspiration for himself and his colleagues in the struggle for independence, because its self-made modernization and its defeat of Russia in 1905 gave them confidence that they, too, could be independent of imperialist tutelage. So in one country at least Japan was held in high esteem; and from that bit of family history Abe developed a serious interest in India, which developed into a personal connection with his natural political counterpart, Narendra Modi, the leader of the center-right Bharatiya Janata Party and Chief Minister of Gujarat. When Modi became Prime Minister of India in 2014, all was set for a rapid intensification of India-Japan cooperation, in everything from intelligence sharing to road-building. Multiple encounters between Abe and Modi, marked by genuine cordiality, were followed by action on the ground, none of it explicitly aimed at China but all of it driven by China's new posture, and all of it bound to increase India's ability to withstand China's power and to cooperate strategically with Japan — for example, in support of Vietnam. The maritime alliance launched by Australia and taken up with enthusiasm by Japan now embraced India as well. With Abe now gone owing to poor health, his hand-picked successor Yoshihide Suga is set to continue the same policies, including prioritizing India in Japanese economic aid.

III

It was not supposed to be that way.

For India's post-independence elite, exemplified by the elegant Jawaharlal Nehru, China was a fellow Asian country that had also emerged from foreign domination; there was little contact with it, but even less conflict. Then very soon, in the winter of 1950, China became the major Asian protagonist in the Korean War, earning much respect as it stood up to the Americans, undeterred by their immense power.

India-China relations were codified through the negotiation of an unusually elaborate friendship treaty in 1954 in which much was made of "The Five Principles of Peaceful Coexistence," which included "respect for each other's territorial unity integrity and sovereignty" and an agreement on trade and pilgrimages between the "Tibet Region of China" and India, which was signed on April 28, 1954. With that settled, Prime Minister Nehru visited Beijing in October 1954, with Mao at his most friendly: "The United States does not recognize our two countries as great powers." he said "Let us propose that they hand over their big-power status to us, all right?" In the Nehru entourage there was an overflow of enthusiasm, now remembered by the slogan *Hindi Chini bhai bhai,* "Indian, Chinese, brother, brother" — the motto of a new era of solidarity between the two most populous nations on earth. The potential for collaboration seemed immense, especially because India's economy was supposed to be centrally planned like China's, so joint projects would not have to depend on the whims of short-sighted businessmen out for quick profits.

The era of good feelings lasted almost five years, even though the two governments did not actually collaborate on anything much, while some of India's many communist parties were either "pro-Chinese" or Maoist, and also dabbled in terrorism. But it was over Tibet that India said bye-bye to *bhai bhai.* On March 30, 1959, with Tibet having exploded in a widespread uprising after Chinese troops entered the country in great numbers to impose Beijing's rule in earnest, the Dalai Lama and his retinue fled through precarious high mountain tracks across India's border into remote Tawang, the seat of a vast Lamaist monastery and the terminus of an interminable track down to the lowlands with their passable roads.

169

Nehru and his government were not sentimental about the Dalai Lama, though they could not drive him back across the border, not with waves of refugees testifying to the brutal repression underway, and so they were forced to host him, provoking Chinese protests. Yet it was something much more fundamental that changed Nehru's and India's attitude to China: so long as Tibet retained its autonomy, it remained a buffer that kept Chinese troops a long way from India, so securely that there was no particular reason to patrol the very long and scarcely accessible Tibetan border segments from the Kashmir cease-fire lines to Nepal, in Sikkim, and then east of Bhutan to the Burmese border.

When oblivion gave way to scouting, patrols, and ground surveys, the Indians made a startling discovery that started a border quarrel which has been dormant for long periods but is still unresolved, and periodically explodes in acts of violence: the Chinese had seized the northern edge of Kashmir's Indian side, the vast 15,000-square-mile Aksai Chin plateau, and built a Xinjiang-Tibet highway across it. They had also intruded in the high-altitude vastness of Ladakh nearby, and also at the opposite end of the Tibet-India frontier in what was then the North East Frontier Agency and is now the state of Arunachal — except that these were not intrusions for the Chinese, who claimed not merely those extremities as their own but almost all of Arunachal till the edges of the Brahmaputra river valley.

Having belatedly decided to monitor the northernmost segments of their British inheritance, the Indians started running into Chinese patrols that disputed their maps, with numerous incidents and some shooting, until — in October, 1962 — the Chinese launched major offensives with tens of thousands of soldiers both in the west against Ladakh and in the east against Arunachal, advancing fast and deep after

170

surprising and overrunning the thinly spread defenders, with thousands of Indian troops killed and captured. Having demonstrated their vast military superiority, the Chinese withdrew from their new conquests within the month, but not from their prior gains in the Aksai Chin. Nehru was utterly humiliated, and his closest associate, the "progressive" firebrand V. K. Krishna Menon, who had served as a peculiarly anti-military defense minister since 1957 (he favored officers who had eschewed combat in World War Two), was driven from office amid public opprobrium that lasted until his death. Mao Zedong would later tell people that his aim in attacking India was not to start a wider war but to end the border incidents and to persuade the Indians to negotiate seriously over what China needed, which oddly enough is still the Chinese position today, because in Beijing they truly, honestly, cannot understand why "poor and dirty" India wishes to defy China.

Notwithstanding all this, India's ruling Congress Party retained an anti-Western core and wanted good relations with China no matter what, all the more so when China's great economic advance seemed to offer opportunities for India as well. With the humiliation of 1962 receding ever more into the past, and with some Congress leaders and officials openly indifferent about exact borders in the trackless and useless high Himalayas, relations gradually improved to the point that by 2011 the new slogan "Chindustan" emerged, amid mutual congratulations, to replace the old *bhai bhai*. There were again heady promises of vast cooperative projects, and also hard-headed calculations that good relations with India would persuade the Chinese to stop giving all their support, and weapons, to Pakistan. Very serious people in India were respectfully heard as they argued that India had to wean itself

171

from American temptations and finally throw its lot in with China, first of all by inviting its vast "Road and Belt" infrastructure projects instead of spurning them.

But that is not how things turned out. Just like Japan before it, India was forced into an anti-Chinese stance by China's irrepressible territorial expansionism, which Xi Jinping only intensified when he came to power in November 2012, posturing in uniform whenever possible. Instead of the renewed hopes of amity of 2011, by the time the BJP won the elections and Modi became Prime Minister in 2014 India was already committed to a pan-democratic alignment with the United States, Japan, and their more operational allies, including Israel in the West and Vietnam in the East (with both of which Indian military relations were intense and important). And this is how matters stand in the wake of the fighting last year in the Galwan Valley and on the edge of Aksai Chin, as India completed its trajectory from hopeful friendship towards China to weary suspicion, ready for outright hostility.

IV

In spite of the clear meaning of all that has happened elsewhere, even now many in Washington provincially take it for granted that American relations with China have been shaped, and will be shaped, by Americans, by the plans of the Biden presidency, by the doings and undoings of Donald Trump, by the Obama Administration before him (whose NSC advisor Susan Rice once declared that she could "shape" China), and indeed by their predecessors going all the way back to Nixon.

It is now a commonplace to assert that American policymakers have been culpably naïve in believing that China's increasing wealth, and the rising standard of living of the vast majority of the population, would necessarily compel the regime to liberalize, eventually leading to insurmountable demands for political self-expression, leading to decentralization and even democracy. At some level the complaint is valid, but it overlooks the vast reality that the regime did liberalize, and to an extent unimaginable when I first visited in 1976, when Mao was still alive, and then again in the aftermath of the violent repression in Tiananmen Square in 1989, until the wholly unexpected reversals that followed the long-expected rise of Xi Jinping in November 2012.

In 1976, Chinese men and women in the countryside could freely wear whatever rags they possessed, but in the cities almost everyone I saw was in blue Mao suits, men and women alike, with no trace of make-up allowed. Ordinary people scrambled along looking neither right nor left, as if on their way to urgent missions. (The most urgent of all was to secure some cabbages to dry on balconies for the winter, without which teeth would fall out on a diet of rice, millet, and sorghum.) Day after day I would wander around Beijing without seeing one person smiling, not even parents with children, and this was true of the other cities I visited, including almost tropical Chengdu and breezy Shanghai, not to speak of Lhasa, where the Tibetans freezing in cotton uniforms walked silently among the Chinese troops who were watching over them. I had been warned that I would have trouble breathing in Lhasa because of its altitude, but the real problem was in Beijing: in Maoist economics, "the night soil" of human excrement was a precious resource collected in buckets all over Beijing and then hand-carted across it on the way to the surrounding farmed fields, so the entire city smelled like a toilet.

By traveling in China I was already exercising a freedom unimaginable for the officials I was meeting: no travel whatever was allowed for them or indeed anyone else, unless under orders, and that was a real hardship for educated couples because the Communist Party preferred to assign husbands and wives to different cities. It also meant that there was no such thing as tourism, no recreational trips to the Great Wall not far from Beijing or the Ming tombs even closer. When I visited those places, they were deserted. As for entertainment, there were occasional Beijing Opera performances and there were color television broadcasts, but in the former the traditional hyper-colorful historical melodramas had been replaced by the grim class-struggle operas imposed by Jiang Qing, Mao's ex-actress wife and one of the Gang of Four then ruling China for the moribund Great Leader. As for television, it offered political tirades against Party enemies (mostly the "capitalist roader" Deng Xiaoping, then under house arrest), more Jiang Qing operas, and brief looks at world news unlike any other version thereof, including Soviet television, which seemed almost normal by comparison. In fact there was no television for most Chinese: color sets were very few and even black and white sets were unimaginable luxuries for single families — they were communal if they were present at all.

In 1989, by contrast, on the eve of the Tiananmen Square demonstrations and massacre, China was a festival of freedom as compared to 1976. In a mere thirteen years, along with the opening of all parts of China to travel and of large parts of the economy to foreign business (even the American defense industry was engaged in joint ventures), there had been liberalization across the board. People could dress as they liked, couples went around holding hands, and there was the beginning of foreign travel, with business types already on jets to London, New York, and Tokyo and Cantonese more modestly riding trains to Hong Kong. Academics invited by foreign universities could and did visit them, and then return and talk of their experiences of academic and political freedom, in some cases lecturing to that effect in universities across China. The opening to China by Nixon and Kissinger in 1972 had been a strictly geopolitical move, and was much needed at a time when the Soviet Union was rising and the United States was sinking into the Vietnam war, but if any of the protagonists had entertained fantastic hopes that liberalization would also follow, they would have been vindicated by 1989.

What happened next, however, was that Beijing's students started demonstrating for democracy and freedom — even as many Sinologists in Western universities were insisting that there was no "Chinese" concept of freedom. To leave no doubts, the students famously built the ten-meter-tall white statue of the Goddess of Democracy and Freedom, whose features were unambiguously European, and placed it in Tiananmen to face the Mao photo on the outer wall of the forbidden city. It was destroyed on June 4, 1989 by the Army troops sent by Den Xiaoping and his Politburo subordinates to drive off the students, with some thousands shot dead, so as to regain control of Tiananmen Square, of Beijing itself, and of China at large, because by then there were student uprisings in many places around the country. In the grim aftermath of the regime's nation-wide intimidation, some things ended that were never resumed, notably American and European arms sales to China; but after the most prominent student leaders were caught or escaped to the West, most aspects of liberalization resumed, notably foreign travel for the ever-increasing number that could afford it — the substantive achievement of a freedom that had been absolutely denied to the citizens of the USSR.

While there was widespread repression after the Tiananmen uprising, there were also limits to the crackdown that were previously unknown. Deng Xiaoping, who had himself been kept under house arrest, and whose son was crippled for life after he was thrown from a third-story window onto the street, was determined to have supreme power in the Party and to keep the Party under control, but he did not murder his rivals as Mao had done, and there were limits even to the punishment of dissidents. Ding Zilin, for example, the Beijing philosophy professor who started the "Mothers of Tiananmen" group together with her professor husband after their son was killed by troops on the square, eventually lost her job (as did her husband), was held under house arrest at times and imprisoned briefly after holding one more protest, and was forced to take a holiday away from Beijing during the 2008 Olympics, but she was not stripped of her pension or thrown out of her university-allocated apartment, and it was not until the ascendancy of Xi Jinping that she was prevented from speaking with foreign journalists.

More broadly, after the regression in 1989, progress in all directions resumed with increasing energy, starting with the economy of course but also culturally, with a rising interest in the Western classics, as testified by the appearance of successive translations of the *Iliad* and the *Odyssey*, both literal and poetical, by commercial publishers out for a profit, who evidently found enough buyers for such books. Hebrew was the other classical language of increasing interest, and this spilled over into Yiddish literature (I saw multiple translations of Sholem Aleichem's tales in the Wangfujin bookstore!) to the extent that there are courses in Yiddish in more than one Chinese university, alongside many more in Hebrew for evangelicals and techies alike.

By 2004 the liberalization of Chinese life had spilled over into foreign policy, with the enunciation by Zheng Bijian, the regime's policy guru then and later, of the "Peaceful Rise" policy, according to which China would become ever more prosperous and more powerful but would nevertheless respect internal norms, starting with international law itself. China would not threaten any foreign country. Taiwan, always a special case, was to "rejoin" the mainland peacefully, and on its own timetable. In retrospect, many view Zheng Bijian's proclamation as deceptive, but I do not: having known Zheng for years, I am quite certain that he was sincere, and all the more so because when I confronted him in 2012 about the multiple intrusions and territorial claims that had disillusioned countries from Japan to Sweden, his answer to my complaint was *"Shīkòng de mǎ,"* or "runaway horses." He was referring to the dangerous arrogance I had seen in Vice Foreign Minister Fu Ying's body language in the wake of the financial crisis in 2009, misinterpreted as the final crisis of Western capitalism and a license to expand China's power in all directions. Zheng Bijian's remark was significant, because some backtracking soon became evident, with a lowering of the temperature on the Senkakus and other territorial claims and a general pulling back that was articulated in a 7,000-character (that is, very long) article by Dain Bingguo, the head of the State Council, which squarely reaffirmed the "Peaceful Rise" doctrine.

In that period there was also a genuine political liberalization, exemplified by the rule of Hu Jintao, who had all three top jobs as Chairman of the Central Military Commission, General Secretary of the Party, and President of China, but who nonetheless interpreted his role as a *primus inter pares,* not another Mao or even Deng Xiaoping, conferring important roles on his colleagues. Hu also allowed provincial bosses wide

177

leeway to develop their provinces — which is how Bo Xilai rose to be the all-powerful boss of Chongqing and its thirty million people, beautifying it very successfully, and frog-marching its municipal employees into obligatory party-hymn singing, while his wife Gu Kailai accumulated wealth until her clumsy murder of a British helpmate. Other provincial bosses were less colorful, but they too went in different directions, and this decentralization, too, was a form of liberalization.

Thus the belief that China would liberalize with increasing prosperity, and thereby become an increasing acceptable participant of international society, was not all a foolish delusion. Even in the administration of justice there was considerable liberalization, as I discovered in backhanded fashion when driving on a long journey with a Chinese friend of a friend. He was a policeman, and soon started complaining about the judges in his city: "my men chase a thief, they finally catch him, and then a few months later he is walking around again, released for good behavior!" Western-style law degrees and lawyers having become important with the opening of China to foreign investors; the Party started appointing lawyers as judges, and they could not help but introduce legal principles, such as better evidence than the confessions of badly bruised defendants. Fortunately, as my companion said, we still execute drug smugglers, and as for foreign spies (he looked directly at me) the Guoanbu still takes them away, that being the Ministry of State Security, the Chinese KGB.

And then, in December 2012, Xi Jinping became the party boss in Beijing, a year later rising to become President of the Republic and Chairman of the Central Military Commission. It

178

was if a locomotive operator simply put the train in reverse, in a process of de-liberalization that has yet to end. The outrages are everywhere: the loss of Hong Kong's erstwhile freedoms, the mass imprisonment of Xinjiang's Uyghurs and Kazakhs in dozens of massive re-education centers, and in foreign affairs a coarse and undiplomatic arrogance ("wolf diplomacy") and a revival of China's territorial quarrels with Japan, Vietnam, and India. As for the United States, Xi Jinping's visit to the United States and to Obama's White House in September 2015 was supposed to resolve the most acute problems — the Chinese theft of American technology and the seizure and militarization of the Paracel islets and the Spratly coral reefs; but Obama discovered that his NSC advisor Susan Rice had been over-optimistic to the point of delusion, and reacted by ordering the first of a series of "freedom of navigation" patrols by American warships that continues still.

Xi's regression had started within the Party itself. The local potentates who had risen under Hu Jintao's deliberately relaxed rule — he had sought locally appropriate polices — were all placed under investigation, with most found guilty of improper enrichment and stripped of everything they had, their families thrown out of Party housing and they themselves detained for long periods if not actually sent to prison or even executed. (The especially egregious Bo Xilai and his wife were given life terms.)

Nor did Xi tolerate the influence of the previous generation of party bosses, as Hu Jintao had done. While Hu himself was not arrested, he was silenced, very visibly so when Xi brings him along for decorative purposes, which happens less and less. As for the non-Han nationalities of China, their very limited rights of self-expression were altogether withdrawn, because Xi is not content with the Party formula that was originally Stalin's: "nationalist in form, communist in content." He wants Tibetans, Uyghurs, Kazakhs, and all the others — most recently including Inner Mongolian Mongols — to stop using their native languages except in domestic settings, and therefore he sees no need for state education in those languages. They are to become Han-Chinese in form as well as Communists in content. Xi Jinping's highest priority is to reaffirm the primacy of the Communist Party's ideology, starting with Marx and Engels (in countless re-enactments and anime showing them in mid-Victorian suits with anatomically correct beards and mustaches) and ending with Mao, whose works are now obligatory reading once again. Mao's very long speech "on protracted war" has been revived as a manual for defeating the United States.

Xi Jinping's very particular devotion to Mao and his all-out attempt to revive Mao's Party is the very last thing I would have expected from him. Since he was parked at the Central Party School before his elevation, Xi received a number of foreign visitors, including a former finance minister of Italy, Giulio Tremonti, once my co-author on a book, and he did converse at length with a faculty member whom I also know well. I heard much about Xi Jinping that was unfiltered. Nobody came right out and said it, but knowing the basic facts of Xi's life it seemed self-evident that he would strive to add legal protections to the Party rules, and would also press for more humane policies, at least within the Party. Those facts are as follows: Xi Jinping's father, Xi Zhongxun, was a very senior party official, who was abruptly purged by Mao and sent to work in a remote factory in 1963, when Xi was ten. Three years later the Red Guards unleashed by Mao's Cultural Revolution closed his middle school, looted the family home, beat up his mother, and treated his half-sister Xi

Heping so violently that she was driven to suicide. His father was recalled from exile to be paraded, shoved, and beaten as an enemy of the revolution, while Xi's mother Qi Xin walked alongside him, herself beaten whenever her denunciations of Xi's father were not loud enough. His seventeen-year-old sister Qiaoqiao was sent off to Inner Mongolia to work on a desolate farm where there was no food, and was saved from starvation by the daughter of her father's friend, the Inner Mongolia party boss.

In 1968 Xi's father was sent to prison, and the next year, when Xi was sixteen, he himself was sent to work and "learn from the peasants" in the remarkably primitive village of Liangjiahe, Wen'anyi district, Yanchuan county, in Shaanxi province, whose capital Xian, of terracotta soldiers fame, is now highly developed but still contains much abject poverty — though not the raw hunger and freezing cold that Xi encountered when he arrived to live in a cave house. Xi was utterly miserable. He ran away, he was caught, he was sent back. But he had one object with him that was his only consolation: the Chinese translation of Goethe's *Faust,* the story of the savant who made a bargain with the devil. Xi read it again and again, learning it by heart. This edition of *Faust* was the only one available in Chinese, translated by Guo Moruo, an eminent writer and high party official, who was himself persecuted by the Red Guards in 1966, escaping worse harm by abject self-criticism, the repudiation of all his previous books, and the denunciation of all his former friends and colleagues as counterrevolutionaries. With that he survived, but both of his sons were tortured until they committed suicide. Aided by a fawning celebration of the genius of Mao's talentless wife Jiang Qing and his utter loyalty to Mao, Guo Moruo was eventually readmitted to high party status, complete with his own luxurious manor house, a staff of servants, a state limousine, and a large collection of antique furniture — a Faustian bargain indeed.

There is no evidence that Guo Moruo himself influenced Xi Jinping, though Guo found his salvation in total devotion to Mao in spite of everything done to him, just as Xi Jinping would do. But *Faust* certainly left a very deep impression. When Xi said as much upon meeting Chancellor Angela Merkel, she probably dismissed it as a bit of cultural flattery, but Xi's devotion was given physical form in 2015, when his own power was fully consolidated: the Shanghai International Studies University was granted funds to translate the immensity of the complete works of Johann Wolfgang von Goethe, novels, poems, plays, memoirs, letters, diaries, treatises, and shorter writings of literary and aesthetic criticism — an ocean of words. The entirety of Goethe is set to appear in Chinese in some fifty volumes containing some thirty million Chinese characters; eighty scholars from six universities and two Chinese state academies are hard at work. And this same Goethean has established concentration camps — one is reminded that Goethe's oak tree stood on the grounds of Buchenwald.

Dealing with Xi's China as a geopolitical threat is proving to be less difficult than anticipated, because its aggressive stance has evoked vigorous responses from allies declared and undeclared, from Australia to India. Dealing with China as a technological competitor is also emerging as a less fearful prospect, because the reverse side of the immense amount of technology theft by China in the last two decades is the weakness of basic science in China, which leaves it bereft when the flow of technology is abruptly cut off by American security measures. But dealing with Xi and his Faustian reversion to a

Maoist interpretation of Party rule will be far more difficult, especially if the destruction of Hong Kong's liberties presages a heightened threat to Taiwan, the one place in the world that the United States must defend by statute. Only one thing can avert greater dangers: China's reversion to the Peaceful Rise policy of 2004, which was very successful while it lasted. We may yet see this, but only after Xi Jinping's fall, which we cannot ourselves bring about, because the fate of China lies in Chinese hands.

ROBERTO CALASSO

The Review Years

"You ask me how *Commerce* began... One day, all of a sudden, Valéry said: 'Why couldn't we continue our meetings by publishing our discussions in a review? As a title I suggest *Commerce*, the commerce of ideas.' That idea delighted all of us there. The editors (Larbaud, Valéry, and Fargue) were appointed immediately. Adrienne Monnier and I took responsibility for putting everything in motion and we started straight away." These are the words of Marguerite Caetani, describing events in 1924. She was born Marguerite Gilbert Chapin, an American who had arrived in Europe in 1902 and married Roffredo Caetani, Prince of Bassiano. In Paris they called her "the Princess," though she signed herself Marguerite Caetani.

Of the three editors, Paul Valéry was the authority, Léon-Paul Fargue a writer admired above all by other writers, and Valery Larbaud a great literary go-between, a mercurial ferryman whenever one spoke in a certain way about literature (as Italo Svevo and James Joyce could testify). Neither Marguerite Caetani, who financed *Commerce*, nor the three editors had anything to proclaim. There was never any question of drawing up a program for the review, nor was it ever raised in conversation with friends, however distant or occasional.

Before the first issue had appeared, Valéry wrote to Larbaud:

> I'm in receipt in Rome of your esteemed letter of the
> 12th which takes me back somewhat to the atmosphere
> of our lunches, infrequent though friendly. The fruit of
> this union is *Commerce* ... The tedious thing is writing.
> ... I would have been very pleased if we had founded a
> review where there was no need to write. You realize
> what advantage! Reader, author, everyone happy.
>
> "Without pressing so far into the perfection of the
> genre, it would have been possible to fulfill what I had
> thought up when I was 23 and had a phobia about the
> penholder.
>
> I wanted to do a review of 2 to 4 pages.
> Title: The Essential.
> And nothing more than *ideas*, in 2 or 3 lines.
> None other than the lean...
> It could be signed with initials, for economy

Marguerite Caetani's name never appeared in the twenty-eight issues of *Commerce*. The review's symbol was a pair of

185

old Roman scales, an image of which appeared opposite the frontispiece of the first issue, beneath the indication of the print run (1,600 copies). Recognizing *the proper weight*: this was the essential premise of the review. Everything not in this balanced spirit was rejected.

It has to be remembered that reviews were those that had *spines* (not the same, therefore, as general periodicals such as *The New York Review of Books, The New Yorker, or the Times Literary Supplement*). They are now largely a matter of the past, since literary reviews are among the considerable number of cultural forms that have gradually disappeared over the last fifty years. Their golden age, it is now clear, was between the two world wars, with notable early examples in the years straddling 1900 (*La Revue Blanche, The Yellow Book, Die Insel*).

Marguerite Caetani was too elegant not to shun like the plague any semblance of a literary hostess. She was a Guermantes, not a Verdurin. This is also why she has generally escaped the attention of many rough and rapacious academics who continue to fill their mouths with "modernism" and "avant-garde." Marguerite Caetani has not been detected by their narrow radar. Perhaps this is why little of importance has been written about her. All the more conspicuous, therefore, is the magnificent portrait of Marguerite (or Margherita, as she calls her) that Elena Croce left us in her memoir *Due città,* or *Two Cities.*

It is a portrait of Marguerite Caetani's years in Italy, when she ran the journal *Botteghe Oscure* between 1948 and 1960 in Rome, a journal much vaunted by Anglo-American expatriates of the time, an excellent review, but which gives the sense of a disaster that has already struck — and can only be read as a colonial version of *Commerce*. To see this, it is enough to put a copy of *Commerce* next to one of *Botteghe Oscure*. The comparison is entirely unfavorable to the latter: poor paper quality, less appealing format and page layout, too many contributors (this was the review's main defect, which risked straying into the realms of well-meaning amateurishness). And yet, as the Italian critic Pietro Citati observed in an interview, "*Botteghe Oscure* was the finest Italian literary review of that time, infinitely finer than *Politecnico, Paragone*, etc. etc., which are much better known."

The writer and poet Georges Limbour wrote an ode to the index of *Commerce*, which began with "Artaud" and ended with "Zen." This was the peculiar wonder of *Commerce*: almost all the names there resonate, they still have something to say. Or at least they stir curiosity. The same cannot be said about *Botteghe Oscure*, where one runs through the names in certain parts of the index as in a telephone directory (there were over seven hundred published writers in five languages). Midway in its lifespan the golden age of reviews came to an end, and no one realized that it had happened. The very idea of the literary review — of the little magazine, as Americans used to call it — had come apart. And *Botteghe Oscure* already seemed more like a weekly almanac than a review.

"Regal" was the word used by Elena Croce — who was generally austere in her use of adjectives — to describe Marguerite Caetani, explaining that "Margherita had alone occupied her almost sovereign role," along with Bernard Berenson, the only possible king in the intellectual geography of an Italy that was now remote and almost undecipherable in the years immediately after World War II. She was bound to him by a friendship that was "almost the emblem of discordant harmony." They were well practiced at exchanging friendly barbs. Berenson said of her: "She is always looking for a new art more ugly than the one before," touching a rather sensitive point about his friend, who lived always "in wait for a completely new 'new.'"

Berenson, a Lithuanian Jew who had emigrated to America and masterfully integrated into the most Waspish part of Boston society, said of himself: "I have spent too much time and money making myself a gentleman" — and he had no intention whatsoever of giving up what he had achieved. Marguerite Caetani, by contrast, had grown up in Boston and her social rise had required no effort. During the years of *Botteghe Oscure*, when a friend observed that the title of the review might be easily misinterpreted, since *botteghe oscure*, which means "dark shops" and refers to the ancient Roman market that once occupied the street on which the review was located, brought to mind, for Italians, the headquarters of the Communist Party far more than the address of Palazzo Caetani, her reply was: "But we have lived here for a thousand years."

Although he rigorously avoided all contact with the world each morning to write his *Cahiers* between five (or four) and seven, when faint noises began to be heard around the house, Paul Valéry was nevertheless a consummate literary strategist and knew perfectly well that associating his name with a review was a delicate operation and bore heavy consequences. This is clearly set out in the letter that Valéry wrote to Marguerite Caetani in April 1924, two months before the first issue of *Commerce* went into print:

> If I had been able to take part in the sittings of the Secret Committee, I would have asked that our program should be stated and all provisions taken to absolutely distinguish this publication from all possible reviews. For there are now so many reviews that there is certainly no need to add another.

It would be essential to acquire an authority, occupying in the World of Letters, or in the confines of this horrible world, a singular strategic position — that of people of absolutely free spirit, who no longer have a need to make themselves known and fire revolver shots at streetlamps, and who moreover are not connected to some kind of system... I think we will have time to talk about it again on my return, in a few weeks. I will do my best to give you a *Letter, on Letters*, since it is your wish, even if I don't know where to find the time to write, considering the engagements (that I don't keep), the inconveniences, etc.

I don't think it necessary to announce the review in the press with a great fuss and to describe it in advance. I take the view that it is pointless mentioning the name of the "editors" on the front cover... It would be my view that we shouldn't have the air of addressing the public, and as if standing on a theater stage, but that we should appear as if among ourselves, with the public authorized to watch from the window... But all of this would need to be discussed orally and in person — I kiss your hand, dear Princess, charging you with all my Roman sentiments for the Prince — and to remember me to Fargue, Larbaud, Léger — if you happen to see them these days.

We open the first issue of *Commerce* and read the table of contents: Valéry, *Lettre;* Fargue, *Épaisseurs* (Densities); Larbaud, *Ce vice impuni, la lecture* (Reading, This Unpunished Vice); Saint-John Perse, *L'amitié du Prince* (Friendship of the Prince); Joyce, *Ulysses — Fragments*. The first three pieces are by the editors, and the fourth is by the review's poet in residence (and constant advisor). The fifth is the only opening by the "Secret

Committee" to the outside world — but it is Joyce's *Ulysses*, and might be enough in itself.

Let us now look at what comes first in this issue, the place usually reserved for programs, manifestos, declarations of intent — the position for all that might be most public and declared far and wide. Here, however, we find the most intimate, private, and secret of forms: a letter. It corresponds to that *Letter, on Letters* previously announced by Valéry to Caetani, but it appears without the clarification "on Letters." Why? And to whom is the letter addressed? To Caetani herself, one might think, seeing that it was she who had asked for the letter. But we find this text reappearing three years later, now with the title "Letter to a Friend," in an enlarged edition of Valéry's *Monsieur Teste*. So it was addressed to Monsieur Teste, the totemic forebear, emblem, and cipher for Valéry himself. And Monsieur Teste was the model — the only one, by definition — for an extreme solipsism. Writing a letter to him meant creating a dialogue inside Valéry's own head. It was a task for his double. From all of this it is already apparent that the opening *Lettre* in *Commerce* was an example of mental dramaturgy, a literary genre invented and practiced by only one author: Valéry himself, on the basis of Mallarmé.

At the same time, Valéry's *Lettre*, via a contorted and specious route, is also — when we read it in the pages of the review — the equivalent of a programmatic declaration, directed at the "World of Letters," at that "horrible world" within whose confines *Commerce* ought to occupy a "singular strategic position." But how is this to be construed? The *Lettre* is presented as though written on a train, on a long night journey toward Paris, "this paradise of the word." The noise of the rails, rods, and pistons mingles with an incessant mental activity. It is the "metal that forges the journey in the darkness"

— and it follows that "the brain, overexcited, oppressed by cruel treatment, necessarily generates, of itself and without knowing it, a modern literature..." This serves to keep at a distance all the avant-gardisms that fire revolver shots at streetlamps.

But there is a more important target: as the train gradually approaches Paris, the city where "verbal life is more powerful, more different, more active and capricious than everywhere else," the "harsh murmur of the train" seems to turn into the "the buzzing of a beehive." It is not just the World of Letters that comes into view, but the whole "western bazaar for the trading of phantoms." And at last Valéry's real target appears: "the activity that is called *intellectual*." At this point he embarks on a game somewhere between persiflage and sarcasm. Valéry claims, in all seriousness, not to know the meaning of the word *intellectual* as an adjective. And he explains to his interlocutor: "You know that I am a mind of the darkest kind."

Yet a sudden clarity emerges when he refers to the noun *intellectuals*. They are the followers of opinion: "Motionless people who cause great movement in the world. Or very lively people, who with the quick actions of their hands and their mouths demonstrate imperceptible powers and objects that were by their nature invisible [...] This system of strange acts, of productions and of wonders, had the all-powerful and empty reality of a game of cards." A diabolical hallucination was gradually taking form, wherein the author of the letter recognized a feeling of being captured as in a web. But at the same time he was implying that one could never be sufficiently far away and separate from it. It was on this intent, suitably disguised, that *Commerce* was founded.

Valéry's inaugural *Lettre* in *Commerce* could be regarded as an apologue, a kind of fable to signify that certain pages, having appeared in a review on a certain day and in a certain company, always have a different significance from that which they assume inside a book. Anyone today, on reading the *Lettre*, which then became *Lettre d'un ami* in the final version of *Monsieur Teste*, would find it difficult to recognize the highly strategic intention that this letter had toward the surrounding world when it appeared one day in the summer of 1924 at the start of the inaugural issue of *Commerce*. Reviews serve this purpose, too: to multiply and complicate meanings.

The *moment*, for a review, is an essential factor. While Paul Valéry was making his night journey toward Paris, Andre Breton was writing the *Manifeste du surréalisme*. *Commerce* made its debut in August 1924, whereas the *Manifeste* would appear in October of that year — and the first issue of *La Révolution Surréaliste* in December. The covers of the two reviews seem to belong to incompatible worlds: *Commerce* in pale beige, its lapidary title with no explanations, accompanied only by the date and place of printing; *La Révolution Surréaliste* in bright orange, with three group photos, the members of the "surrealist headquarters" photographed by Man Ray, as in a school photo, and then the names of a throng of contributors in the summary, and in the middle a striking sentence: "A new declaration of human rights has to be reached," about which there was no corresponding piece in the first issue. Benjamin Péret, the Surrealist poet who was one of the two editors, had wanted the graphics to resemble a popular science review called *La Nature*. The printer of *La Revolution Surrealiste* generally produced Catholic publications.

Two faraway worlds, one might say, with little in common.

And yet, starting from Cahier II, or the second issue, of *Commerce*, important texts by the surrealists are included among not many other pieces: Louis Aragon, *Un vague des rêves* (A Wave of Dreams), in Cahier II, which is also an account of the birth of surrealism, and Andre Breton, *Introduction au discours sur le peu de réalité* (Introduction to the Discourse on the Inadequacy of Reality) and *Nadja*, in Cahier III and XIII — and also writing by such reprobates as Antonin Artaud, *Fragments d'un journal d'enfer* (Fragments of a Journal of Hell), in Cahier VII and divergent figures such as the surrealist and 'pataphysical writer Rene Daumal, *Poèmes*, in Cahier XXIV. Viewed retrospectively, one might say that these texts are filtered through a close mesh, as well as being among the few still fresh works in the plethora of largely vacuous writings of the group. Surrealism was a spice added to the *Commerce* marketplace, purified of dross and of any fanciful ambition to shoot at the streetlamps.

What happened in 1924? According to Aragon, who was its visionary and astute chronicler, that year was swept away by "a wave of dreams" (the title of his long essay in *Commerce*): "Under this issue [1924] that holds a net and drags a haul of sunfish behind it, under this issue adorned with disasters, strange stars in its hair, the contagion of the dream is spread across the districts and the countryside." This explains the fact that *La Révolution Surréaliste*, making its debut at the same time that Aragon's piece was published in *Commerce*, would aim everything, even in the most childish manner, at this word: *rêve, rêve, rêve* — dream, dream, dream — as though it were heightened through repetition.

But Aragon himself was a shrewd cultural politician and he immediately compiled a list of "Presidents of the Dream Republic" where — alongside the writer Raymond

Roussel, the anarchist assassin Germaine Berton, Picasso, De Chirico, and Freud — were the names of Léon-Paul Fargue and Saint-John Perse, founding members of the "Secret Committee" of *Commerce*. Even though they were surrealists, these literati did not forget the old ways. There was a subcutaneous circulation from the start between *Commerce* and *La Révolution Surréaliste* at the very moment of their launch. The proof? The phrase on "human rights," which dominated the cover of the surrealist review, was taken from Aragon's *Vague des rêves*, which appeared in the autumn of the same year in *Commerce*, where only there is a hint of explanation found. "All the hope that is still left in this desperate universe will direct its last delirious looks toward our pathetic stall: *'It's a matter of reaching a new declaration of human rights.'*" The road toward that "new declaration" must have been long indeed, since nothing more was heard about it.

Fifteen surrealists met on two evenings, in January 1928, to conduct an "Inquiry on Sexuality," the results of which would appear two months later, with the same title and in the form of a multiple conversation, in issue number 11 of the group's review *La Révolution Surréaliste*. The conversation was begun by Breton with a question: "A man and a woman make love. To what extent does the man take into account the pleasure of the woman? Tanguy?" An old question. Puzzled responses. Yves Tanguy: "To very little extent." Others intervene. Breton steers and comments: "Naville considers therefore that materially the pleasure of the woman and that of the man, in the event of these happening simultaneously, might be translated into the emission of confused and indiscernible seminal fluids?" Pierre Naville confirms. Breton replies: "It's impossible to verify it, unless one entertains highly questionable verbal relations with a woman."

Nothing more is explained: we will never know what these "highly questionable verbal relations" are. They then move on to homosexuality (here called pederasty), about which Raymond Queneau ventures to say that he has "no moral objection whatsoever." Protests. Pierre Unik declares: "From the physical point of view, pederasty disgusts me in the same way as excrement and, from the moral point of view, I condemn it." Queneau comments that he has observed "among surrealists a particular prejudice against pederasty." At this point Breton has to intervene, to put things in place: "I accuse pederasts of proposing a mental and moral deficit to human tolerance that tends to form systematically and paralyze all the enterprises that I respect. I make a few exceptions, a separate category in favor of Sade and one, more surprising so far as I'm concerned, in favor of Jean Lorrain." (The latter was an openly gay writer and dandy of an earlier generation.) Doubts over these exceptions: "Then why not priests?" Breton explains: "Priests are the people most opposed to this moral freedom."

And they move on, from point to point. Jacques Prévert says he would not be interested in making love in a church "due to the bells." Péret, always extreme, says: "This is my only thought and I have a great urge to do it." Breton agrees and explains: "I would like it to include all possible refinements." Péret then reveals how he would intend to behave: "On that occasion I would like to desecrate the hosts and, if possible, defecate into the chalice." But on this Breton makes no comment. They move on. It is established that "no one is interested in bestiality." Breton takes over, asking: "Would it be pleasant or unpleasant for you to make love with a woman who doesn't speak French?" Péret and Prévert have no objection at all. But Breton exclaims: "Unbearable. I have a horror of foreign languages."

195

Almost a century later, one cannot avoid noting the unfortunate lyrical affectation of all the surrealists in what they were writing then, as if a dull screen were preventing them from recognizing the childishness of their excessive imagery, as well as their wild aspirations — a kindergarten bordering on a charnel house, from which they had only just emerged, while another was being prepared.

Still, all that — and more — on the first evening. We could easily continue with the second, which followed four days later. But the point would be the same: *certain things are discovered only if a journal is established.*

T. S. Eliot, who was Marguerite Caetani's cousin, launched *The Criterion* in 1922 in a situation that was the opposite of what was happening in Paris. For him, in London, it was not a question of too many literary reviews but of too few, especially those with a cosmopolitan character.

The first person he turned to — not surprisingly — was Valery Larbaud: "I am initiating a new quarterly review, and am writing in the hope of enlisting your support. It will be small and modest in form but I think that what contents it has will be the best in London [...] There is, in fact, as you very well know, no literary periodical here of cosmopolitan tendencies and international standards." The first piece Eliot requested was Larbaud's lecture on Joyce. The next day Eliot wrote to Hermann Hesse asking him for "one or two parts of *Blick ins Chaos.*" And he added: "You don't know me: I am a contributor to the 'Times Literary Supplement' " as well as "English correspondent [...] for the 'Nouvelle Revue Française'; lastly, the author of several volumes of verse and a volume of essays."

The Criterion also had a patroness, Lady Rothermere, of whom Ezra Pound disapproved (as moreover he scorned everything else about England): "Do remember that I know nothing whatever about Lady Rothermere, save that she, by her name, appears to have married into a family which is *not* interested in good literature. I am interested in civilization, but I can't see that England has anything to do with any future civilization." What a shame that in the same letter Pound indicated that the "real voice of England" was the *Morning Post*, a newspaper that attributed all kinds of evils to Jewish conspiracies.

When, in January 1926, *The Criterion* became *The New Criterion*, moving from the administration of Lady Rothermere to that of the publishing house Faber & Gwyer, Eliot felt he had to show his cards and wrote an essay that began with these words: "The existence of a literary review requires more than a word of justification." It is rarely wise to ignore Disraeli's maxim "never explain" — nor was it in this case. Like a diligent schoolboy, Eliot set out along the path of good sense. The number of contributors should never be too many or too few. Another error to avoid would be "including too much material and representing too many interests, which are not strictly literary, or on the other hand by sticking too closely to a narrow conception of literature." There should not be a "program" but rather a "tendency." Authors should follow that tendency, but they should not be in too much agreement either.

So far, it is hard to disagree. But cracks suddenly start to appear in the sensible and fair-minded approach. One notices an oblique swipe at *Commerce*, without naming it, which Eliot would condemn as a "miscellaneous review," whereas the review that Eliot has in mind "should be an organ of documentation. That is to say, the bound volumes of a decade should represent the development of the keenest sensibility and the clearest thought of ten years." At this point it becomes ever clearer that Eliot is no longer playing the role of an unbiased director but, on the contrary, is anxious to show exactly where he stands — above all that there are those whom he wishes to exclude from his review: "I believe that the modern tendency is toward something which, for want of a better name, we may call classicism." A tendency that, under that awkward and inappropriate name, was certainly not about modernity but was about Eliot at that moment in his life.

And he did not stop there. He had to declare who was to be followed. With a sudden candor, Eliot draws up two lists, of good and bad. The bad ones are humanitarian liberals: H. G. Wells, George Bernard Shaw, Bertrand Russell. Fairly predictable. But who are the good ones? We discover that the first two approved books are *Réflections sur la violence* by Georges Sorel and *L'avenir de l'intelligence* (The Future of Intelligence) by Charles Maurras, and they are followed approvingly by Julien Benda, T. E. Hulme, and Irving Babbitt. The striking name is Maurras, since he was synonymous with Action Française, the political movement of the extreme right in France. It was a very peculiar version of "classicism," then, that Eliot was advocating.

In the opening lines of *Barbarie et poésie*, published a few months earlier, Maurras had written: "We have had to add to literary criticism action in the public square. Who is to blame? It was no one's fault that the barbarian realm was founded outside the Spirit, in the very structure of the City. The Barbarian down below, the Barbarian of the East, our Demos flanked by its two friends, the German and the Jew, made an ignoble yoke weigh heavily on the intelligence of the nation." As for the Jew, "the right word seems to have been spoken at a famous meeting between Catulle Mendès and Jean Moréas:

— To take Heine for a Frenchman! said the Jew, scandalized. — *There's nothing French about him,* replied the Greek, delighted. — *But,* Mendès observed, *neither is he German! — The truth...,* Moréas began, hesitating somewhat. — *The fact is that he's Jewish,* Mendès exclaimed. — *I didn't dare say it to you,* replied Moréas."

Eliot certainly was not proposing, like Maurras, to "add to literary criticism action in the public square." But about the Jews he agreed with Maurras. For his part, Valéry, whom Eliot regarded as a "profoundly destructive, even nihilistic mind" (though this did not prevent him from thinking that Valery was also "the symbol of the poet in the first part of the twenty-first century — not Yeats, not Rilke, nor anyone else"), would continue to steer the miscellaneous *Commerce* without falling into the trap of *taking a position.* Even "classicism" was not an appropriate formula for him. But until its end in 1939, when taking a position became obligatory, *The New Criterion* continued to "illustrate, in its limits, the period and its tendencies."

〰️

One might wonder when and how the numinous and ominous figure of the female surrealist first appeared. A starting point is found on page 17 of the first issue of *La Révolution Surréaliste*: a series of small square photos of twenty-eight young men, without their names and in alphabetical order. At the center, larger and once again in square format, there is a photo of a woman with no name. Below, in italics, are the words: "Woman is the being who casts the largest shadow and the brightest light in our dreams. Ch. B.," indicating Charles Baudelaire, first among the prophets.

Who are the twenty-eight men? The surrealists of the

moment, together with their chief patrons: Freud, De Chirico, Picasso. In second place, in sequence, Antonin Artaud "handsome as a wave, likeable as a catastrophe," according to Simone Kahn, Breton's wife. And then René Crevel, "the most handsome of the surrealists"; Jean Carrive, the youngest surrealist (sixteen); toward the bottom Man Ray and Alberto Savinio. But who is the woman in the middle, in a police identity photograph, with the sad piercing gaze?

She is Germaine Berton, described in modern encyclopedias as a "worker, trade unionist, anarchist." On January 22, 1923 she killed Marius Plateau with a shotgun at the headquarters of Action Française, where he was a secretary. He was killed by mistake. The assassin had someone more important in mind, Charles Maurras or Léon Daudet — both political leaders who started out as influential men of letters. During Berton's trial for murder, Aragon wrote in defense of the accused that it was legitimate "to resort to terroristic methods, in particular to assassination, in order to safeguard, at the risk of losing everything, that which appears — wrongly or rightly — more precious than all else in the world." Germaine Berton was acquitted, and in 1924 she gave a series of tumultuous anarchist lectures that led once again to her arrest. Not much is known about her life after that, until her suicide in 1942.

So the female surrealist's star rose with an aura of blood and death. But there was an alternative image. In the first issue of *La Révolution Surréaliste* there was also a magnificent photo on page 4, taken by Man Ray, of the naked headless torso of Lee Miller shaded with zebra stripes. The female surrealist would comprise the alarming gaze of Germaine Berton and the recognizable torso of Lee Miller.

Breton's *Manifeste du surréalisme* came off the press on October 15, 1924, and three days later a jointly written pamphlet titled *Un cadaver* appeared with a text by Breton. What had happened in the meantime? The funeral of Anatole France. Janet Flanner, the most effective and chic of Paris news reporters with her pieces for *The New Yorker*, noted: "I recall that at Anatole France's funeral procession, the first of these official honorary ceremonies that I had ever seen, the cortege was followed through the streets by a group of disrespectful Surrealists, who despised his popularity and his literary style, and who shouted insults to his memory ('*Un cadavre littéraire!*') in unison every step of the way. This was possibly the first of their sadistic street manifestations and was considered a scandal, since Paris has so long been noted as a great appreciator of its intellectual figures."

Breton contributed to the surrealist pamphlet a short piece of which he must have been proud, since it reappeared a decade later in his book *Point du jour* (Break of Day), where he wrote that the year 1924 could be considered fortunate because it had seen the death of Pierre Loti, Maurice Barrès, and Anatole France: "the idiot, the traitor, and the policeman." And he did not stop there: "In France a little human servility has gone. Let there be celebration on the day when cunning, traditionalism, patriotism, opportunism, skepticism, realism and heartlessness is buried! Let us remember that the lowest comedians of our time have found a stooge in Anatole France and we won't forgive him for having adorned his smiling inertia with the colors of the Revolution. To close up his corpse, why not empty — if anyone wishes — one of those shacks on the *quais* with those old books 'he loved so much' and throw the whole lot in the Seine? Once dead, this man ought not to produce any more dust." Such a miserable point had perhaps never before been reached in the highly complex history of the avant-garde.

In contrast with the commotion during the funeral of Anatole France, five years later, as the decade and a whole way of life was drawing to a close, there was silence at the funeral of Hugo von Hofmannsthal, perhaps the only writer who could be rightly called European, among the many who claimed to be. Rudolf Kayser gave an account of it in *Bifur*, which sought to vie with *Commerce*: "We attended the funeral of Hugo von Hofmannsthal. In a small baroque village church, we were there, black and silent before that casket, around which the incense, the music, the Catholicism reigned funereal and heavy. Then we went out into a hot summer day. The dead poet and friend guided us, a small procession of people dressed in black. But along the edges the people were lined up, there were thousands of men, women, children who flowed with us into the cemetery. They knew nothing about him, nothing other than his destiny, nothing other than his name. At the graveside, beside the priests, there were some film cameramen. This was our goodbye."

What was there before the word "revolution" inevitably thrust itself into the title of the surrealist journal, which in 1929 became *Le Surréalisme au service de la Révolution*, and finally insisted on being served? There was *Littérature*, a monthly review, first issue in March 1919, with unremarkable graphics, title underlined, poetry in italics, prose in roman. Looking back, Breton claimed that the title ought to be construed "antiphrastically, in a spirit of mockery." After the shock of Dada, recently arrived from Zurich, nothing could be treated with proper respect, especially literature.

But this was not the case. Indeed, here everything has the air of transition, of a judicious blend of established powers and emerging powers, of notables and new recruits. It is enough to glance through the names on the contents page of the first issue: Gide, Valéry, Fargue, Salmon, Jacob, Reverdy, Cendrars, Paulhan, Aragon, Breton. They are all there, those who would continue on for another twenty years, old men and subversives, neoclassicists and presurrealists. And there is, in the table of contents, a deft game of precedence. Heading them all were Gide and Valéry, who were now established names. Then the others in random order, to Breton, who was already hoping to call the shots. It is bewildering to read the issue from start to finish, skipping nothing. At the start Gide produces fragments of his new *Fruits of the Earth*, with an epigraph in bold, imperious, that will be cherished by lovers of *bonheur*, an ideal motto for future Gentils Organisateurs of the Club Méditérranée: "*Que l'homme est né pour le bonheur, / Certes toute la nature l'enseigne*" (All of nature teaches that man was born for happiness). Then comes Valéry's poem *Cantique des colonnes*, "Song of the Columns," which now sounds fairly vacuous.

But try looking through the rest of this issue of *Littérature* and an embarrassing feeling is gradually confirmed: it is as though everything has been sketched out by the same hand and a hand with no conspicuous talent. Even writers such as Fargue or Cendrars, who could hardly have been confused with others, are flattened, toned down, as though they were wearing a regular uniform. All of them make improvident use of jumbled images and have a shared incapacity to explain what they are talking about. Exactly a century later, little remains of that *Littérature* about which they write. Yet we are still struck by the diplomatic aspect: the group photograph, a fleeting convergence of certain names that would soon vanish from the scene, with a canny game of swapping, adding in and taking out.

The rule of the good neighbor does not apply just to books in libraries, but also to pieces in literary reviews. Indeed, it

203

could be a criterion for testing their nature or quality. Every issue of a review can be seen as a whole, where different voices are intersected and superimposed within a pre-established landscape, with its hedgerows, avenues, fountains, and wild areas. And over time the physiognomy of the place can radically change, as if in a grotesque game. *Littérature*, which some of its authors regarded as a rash and ruinous enterprise, proved in the end to be a collection of bland lyrical texts, where the factor of novelty ended up almost stagnant and certainly tedious.

It was the age of *plaquettes*, those slim volumes, no more than a hundred pages, sometimes less than fifty, often graphically elegant, printed in few copies, generally numbered, by publishers who did only that (Au Sans Pareil, K, GLM, L'Âge d'Or, among others), a dust wafting around normal books, which were very often published by Gallimard, or by the N.R.F. as it was still called. Writers could be authors of various *plaquettes* and of no book. There were already collectors of *plaquettes* and of autographs. Max Jacob was caught diligently copying out several examples of his poetry which were then to be offered as original versions for various expectant collectors. And they were searching above all for *grands papiers*, rare copies on special paper. That was the final period of a parallel and morganatic publishing trade, on which various antiquarians-of-the-new lived for a long while, in whose shops, in paper wrappings, there was much to explore. Those *plaquettes* then re-emerged, as if embalmed, in the windows of the great Parisian bookshop and gallery La Hune, well displayed, when month after month, year after year, someone was rediscovered, Artaud or Crevel or Desnos or Vaché or Cravan. It was a long paper-trail that remained in evidence until the end of the 1970s.

Commerce came to an end in 1932. But its model, especially typographical, continued to spread throughout the 1930s. The format generally square, the title evocative and alone on the frontispiece, the absence of any preface, the names of the editors opposite the frontispiece, the predominance of new texts blended in each issue with something from the past, as well as something exotic or "oriental": those are the characteristics of *Commerce*, which reappear in *Bifur* and *Mesures*. Both *Bifur*, which was founded in 1929, and *Mesures*, which was founded in 1935, would rely, as *Commerce* did, on foreign writers previously unknown in France, who became a sort of emblem for the review: Gottfried Benn for *Bifur*, in the first issue, and Constantine Cavafy for *Mesures*, introduced by Marguerite Yourcenar as "one of the most celebrated poets of modern Greece, and also one of the greatest, as well as the most subtle, and perhaps the most singularly new, and at the same time charged with the richness of the past," followed immediately, by fortunate coincidence, by a part of *Mount Analogue*, a novel by René Daumal. And the cosmopolitan nature of the enterprise is declared in the list of "foreign advisors" for *Bifur*: Bruno Barilli, Gottfried Benn, Ramón Gomez de la Serna, James Joyce, Boris Pilnyak, and William Carlos Williams (only the last of these made a recognizable contribution). The list is varied and outstanding, but it isn't easy to be cosmopolitan.

The film critic Nino Frank, the real inventor of the review along with the artist and poet Georges Ribemont-Dessaignes, was thinking about spending some time in Berlin, for sentimental reasons, when news broke of the burning of the Reichstag. It was a good excuse to get the "Paris Journal" to commission a series of articles. But — Frank explained —

205

by the morning of his departure "I had already forgotten the official reason for my journey." He found that he was the only passenger in the plane. At Tempelhof he was immediately stopped and questioned, abruptly and politely. Berlin seemed to him like a city of people who "passed without looking, except for certain women, still forlorn and nervous," while he noticed a sound in the background: metal boxes rattled by the SA, who expected donations.

Before leaving, Frank had one more visit to make, also connected to *Bifur*. He recalled: "A few years earlier, a respectable and portly, bald-headed man, his eyes shielded by gold-rimmed glasses, rang my doorbell. I am always ill-disposed to such intrusions. We couldn't understand each other since he spoke only his language, and I spoke everything apart from German. It was Gottfried Benn, with whom I had exchanged letters and with whom, in the absence of anything better, I exchanged firm handshakes." Frank knew only that Benn was "the only poet in his country who had, toward the start of the 1930s, some density, who published little, and things of a fairly glacial incandescence. Untranslatable, they told me, and the same was said, more or less in the same years, about Boris Pasternak."

Invited to his house, Frank found himself "in a poor street where on the door I read that I was about to ring at the office of Doctor Gottfried Benn, a specialist in venereal diseases. A nurse took me to his room, where I met him again, dressed in a long white coat, the man with the gold-rimmed glasses: his manner was friendly and vaguely formal and, between one patient and the next, we had an unusual conversation." Frank wanted to know something about the state of things in Germany, but Benn spoke about his "poetical itinerary." He stopped from time to time, "casting a rather cloudy gaze, then began talking again about Dehmel and Hofmannsthal: 'Pessimisme héroïque' he said in French, with a heavy accent. Since I took the opportunity immediately to mention once again Hitler and the Reichstag, he shrugged these off with a gesture of slight irritation. Then, seeing my surprise, he hinted that it was a question of leaving things alone, of accepting without censure, of seeing whether these might manage to do better than the others." But something about the conversation didn't add up. "With a pirouette unexpected in a person so solemn," Benn suddenly started talking about gonococcus and treponema. Syphilis, he said, was no great problem, whereas gonorrhea was. Meanwhile "the windows vibrated heavily at the hum of the engines at the nearby airport."

Politics was pressing. Hitler had already appeared in *Bifur* in December 1930, in the form of a misspelling. "On the one hand, the multiplication of bourgeois parties and their collapse, on the other the expansion of the Hittler movement, were the characteristics of the Reichstag elections": this was reported, at the beginning of the issue, in Franz Carl Weiskopf's article on the recent German elections, the review's first intrusion into current affairs. Weiskopf was a member of the Association of Proletarian Writers and his article was most probably imposed by Pierre G. Lévy, the review's financial backer, a prosperous bourgeois and follower of modernity who "was leaning ever more toward militant Marxism" (in the words of Ribemont-Dessaignes) — but at the same time, in his indefatigable snobbery, had launched the journal to emulate in some way the Princess of Bassiano who ran *Commerce*.

Others were also chomping at the bit, thirsting for political trouble. A few lines after Weiskopf's article there appeared twenty-five-year-old Pierre Nizan, who described himself as a "philosopher, traveler and communist," and wrote: "But why should I hide my game? I say simply that there's a philosophy of the oppressors and a philosophy of the oppressed." The 1930s were now in the air. There was a shrillness about everything. A great contest was under way to find the worst oppressor, always in furtherance of some oppression suffered. The next issue of *Bifur* began with the religious scholar and thinker Henry Corbin's translation of Heidegger's "What is Metaphysics?" which Alexandre Koyré introduced with these words: "In the philosophical firmament of Germany, the star of M. Heidegger shines with supreme radiance. According to some it is not a star but a new sun that rises and with its light eclipses all its contemporaries." A whole variety of games was being played all at once.

There was also the announcement of a Great Game that is still open. "*Le Grand Jeu* is irremediable; it is played only once. We want to play it at every moment of our life. And moreover 'he who loses wins.' Because it's a question of losing. We want to win. Now, *Le Grand Jeu* is a game of chance, namely of dexterity, or rather, of 'grace': the grace of God and the grace of gestures." These are that words that Roger Gilbert-Lecomte used to launch the first issue of *Le Grand Jeu* in the winter of 1928 — words that escaped the Surrealist web. The words "grace of God" were unthinkable elsewhere, and also "grace of gestures." This was the point that most irritated Breton and Aragon, who in their response to the new journal were temporary reincarnations of Monsieur Hommais. In their view, those words transformed the youngsters of *Le Grand Jeu* (Daumal was twenty, Gilbert-Lecomte twenty-one) from potential allies into certain reprobates. The most serious charge against the new journal was "the constant use of the word 'God' further aggravated by the fact that one of the articles states that it is referring to a single God in three persons." To this charge was added "a blunt remark that declared the preference given to Landru [a French serial killer of women] over Sacco and Vanzetti."

Here was the sound of something radically divergent, ready to strike out in a different direction. This was no longer a literary dispute or a clash between avant-garde sects. The new review was interested in identifying a "fundamental experience," as Daumal would call it, from which everything else had to follow, including Scripture. And of course the review itself. Only three issues of *Le Grand Jeu* appeared; the journal closed in the autumn of 1930. But from its very first lines one sensed an "air of other planets." It was a review that was taking its leave from the world of reviews. And in particular, before even being expelled from it, it was distancing itself from the Surrealist atmosphere that now pervaded everything (an everything that broadly coincided with the Sixth Arrondissement). The definitive sign of that separation can be found, perhaps, in two pages by Daumal that appeared in the second issue of the journal, called "Once More on the Books of René Guénon." One reads there that Guénon, "if he speaks of the Veda, thinks the Veda, he is the Veda." More than describing Guénon, a French mystic and esotericist who wrote about Hinduism and converted to Islam, those words foretold what Daumal himself would become, as a writer and an interpreter and translator of Sanskrit texts, right to the end.

Why did the season of the reviews come to an end? Mainly because the irresistible attraction of the *new* fell into decline, steadily fading and vanishing. "*Au fond de l'Inconnu pour trouver du nouveau*," to the depths of the Unknown to find the new: it is always a line or a phrase of Baudelaire that signals the essential features of modernity. The *new* that Marguerite Caetani was seeking, and that she found at the start of *Commerce*, was not the same *new* that she sought and failed to find twenty-five years later when *Botteghe Oscure* began. Everyone continued to pose as new, but this was now only a sign of social recognition. And even when the new was really new, it was not always what it claimed to be. Around a century later, it is striking how all the avant-gardes were weighed down by what was already old. Everything was sustained by an amalgam of art and snobbery. But the formula gradually fell apart. Everything proceeded "carrying its own corpse on its back," in the words of Roger Gilbert-Lecomte, the poet who was one of the founders of *Le Grand Jeu*, and the most lucid of the mutants. They had to "change level," said Daumal, the first who managed to do so, and devoted himself to steering toward Mount Analogue, the inaccessible summit of his spiritualist novel of that name, whose subtitle is *A Novel of non-Euclidean and Authentically Symbolic Adventures in Mountaineering*. Having reached that empyrean, there was no more talk of literary reviews — and no need for them.

Obviously during those years, between 1920 and 1940, some notable reviews flourished in other countries, too — in Germany, England, Italy, the United States. But in Paris there was a concentration of journals that found no equivalent elsewhere. It all happened inside the boundary of the Sixth, with occasional forays into the Seventh and the Fifth. It was said that the editors of *Bifur* had only to spend each day at Café de Flore and Les Deux Magots to fill the table of contents of their journal.

The Paris reviews had spawned other significant offspring during the 1930s. Each was a variant of the classic format of the Parisian review: anthropological (in the style of Marcel

Mauss) with *Documents*, edited by Georges Bataille; militant-delirious with *Acéphale*; smugly modernist with *Minotaure* (based in Geneva with Albert Skira, though still Parisian); the progeny of *Commerce* and *Mesures*. But the concept and the intent of the review remained unquestionable: it was created by a few and for a few, yet its ambition was absolute and limitless. This aspiration was gradually lost, until it more or less disappeared after 1945. A common thread tended no longer to be there. Literature was preparing to become what it would be in the new millennium: a matter for individuals, stubbornly separate and solitary.

In the first issue, in March 1964, of *Art and Literature*, which described itself as an "international review," and indeed was, there appeared a piece by Cyril Connolly called "Fifty Years of Little Magazines," which reads like an epicedium, a dirge, to literary reviews:

> Little magazines are the pollinators of works of art: literary movements and eventually literature itself could not exist without them. Most of the poetry of Yeats, Eliot, Pound and Auden appeared in magazines, as did *The Portrait of the Artist* and *Ulysses, Finnegans Wake,* and nearly all of Hemingway's short stories. A good magazine brings writers together, even the most isolated, and sets them influencing their time and, when that time is past, devotes a special number to them as a funeral.
>
> Little magazines are of two kinds, dynamic and eclectic. Some flourish on what they put in, others by whom they keep out. Dynamic magazines have a shorter life and it is around them that glamour and nostalgia crystallize. If they go on too long they will become eclectic, although the reverse process is very unusual. Eclectic magazines are also of their time, but they cannot ignore the past nor

211

resist good writing from opposing camps. The dynamic editor runs his magazine like a commando course where picked men are trained to assault the enemy position; the eclectic editor is like a hotel proprietor whose rooms fill up every month with a different clique.

To give some examples: *The Yellow Book* was eclectic, *The Savoy* dynamic, *The Little Review* dynamic, *The Dial* eclectic, *Transition* dynamic, *Life and Letters* eclectic *(also The Criterion and The London Mercury), Les Soirées de Paris* dynamic, *La Nouvelle Revue Française* eclectic, [...] *Verve* eclectic, *Minotaure* dynamic, etc.

An eclectic editor feels he has a duty to preserve certain values, to reassess famous writers, disinter others. A truly dynamic editor will completely ignore the past: his magazine will be short lived, his authors violent and obscure. The eclectic will be in constant danger of becoming complacent and middlebrow: he lasts longer and pays better. Most quarterlies are eclectic: they have so many pages and are less agitated by the time-clock.

There is very little to add, almost sixty years later, except that it has now become unlikely that there could exist a magazine that would even publish a eulogy such as this, which was after all solidly based on facts, since Connolly himself had edited *Horizon* between 1939 and 1949, which is to say, during the closing years of this short history that has the advantage of a clearly defined beginning and an end, like certain short stories by Nathaniel Hawthorne.

ISHION HUTCHINSON

Chorus of the Years

Why won't you let me be glory, standing
there in the mountainous half-bright shadow,
fallen step-by-step down the staircase where
a bad smell, urine and something else,
unarguably an ultimate flaw,
good to ignore years before but now not,
not with you there above me, looking down,
hardly clear, hard silent, except for cricks
on the landing I strain to count, losing
each, for what, for glory and motion,
which can't be claimed, neither can—*I know it,*
this frowsiness we ascend by, descend
fast to register but not recognise,
being that it is a malevolent malice
I left behind in brackish St Thomas,
that ash earth place, where dark glares in vials
and parchment with names are put in shoes to
turn minds spider (it happened to mom),
where speartips of cane-flags pointed at hearts
set whole hills in tears, and rage, Jesus, rage
evening after evening drags—let me stop
now, halfway up the stairs; the arc's broken
like an hiatus at fresh water gapes
back at the chorus of early days
when, of course, you were the only singer,
lifted up, granted, like fire in coal
broken through, at last, one black ice nugget.

Crowns

i.m. Donald Rodney (18 May 1961 — 4 March 1998)

Emblems of countless martyrs
devoured by the Atlantic,
who remembers that slavery was monarchical,

that historical atrocity
came directly from the divine head,
that gravity cannot be numbered.

Do not seek to be venerated
or to win the appraisal of civic awe,
like for instance Basquiat's crowns.

Estimates have been made — "about 15 million" —
but you didn't allow your body
to conform to that illness;

you transformed that. But into what?
Emblem of power and of savage mockery?
Vehemence yet no vengeance? And yet,

ever at the fulcrum
like that ocean, bleak plain ink which echoes
the aftermath of your rage

which achieved the most difficult
grace in the election of urgency (which is *grace*).
Turbulent saccharum officinarum: you transformed all that.

Obsessive sketching of that.
The immense, miserable aftermath of that.
Concentric abyss that your crowns

turning wheels within time
inexhaustible after a splash opens
the death clinic chasm, turning

the aftermath of surgery and slavery,
growing irrepressibly without end, blood's
real provenance of what survives. And what survives

is diaspora. (Braced, sotto voce, in this
parenthesis, is your perpetual rage.)
All else constitutes a lived fable.

Zungguzungguguzungguzeng

All me sparks fly all night;
all my mouth axle bright, wheel
the true guillotine serpents' fleck
amber sweat off my waistline,

sibilant as touch-me-nots'
shuttered leaves rattling Death
in the Arena. Honey Blight
and Armageddon. I am Thorn

Tongue, bare sprite-child nerved
against neon slush and ants trap,
I squeal, bitten, "Mother O mother...
come!" No one but echo and ice.

Day fevers dusk a Midas
wisp. Torched corona. I am adagio,
brisk, cool, and deadly onstage.
My visible black flares yellow,

speckled lava. All me manna
chrome, stigmata's tingling
rush turns the purging
cassia spokes ripe, ripe music.

WALTER SCHEIDEL

After Covid

Paleontologists disagree about whether dinosaurs were thriving or had already entered a long decline when an extinction event finished them off sixty-six million years ago. Depending on who is right, the asteroid that struck Earth either radically changed the direction of evolution or merely accelerated an established trend. Disasters that target the currently dominant species invite similarly divergent interpretations. Their capacity to jolt us out of our complacency is not in doubt. But in so doing, do they truly redirect the course of human history, or do they merely act as catalysts of ongoing change? Covid19 is just the latest in a long series of crises that have raised this perennial question.

And how it has been raised! Since the pandemic began, journalists, pundits, scholars, and pundit-scholars speak as if the pandemic will itself periodize history, into the "Before Time" and the new world that we have entered. They have fallen over each other predicting all manner of dramatic change. But what kind of change, exactly? A big divide separates the realists and the continuationists from the aspirationists and the disruptionists. The former prefer to view the coronavirus crisis as an amplifier of present shifts and enhancer of familiar structures. The latter consider it a transformative force, a crisis that is an opportunity, a source of novel remedies for assorted societal ills thought to be in urgent need of correction.

The continuationist position has much to commend it. After all, a great many of the crises highlighted by the pandemic were already underway. Nationalism and anti-globalist sentiment were on the rise. International indices of freedom were declining. Digital tracking and surveillance had become ever more invasive. Economic inequality was already unprecedented. Corporate debt had already reached record highs, and central banks had already begun to drive more of the economy. Tensions between the United States and China were already mounting. Iran had long been in trouble. China's strategic ambitions were already obvious, and its growth had already begun to slow, as had India's. Oil prices were already too low to sustain the bloated budgets of the petrostates. The European establishment was already eager to go green even before the EU's covid-recovery package unleashed a torrent of funding for salient projects. Online shopping had long been eating into retail's market share, and remote instruction and telecommuting had been expanding for many years. Millennials had already been dealt lousy cards by the Great Recession and austerity. African-Americans led shorter and unhealthier lives even before they succumbed in disproportionate numbers to the coronavirus. And even the "novel coronavirus" is not as novel as it has been made to sound: multiple outbreaks of SARS and MERS have been recorded since 2002.

In all these and many other respects, the crisis has served as an accelerator and an amplifier. Sometimes the push was felt to be sudden and hard: the head-over-heels transition to remote work and teaching is a prime example. But even that apparent rupture was firmly rooted in technological shifts that had long prepared the ground. This kind of historical acceleration has a long pedigree. The World Wars and the Great Depression spawned unprecedented mass mobilization (for war and revolution) and economic shocks. Taxes soared, the right to vote spread, colonial empires trembled, and welfare states bloomed. Capitalism was temporarily tamed, suspended, and sometimes even abolished. Yet none of this came out of nowhere: well before 1914, there had already been pensions, progressive taxation, labor unions, public schools, suffragists and suffragettes, and independence movements. What these crises did was give an enormous boost to initiatives that were already in progress.

The dramatic empowerment of the masses was rooted in the modernizing institutional and economic transformations of the previous century or two. Even purposely radical communist regimes built on nineteenth-century ideas and embraced generic schemes such as industrialization. Genuine detours from the modernizing script — such as the Khmer Rouge's murderous evacuations of urban residents to the countryside — remained exceedingly rare and unsuccessful outliers.

Nor had historical pandemics been genuine game-changers. It is hard to imagine disasters more disruptive than the Black

219

Death of the late Middle Ages and the pandemics of smallpox, measles and influenza that ravaged the Americas after European colonizers introduced these pathogens after 1492. Yet even the medieval plague frequently intensified earlier trends, from urbanization and the erosion of serfdom to challenges to Catholic unity and papal supremacy. In the New World, the decimation of the indigenous population greatly assisted the Spanish conquests, but even that process was ultimately a mere acceleration, however monstrous in scale and style. The ultimate outcome had hardly been in doubt: witness the wide and rapidly expanding disparities between the fiscal-military states of Europe and the largely Copper Age societies of the Americas, the fissions that had already opened within the most powerful American empires of the day, and the conquistadors' zeal to out-colonize their fellow European competitors.

Nothing quite as dramatic has happened since, even as epidemics remained common. When bubonic plague intensified one more time in seventeenth-century Europe, the most dynamic economies — most notably Britain and the Netherlands — weathered it quite well. In the nineteenth century, massive outbreaks of cholera and yellow fever famously raised support for ambitious public health measures but cannot rightly be viewed as their root cause. After all, the counterfactual of ever richer and more knowledgeable societies persistently failing to invest in sanitation is hardly a plausible one. However much repeated health scares shaped the pace and scale of intervention, it was economic growth and science that made it possible in the first place.

A century ago, the Spanish Flu was as global in its reach as Covid19 is today, but it turned out to be much more lethal. It targeted not only the elderly but also infants and, most crucially, people in their twenties and thirties — workers in the prime of life who often had just started a family and who left behind spouses and small children. Vast numbers of people died: perhaps forty million, or 1 in 50 people on earth, equivalent to more than 150 million today. Yet in the end, little tangible change resulted from this catastrophe. Improved coordination of international health monitoring was well in line with the overall consolidations of the League of Nations period and fairly unremarkable.

This is not to say that crises never reroute trajectories of development. But such outcomes are made all the more noteworthy by their extraordinary rarity. A few years ago I was able to identify a clear example: the attenuation of income and wealth inequality through major disasters. I found a pattern that has held true across recorded history: massively violent ruptures were the only events that have ever greatly shrunk the gap between rich and poor. Those events, I found, came in four flavors: the collapse of states, catastrophic pandemics, mass mobilization warfare, and transformative revolution. The latter two were especially characteristic of the twentieth century.

State collapse was the most ancient leveling force, dating back to Old Kingdom Egypt. It was also the most dependable. Early states were designed as powerful engines of inequality: whenever they unraveled, they took elites and their accumulated wealth and power down with them. While most people ended up worse off, the rich had the most to lose. Pandemics, by contrast, equalized by different means, administering a harsh Malthusian solution to demographic pressure. When they carried off a sufficiently large enough share of the population, labor became scarce and wages rose, while demand for

221

land fell, reducing its value. The masses who sold their labor found themselves less poor while the rich who controlled capital lost some of their income and wealth.

There occurred, in these cases, a kind of egalitarian intermission in history. Such shifts are faintly discernible during the first pandemic of bubonic plague at the end of Roman antiquity, are amply documented in Western Europe in the wake of the Black Death, and have also been observed in seventeenth-century Mexico, where real wages increased once indigenous population numbers had dropped to record lows. But these violent levelings — these adjustments by catastrophe — never lasted. As states were rebuilt, greedy elites returned. As plagues faded, population recovered, wages fell, and fortunes grew. Even so, the egalitarian intermissions could go on for generations, providing rare relief from plutocratic dominance. At the very least, they proved to the world that life did not always have to be the way it usually was.

The unique ruptures of modernity drove home that message with even greater force. In the World Wars — especially the second one — returns on capital plummeted, and governments launched aggressive interventions in the private sector and raised taxes on large incomes and estates sky-high. Conscription and the war effort boosted the bargaining power of workers and unions thrived. After the war, social solidarity and the newly grown fiscal and organizational capabilities of government underwrote welfare states. During the 1950s and 1960s, and occasionally even the 1970s, economies grew, middle classes expanded, and inequality was kept at bay.

Those societies were the lucky ones. Others experienced violent upheaval that led to far more dramatic change, as in Russia after World War I and in China after World War II. Communism actively pursued economic equality by the bloodiest of means. But that grand and grotesque experiment merely created new social hierarchies. The compression of wealth and income distributions persisted only as long as violent regimes survived or remained committed to that goal. The moment restraints were relaxed, material inequality soared to previously unknown heights, from Russia to China and beyond. In the West, where equalization had been less radical, its reversal was also more muted, but it has proven equally persistent. Since the 1980s, large economic policies and processes such as globalization, deregulation, financialization, and automation have rewarded some more than others, to put it mildly. In the United States, this process has gone further than among its Western peers, creating economic disparities not seen since the 1920s. Seemingly impervious to political preference, this process has continued under Democrats and Republicans alike.

So will the pandemic prompt a change of course? Recent history gives us little reason to think so. Although the Great Recession of 2008 battered the One Percenters, they soon recovered, while many others continued to struggle. This time does not look notably different. Inequality has gone up, in the United States and elsewhere. Job losses have disproportionately hit the young, the poor, the less skilled, and traditionally disadvantaged groups. And economic inequalities have been replicated in other domains, from worse health outcomes for the least protected and inferior learning opportunities for poorer students.

Meanwhile, at least so far, the super-rich have recovered with astonishing speed. Bloomberg's index of American fortunes among the world's top 500 reveals the most V-shaped of recoveries: in 2020, a steep plunge between mid-February and the third week of March followed by an almost complete turnaround by early June. Jeff Bezos, the leader of the pack, is richer than ever before. To the relief of non-billionaires, the S&P 500 has closely tracked this plutocratic V. Yet while that has been good news for portfolios of all sizes, key indicators of economic health and general welfare, such as GDP or employment, are lagging far behind.

Taken together, these developments fit the continuationist template: existing inequalities have been brutally exposed, or have grown, or have made themselves more painfully felt, or all of the above. But there has been no change of direction. What does this mean for the future of inequality — or climate change, or "late capitalism," or the "neoliberal world order?" What, in other words, are the odds of seizing progressive change from the jaws of ... more of the same?

A genuine re-direction, a bold new course for society, may be accomplished by peaceful or violent means. Aspirational disruptionists hope for the former. Their message is simple: this is the time. At long last, the coronavirus crisis will make it impossible for us to avert our gaze from society's ailments. It will shake us out of our customary stupor and jolt us into action, ready to combat inequality and systemic racism while shoring up health care and worker protection and infrastructure and the environment. This perspective, popular in large parts of punditdom, involves a bold leap from trigger (virus) to outcome (transformative change). The proximate mechanisms that are supposed to generate such sweeping change tend to be rather less well defined. During the Democratic primary, Bernie Sanders' vague allusions to a "movement" that would somehow ensure implementation of far-reaching programs were emblematic of the magical thinking employed to bridge that chasm. The path to a grandly upgraded social contract or a Green New Deal seems similarly obscure. Yet the more

224

ambitious and game-changing the goals, the more clearly formulated the way to reach them needs to be. At least for now, the needed clarity is absent.

The current buzz of progressive energy in politics may prove deceptive. The election of Joe Biden was a relief of historic proportions, but with mainstream politics stuck in crisis-management mode, drastic re-directional change would seem less plausible than ever. The results of our recent election, which highlighted persistent polarization and all but guaranteed a prolonged stalemate, confirm this impression. (Old news alert: Democrats and their allies enjoyed a 26-seat margin in the Senate when the New Deal got underway, and a staggering 63-seat margin when FDR's Supreme Court packing plan failed. Obama dropped the "public option" from the Affordable Care Act when his side in the Senate was 18 seats ahead. Enough said.) American institutions have focused on keeping everything afloat, as have the leaders of European countries and others elsewhere. If such efforts bear fruit, the prospect of radical transformation will once again recede.

That would not come as a surprise. Historically, transformative change has been born of extraordinary violence. Yet Covid19, for all its terrors and mortality rates, is not particularly violent at all. Worldwide, the 1.25 million or so lives lost as of this writing equal about a week of normal mortality (which averages 165,000 per day) — or rather a few days more, allowing for undocumented deaths; and they were for the most part gleaned from among those already well advanced on their journey to the sweet hereafter. This is a far cry from the fall of ancient Rome, which set back civilization by centuries, or the Black Death, which took one in three Europeans, or the world wars and communist takeovers, which ruined entire countries and killed many tens of millions of all ages.

After Covid

Looked at from that angle, the notion that we might achieve re-directional change without comparably massive dislocations seems more wishful thinking than realistic strategy. At the very least, it is squarely at odds with what history teaches us. There is no historical precedent and no obvious contemporary mechanism for making that happen. While we cannot rule out anything — what if the 2020s are different after all? — this should certainly give us pause.

But what of the alternative? What is the potential for ruptures dramatic or violent enough to upend the established order and open up space for transformative change — for upheaval so severe that it cannot fail to force us off the beaten path?

My answer will be sobering for those who crave radical change. Conservative forces are more powerful than they have ever been. The four violent leveling mechanisms that have been operating in the past are now kept at bay by four robust stabilizers of the established order. Mass affluence is the most basic one. It is hard to find societies with a per capita GDP of more than $5,000 or $6,000 (measured in 2011 standardized dollars to ensure comparability) that have experienced societal breakdown or revolution. By some measures not even Yugoslavia in the 1990s cleared that fairly modest threshold of prosperity.

While this lack of precedent does not rule out truly violent dislocations in Western countries or their peers, it strongly suggests that the likelihood is low. Moreover, economic achievement tends to lower fertility and age populations: the resultant paucity of desperate young men — the most plausible agents of revolutionary struggle — imposes a pacifying constraint. Those concerned about secession, armed conflict, and collapse will have to cite the likes of Syria, Yemen, and the two Sudans rather than the United States.

Such outcomes are qualitatively different from the anti-government protests and riots that have become more common in the United States and some European countries over the last decade. Rooted in the Great Recession and its social consequences, these protests have mobilized growing numbers against austerity, globalization, and more recently climate change. The wave of activism and unrest that started in May 2020, while triggered by particularly jarring instances of racial injustice, would likewise seem hard to disentangle from the Covid19 lockdowns and the sudden economic downturn that disproportionately hurt the young. Once again, the pandemic amplified existing discontent.

It is true that this need not be the whole story. In pioneering work that seeks to identify regularized patterns across history, Peter Turchin has argued that these events are not merely responses to acute crises, but are meaningfully correlated to gradual shifts in destabilizing variables from political polarization to immigration and inequality over the long term. He envisions a cycle moving from relative stability after American independence to a peak of destabilizing factors from the 1860s to the 1910s, and then on to another minimum in the 1950s followed by a renewed and ongoing rise. At least so far, however, the overall intensity of unrest has been much lower than it was in the past, when society was poorer and less well buffered against privation. The United States seems a long way from the riots of the late 1960s, let alone the bloody labor conflicts of the 1910s and 1920s — not to mention the Civil War. This will come as bad news to radicals.

This is not an accident. Other stabilizers have been contributing to this striking attenuation. The social safety net has helped tame the fallout from crises. Europeans woke up to the virtues of welfare when the mobilizations of the Great War and the Bolshevik revolution shook the foundations of the old order. Although America briefly lagged behind, the Great Depression quickly forced it to follow suit. Support schemes have been expanded ever since, from Johnson's Great Society to the second Bush's prescription drug benefit and Obama's Affordable Care Act. Threadbare though this system may seem to admirers of the most generous European welfare states, it largely manages to stave off mass immiseration and serious social unrest, especially as ad hoc patches — such as the $600 weekly supplement to unemployment benefits this spring — can be applied as needed.

The third and fourth great stabilizers — the other impediments to cataclysm — are more recent in origin. Quantitative easing — whereby central banks expand the money supply by buying government securities — has come to play the role of a miracle drug that promises to shore up businesses and markets without the need for austerity or punitive taxation. Thus far, this torrent of keystroke money has been good news for investors and bad news for progressives. The aforementioned V-shaped recovery enjoyed by the former would not have been possible without this intervention. And the final stabilizing force is science, and its particular potency in the face of a pandemic. During the Spanish Flu, there was no flu vaccine and DNA was unknown. A century later, the SARS-CoV-2 genome was sequenced mere weeks after the first report in Wuhan, and its mutations are now carefully tracked around the globe. Within months, more than a thousand drug and vaccine trials were underway, fast-tracking has cut development time to a fraction of the usual slog, and pharmaceutical production capacity was ramped up on spec.

Of course we still do not know how all this will work out, especially as the efficacy — and the popular acceptance — of new vaccines and treatments remain uncertain. Yet a measure of cautious optimism seems warranted. The sooner science delivers the goods, the better are our prospects of a return to some version of normal, if indeed that is, or should be, our goal.

Yet modernizing development is not a one-way street toward greater resilience. At the same time as it buttresses the established order with growth, welfare, finance, and science, it also undermines the status quo, rendering it more socially and economically fragile as a direct result of progress. Governance is the main exception. In rich countries, the state and its agents are firmly entrenched. If push came to shove, we would soon realize just how far their instruments of surveillance and repression surpass anything available in the past. The only restraint resides in the political will to employ these means.

Welfare matters even more. States that capture and redistribute between a third and half of GDP cannot be dislodged, at least not without bringing down everything else. There is no plausible alternative. Bloated in their bureaucratic complexity and persistent in their insinuation into every conceivable aspect of our lives, they are hard to capture, harder to restructure, and impossible to overcome.

Fragility lurks elsewhere now, above all in the economic domain. Advanced economies have become vulnerable in new ways. Three principal reasons stand out, all of them direct consequences of development and progress. First, there is

229

globalization in the broadest — and most de-politicized — sense of the term: the interconnectivities and interdependencies that govern production and exchange. This is, empirically, how economies now work. A chain with many links has many vulnerabilities. Yet despite initial worries about vulnerable supply chains, this intricate web seems to have passed the latest test.

The second is the growing importance of the service sector, which expands at the expense of farming and manufacturing as societies grow richer. In normal times, retail, hospitality, and entertainment account for a tenth of America's GDP. The greater the role played by these services, the more lockdowns and social distancing drag down the overall economy. When the Spanish Flu struck, there was far less to shut down than there is now, from airlines to resorts.

But this time we also caught a lucky break. Fully a third of official economic output is generated by finance, insurance, the real estate business, and all manner of financial and business services. Well suited to remote work, these crucial white-collar sectors were spared major devastation. Had Covid19 appeared twenty years ago, they would have been much harder hit, with dire consequences for economic life more generally. (All we got was the pathetic Y2K scare.) This in turn underscores the stabilizing potential of science and technology well beyond virology. Information technology has truly been a savior.

Overall, these vulnerabilities have been rather well contained by some of the same technological and economic innovation that has brought them into being. This leaves a third and altogether different source of fragility: our valuation of life and our attitude to risk. Given short shrift in current discourse, it deserves far more attention. All other things being equal, a society more inured to morbidity and death would be considerably more resilient in the face of a pandemic, and so would be its economy.

To be sure, humans have always feared disease and the end of life. Yet no matter how fundamental and invariable such attitudes might seem to be, they are sensitive to overall development. For most of history, life was short. Two centuries ago in the West, and a century ago or even less elsewhere, average life expectancy at birth was a third of what we now take for granted. Perhaps one in three babies did not survive their first few years. The ranks of adults were whittled down in a steady drain of attrition. And even as some lasted to a ripe old age, they were vanishingly few in number. No one thought that odd or even remarkable. Much of the underlying suffering was frightfully mundane, driven by childhood diarrhea and dysentery and typhoid and tetanus. Epidemics merely added further uncertainty to the mix.

When great plagues struck ancient civilizations, there was nothing to be done. The basics of infection long remained a mystery. In Europe, the Black Death of the late Middle Ages inspired early experiments with quarantines. An improvement over helpless laissez-faire, those early lockdowns nevertheless failed to solve the problem: waves of plague pounded Europe for more than three centuries. In the 1720s, when Marseille was sealed off from the outside world for two years to prevent a plague outbreak from spreading inland, half of its residents perished. And the disease slipped through anyway: not even the seventeen miles of actual stone walls that had hastily been thrown up cross-country managed to stop it. When Yellow Fever swept Philadelphia in 1793, the federal government shut down and almost one in ten residents lost their lives. Residents blamed a variety of causes from rotting coffee and lightning rods to that old mainstay, divine punishment.

But then the world finally changed. In the centuries that followed, successive breakthroughs in epidemiology gradually rendered human life more predictable and less vulnerable. Modernity's crackdown on smallpox and typhus, on cholera and typhoid, on tuberculosis and yellow fever, on polio and measles set us free us from much misery and early death. This was without precedent. Science did not restore a better world we had lost. It cleaned up and increasingly secured a world that had always been a dirty, dire, deadly mess.

It has been all too easy to get used to the blessings of that epochal clean-up, and to take them for granted. Now is the first time they are slipping from our grasp, and the first time we count on science to retrieve them. Gone are the low expectations of even a hundred years ago. When the Spanish Flu appeared back in 1918, global life expectancy at birth was only half of what it is today, and the Grim Reaper was still a constant companion in ways we now find hard to fathom. Vaccines for tuberculosis, typhus, tetanus, measles, and polio had yet to be developed. Viruses raged largely unchecked. In that world, a new strain of influenza was simply one more refugee from Pandora's well-stocked box. And when that pandemic departed as abruptly as it had arrived, scientists could not take credit.

2020 was very different. Cradled by the comforts of peace, penicillin, Prozac, and prosperity, we have grown far less tolerant of hazard than our toughened ancestors. Economies wither under anxious distancing even as case fatality rates fall far short of those wrought by historical pandemics and greatly favor those with most of their lives still ahead of them. This makes our pandemic above all an economic crisis, with all the social, psychological, and political repercussions that entails. Economic activity hinges very much on perception — not just on bare needs (long met by modernity) but on the confidence that has us demand and consume all those superfluities that prop up employment and GDP. But now, unlike in the past, that confidence has been shaken.

Every year about 2.8 million Americans die from all causes. As of this writing, Covid19 had raised this tally by a little over 8 percent, or a bit more if all likely deaths are included. And these bare numbers inflate the pandemic's overall impact. In the United States, the mean age of death of or with Covid19 has been around 75 years, an age at which remaining life expectancy averages 12 years (or rather less for those with pre-existing conditions, which are overrepresented among those who do die). This is very much worth putting in perspective. Recall the morbid excitement of the media when, last spring, Covid19 fatalities passed the toll of the Vietnam War of a little over 58,000 — a false equivalence if there ever was one. Average age at death among those soldiers was 23 years, at which point the average man could expect to live another 48. A total of 2.8 million years of life were lost. The official Covid19 toll did not reach that mark until around Election Day. And even that calculation ignores the fact that these young soldiers were cut down with their whole lives ahead of them and before most of them had a chance to start a family. If we found a way to factor that in as well, the weight of loss would appear even more staggering.

And yet our response is different, our fear more palpable. How would we feel today if 2.7 million young Americans were drafted to go fight overseas, as they were then? (Or rather 4.5 million, adjusting for today's larger population.) Would that even be possible? Yet just fifty years ago they mostly went, even if some claimed bone spurs or went to Canada. Over 26 million Americans served in the two World Wars and in

Korea, without major resistance at all. In the Civil War, 1 in 50 Americans was killed. The shift away from treating lives as expendable and fellow citizens as cannon fodder is a fairly recent one.

Good riddance, we might say: few if any of us will pine for that bygone age. But our growing commitment to safety, and our ability to honor it, have come at a price. Some economists have cooked up an unappetizing concept known as the Statistical Value of Life. Working from dubious premises, they inform us that an American life is currently worth close to ten million dollars. Government agencies eagerly seize on this number to impose costly safety regulations on private industry but conveniently ignore it when compensating the families of service personnel killed in action, who are usually fobbed off with a million or two in lifetime support. Callous as it might seem, that latter approach at least has the virtue of being more realistic than the high-end price tag that signally fails to align with other metrics: equivalent to twice average lifetime per capita GDP in the United States, it values all Americans, who account for a paltry 4 percent of humanity, at more than 3 quadrillion dollars, or close to ten times total global wealth.

Such absurdities are but a pale reflection of a broader revaluation of values. We no longer fight fear, we promote it. We seem transfixed by our fragility. Summary school closings, which wreak havoc on countless working parents, are hard to reconcile with the minuscule health risks faced by the very young. Let us grant that they are designed to protect those parents and not just unionized teachers. But plenty of parents have also been wary of letting their children return to college, despite the fact that only 0.1% of Covid19 deaths have occurred between the ages of 18 and 22. One cannot help wondering how the families of the 26 million Americans who served in the two World Wars and in Korea would have felt about that.

During the Spanish Flu in the fall of 1918, male college students trained for the war in France. And even as this pandemic took more than half a million American lives, its economic consequences were ultimately minor. Shutdowns were haphazardly imposed and retail was not greatly affected. For the most part, people just plowed on — partly because working from home was not an option and welfare was almost non-existent, and partly, perhaps, because it did not actually occur to them not to. The notion that the preservation of life justifies almost any cost —widely if unevenly embraced by a citizenry ready to pull back regardless of government fiat — had not attained its present dominance.

This collective anxiety, and the open-ended distancing and recession it spawns, places an especially heavy burden on the fourth great stabilizer. Well beyond warding off mass mortality and morbidity, science must now restore the sort of confidence that governments cannot decree. Our trust in the blessings of modern medicine has eclipsed traditional religious beliefs as well as faith in government — at least in much of the population. Last year, a Pew Research Center survey found that more than twice as many Americans had confidence in scientists than in elected politicians. And why wouldn't they? Unlike the uneasy compromise of life with rampant Covid19, the renewed freedom of life after — or rather alongside managed — Covid19 is entirely the gift of the high priests of science. And the more we value life, health, and safety, the more we rely on that gift to get everything back on track.

This is all the more true as reactions to containment measures vary, driven by factors as diverse as vulnerability, political preference, and class. The pandemic has even provoked a new know-nothingism, an unembarrassed hostility to science, that reached all the way into the White House. This variation in responses to the crisis fosters acute tensions — between young and old, between red and blue, between rich and poor. The longer the viral threat lingers, the more corrosive these tensions are bound to become. Government must help us stay afloat while the pandemic rages. It also has a crucial role to play in subsidizing and distributing medical remedies. At some point it might even have to mandate their use. In the end, however, only science can deliver us.

The coronavirus shock has been both amplified and checked by modernity: by global connectivity and fragilities on the one hand, and by financial relief, Zoom, and medicine on the other. It bears within it both boost and restraint. This is something it has in common with a greater crisis to come. Neither the Paris Accord nor Greta Thunberg will save us from climate change. Geneticists, physicists, and engineers are our only credible line of defense.

Much has already been accomplished, from drought-resistant genetically modified crops to the ever more effective harnessing and storing of renewable energy. Nuclear power, an even more powerful redeemer, has been at our disposal for almost eighty years, even as misguided politicians around the world are doing their craven best to snuff it out. But more will be needed to sustain mass affluence in the First World and to spread it elsewhere. If nuclear fusion remains a pipe dream, geoengineering may well have to come to the rescue. Yet whatever the precise configuration of techniques that will

236

keep us on track, all of them will share the same source: science.

We can argue to our heart's content whether the twenty-first century will be America's or China's. But that debate is moot. We already know that this will be the century of science. For the first time in history, it will not be enough for scientists to make the world smarter and richer. Now they will be called upon to make sure that it does not slide back into the dark days when germs held humanity hostage, and to enable us to square the circle by reconciling environmental protection with ongoing growth.

Modernity has long struggled to contain the forces it unleashed. Smog had to be tamed. Nuclear war — the ultimate genie-out-of-the-bottle hazard of modernity — had to be averted. HIV, Ebola, and the SARS outbreak of 2003 had to be contained. The current challenge has not introduced a new dynamic: it is simply the latest in a long line of challenges brought forth by progress. As a challenge, the coronavirus crisis ought to be manageable enough to be overcome even as it accelerates ongoing shifts and trends, not all of them equally worrisome. Yet this need not be true of the next "novel" virus, be it natural or man-made — let alone of the much more complex and daunting process of environmental degradation.

It may seem strange, even a little morbid, to marshal an ongoing crisis to ponder future ones. But that is exactly what we must do, once we appreciate that Covid19 is unlikely to serve as that rarest of agents, a genuine historical disrupter. But the post-Covid19 continuities, for better and for worse, should not make us complacent about the volatility of late modernity. The most positive spin we might put on our epidemiological calamity is that it has provided us with an invaluable trial run for the more enormous crises that await us. Just as coronavirus outbreaks in the early 2000s and the financial crisis of

2008 taught us lessons that have come in handy (or would have come in handy had they been heeded), the more we are willing to learn from the present pandemic the better equipped we will be to deal with worse travails down the road.

In the end, this might well turn out to be the most important legacy of Covid19: an enlargement of our imagination of disaster, a sober preparedness for the perils that surely await us. Do not expect the virus to re-make our world. It will not force us to solve our most pressing problems; only we can force ourselves to solve them. There was a touch of wisdom in Michel Houellebecq's sardonic prediction that the post-Covid19 world "will be the same, just a bit worse."

HELEN VENDLER

Strangering

According to Wallace Stevens, "Every poem is a poem within a poem: the poem of the idea within the poem of the words." We often put "the idea" in a brief phrase: "the evils of war." We rarely talk about the *poetry* of the idea. By itself, the theme, the idea, is always banal: it has to be recreated by the poet's imagination into something animated. (And since the poet at hand is male, I'll call him "he" in what follows.) And then, how is he to arouse a glow of personal vividness within the language, and create "the *poem* of the words"?

Suppose the poet wants the "idea" of his poem to be "the disparity of cultures." What might "the *poem* of the idea" be?

This particular poet's imaginative move is to locate his two cultures in cosmic space, on two different planets, one of which is Planet Earth. And how will the words be made into "the *poem* of the words?" An answer occurs to him. What if a visitor from outer space had studied English, but could not escape mistakes in using it for the first time? At this initial stage, there remains a great deal to be done, since both the poem of the idea and the poem of the words are still sketchy and unfulfilled. But at least the poet now has the two poetries to work with. And the poet, Robert Hayden, an Afro-American (his preferred term), is convinced that a poem written by a minority poet has to be as strong in the poetry of its words as in the poetry of its idea. In "Counterpoise," a group-manifesto that Hayden published in 1948, he declared emphatically, "As writers who belong to a so-called minority we are violently opposed to having our work viewed, as the custom is, entirely in the light of sociology and politics."

Let us suppose that it is 1978, and in a new book of poems a reader is seeing an odd entry, bizarrely bracketed fore and aft to show that the title is an editorial addition: "[American Journal]." Who, the reader asks, kept the journal; for whom was it intended; who attached the subsequent title implying, by its non-authorial initial capitals, an editor familiar with written-English usage? The answer is suspended. As the poem opens, the reader sees a series of totally unpunctuated sentiments flowing down the page in hesitant and unequal paragraph-stanzas halted intermittently by pauses. The journal-speaker is fluent, but not error-free, in English. The reader is in fact encountering the internal stream of consciousness of an extraterrestrial, dispatched by his rulers ("The Counselors") to spy on, and report on, a group of brash new planetary invaders calling themselves "americans."

We see that the spaceman has learned only oral English, and knows none of the conventions of written English such as punctuation, apostrophes, and upper-case letters; but there must exist in his own native language some sort of honorific distinction reserved for the rulers, "The Counselors" (the honorific is translated in his journal by its sole and singular use of capital letters). In the poem's prologue, the extraterrestrial muses on his new situation:

here among them   the americans   this baffling
multi people   extremes and variegations   their
noise   restlessness   their almost frightening
energy   how best describe these aliens in my
reports to   The Counselors

disguise myself in order to study them unobserved
adapting their varied pigmentations   white black
red brown yellow   the imprecise and strangering
distinctions by which they live   by which they
justify their cruelties to one another

charming savages   enlightened primitives   brash
new comers lately sprung up in our galaxy   how
describe them   do they indeed know what or who
they are   do not seem to   yet no other beings
in the universe make more extravagant claims
for their importance and identity

The spy, disguised and passing as a fellow-citizen, studies the unfamiliar new tribe, noting its heterogeneity, its "strangering" distinctions, and its repellent moral justifications. Little by little the inner voice of the spy reveals his burden: he must compose a report for The Counselors, and he feels inadequate to the task. Although the planet of the "aliens" belongs to the same galaxy as his own, he knows no group in the entire universe who regard themselves so insolently, so proudly, as these "savages" do. So far, the extraterrestrial voice has offered relatively little information about its own powers and intentions; only later — during a visit to a rough tavern — does it reveal that it has masked itself (at least in the tavern) as male. I am calling the voice "he," but it has the power to exist in different genders and can adopt local skin-pigmentation at will.

Since the planetary visitor is addressing himself, we can only guess, from his own categories and judgments, what sort of person is generating these words. We learn that he is frightened by lawless energy, by noise, by unpredictable restlessness, by multiple skin-colors: in disguise he has "adapted" — but he means "adopted" — various pigmentations depending on his social context. "Adapted" is one of his linguistic falterings, like "strangering" (in lieu of "strange"). He has strong moral views, and is revolted by the cruelties he sees among these "savages" (however charming); he has equally strong intellectual views, judging the newcomers as "primitives" (however sophisticated their technology). To him, the "americans" are aliens incapable of introspection or self-analysis yet ever-boastful in their claims to importance and to a unique identity.

Hayden's 141-line "[American Journal]" has attracted a good deal of contemporary attention, but its imaginative swirls of inconsistent "american" ideologies and behaviors have provoked more critical observation than its equally imaginative flights of language. I want to reflect here on Hayden's imaginative interest in creating a spaceman's mind and forms of expression. "The Counselors" on the spaceman's planet apparently maintain a training laboratory for spies, providing language-tapes of any culture they intend to investigate. Two sets of these tapes are labeled "English," one transmitting British English and the other American English, and the spy has been afforded both sets for his diligent preparatory study. One of the most entertaining aspects of this nonetheless serious poem is its presentation of the verbal and interpretive blunders that any visitor to a foreign land is bound to commit when he finds himself embedded in a bewildering unknown culture. Hayden must have taken intense pleasure in thinking up, all through, the multi-faceted "poem of the words" used by the alien.

"[American Journal]" presents itself as a quasi-symphonic poem, advancing with the fluidity of musical movements in the spaceman's successive choices of aspect: scenes, emotions, distinctions of pacing, degree of self-distancing. After the opening prologue, the voice (perhaps to reassure The Counselors) begins to liken this brash new species to his own tribe; "like us," he says, they have advanced technology and have traveled to the moon (grossly leaving their "rubbish" behind); and apparently they too worship "the Unknowable Essence" (but how do they define their Unknowable?). In lieu of shamans they have "technologists" (a native speaker might have said "scientists"). The observer tallies geographical and meteorological earth-features that he recognizes from his own home-planet, including the temporal feature of the sun by day, the moon by night:

> oceans deserts mountains grain fields canyons
> forests   variousness of landscapes weathers
> sun light moon light as at home

Strangering

Nostalgia for "home" has made him begin his observations with familiar perceptions, but he is as yet a novice in English pronunciation: he separates the word "sun" from "light" and "moon" from "light," as though his overarching category "Light" has separate subordinate categories, that of the sun and that of the moon. With him, the light has not, as in native English voicing, been absorbed almost silently into the polysyllabic "moonlight" and "sunlight."

The observer, we are pleased to see, has an aesthetic sense resembling our own, responding instantly to "red monoliths" like those of his remembered "home":

much here is
beautiful   dream like vistas reminding me of
home   item   have seen the rock place known
as garden of the gods and sacred to the first
indigenes   red monoliths of home

For the first time, an actual American name has at this point made its way into the spaceman's report: the so-called Garden of the Gods in Colorado Springs is a stark terrain of red monoliths held sacred by Native Americans. The name points us to an incident in the life of Robert Hayden. In 1975, five years before his death, the day after his reading at Colorado College, Hayden visited the Garden of the Gods at the invitation of a young MFA student whom he had met the night before. A few years afterwards, that student — Yusef Komunyakaa, later a distinguished poet himself — recorded their walk:

Hayden had to be assisted closely along the rocky paths up the beautiful hills. He seemed nearly blind. . . . Soon we were in the heart of the Garden of the Gods, beside

a formation called Balanced Rock—a smaller stone
supporting a larger one, massively depicting a visual
mathematics too subtle for words. Hayden stopped,
looked around, and said, "I love this country."

In "[American Journal]" Hayden bestows his own warm response to the grandeur of the scene on his extraterrestrial, fusing himself and the surreal cosmic visitor.

A reader aware that Hayden is African-American may suspect that he is satirizing, in the response of the technically sophisticated alien contemplating the americans, the discourse of a "civilized" white gazing, with simultaneous denigration and envy, at a "primitive" Black culture. But by now enough ink has been spent on the poem to discourage any idea that its "message" is without subtlety; a number of identity-determinants national, linguistic, gendered populate the poem. Although the spy celebrates the landscape so like his own, he is not free to mention in his report the sensuous appeal of the americans themselves. After his search for the right adjective to describe them—"i am attracted to / the vigorous americans disturbing, sensuous"—he becomes ashamed, adding "never to be admitted," meaning, surely, not even to himself.

The next movement of the poem is a scherzo, in which the alien-in-disguise has a conversation in a tavern with an american. When he asks what is meant by "the American dream" the "earth-man" answers in ignorant colloquial language (with its crude "irregardless," its unthinking alliance of "sure" and "i guess"). The alien, never having read written English, is mistaken in substituting two words for the proper English single word, as in "night mare" and "every body"), and he is baffled by the redundant insertion of the all-purpose American linguistic filler, "okay." The "earth-man" says, of the American Dream:

245

                    sure
we still believe in it i guess… irregardless of the some
times night mare facts we always try to double
talk our way around   and its okay the dreams
okay and means whats good could be a damn sight
better   means every body in the good old u s a
should have the chance to get ahead or at least
should have three squares a day   as for myself
i do okay   not crying hunger with a loaf of
bread tucked under my arm you understand

The alien's dutiful previous listening to the tapes of
spoken English does not equip him to understand the torrent
of incorrectness, slang ("double talk," "three squares"), and
abbreviations ("u s a") uttered by the "earth-man." He puts forth,
in reply to this barrage of American dialect, his courteous
British reply (deriving from his alternate set of language-
tapes, the British one): "i / fear one does not clearly follow." His
tavern-mate becomes suspicious:

notice you got a funny accent pal   like where
you from he asked   far from here I mumbled
he stared hard   I left

The tavern-dialogue teaches the alien that his linguistic
mimicry is still imperfect:

must be more careful   item   learn to use okay
their pass word   okay

After the comic interlude of the tavern scene, however,
"[American Journal]" suddenly turns savage, as a street riot

erupts, alive with new unintelligibility. The alien sees people he characterizes as "sentinels" — a literal translation from some word in his native tongue, since he hasn't learned the correct English word for "police." The "sentinels" are disturbingly re-characterized by the crowd — "pigs / i heard them called"--as the police retaliate "with flailing clubs":

> unbearable decibels   i fled lest
> vibrations of the brutal scene do further harm
> to my metabolism already over taxed

A biological fact about the alien — that under the rule of The Counselors the capacity to tolerate violence has been genetically bred out of his metabolism — leads him to side with the police, as with the primary authoritarian decisions that have created and socialized him. His voice becomes that of a repressed creature unconscious of his own victimization, incapable until now of any mental act not channeling the opinions of The Counselors. Yet his equilibrium has been so shaken by the violence of the riot that the very word "serenity" shatters into linguistic fragments over a line-ending:

> The Counselors would never permit such barbarous
> confusion   they know what is best for our sereni
> ty   we are an ancient race and have outgrown
> illusions cherished here   item   their vaunted
> liberty

His (temporary) identification with The Counselors allows the alien to parody the earth-men's truculence:

> no body pushes me around i have heard
> them say   land of the free they sing   what do
> they fear mistrust betray more than the freedom
> they boast of in their ignorant pride have seen
> the squalid ghettoes in their violent cities

(Nowhere does the alien sound more like a white supremacist than here: he has learned, and uses, the abusive word "ghetto.") And he wonders, returning to the word "paradox" from an earlier summary:

> paradox on paradox   how have the americans
> managed to survive

After the deafening street riot there arrives a louder scherzo than the earlier tavern-interlude: now it is the "patriotic" spectacle of the Fourth of July. As "earth-men / in antique uniforms play at the carnage whereby/ the americans achieved identity," the alien reveals that on his own planet they indeed do study American history in its origins:

> we too recall
> that struggle as enterprise of suffering and
> faith uniquely theirs

But what has happened in the vulgar modern era to the noble independence celebrated on the Fourth? With mockery the alien sees its debasement into a craven nationalism:

> blonde miss teen age
> america waving from a red white and blue flower
> float as the goddess of liberty   a divided

Liberties

people seeking reassurance from a past few under
stand and many scorn

"A past [that] few understand and many scorn": in these
high-minded words the alien exhibits his own superior
wisdom as he judges American ignorance and political decline.
And hearing contemporary skeptics dismiss the Fourth of July
parade ("why should we sanction / old hypocrisies"), the alien
returns to his "native" moralizing and irritated scorn. Yet his
anxiety exhibits itself afresh as the revered word "Counselors"
breaks into pieces at a line-end:

> The Counse
lors would silence them

> a decadent people The Counselors believe   i
> do not find them decadent   a refutation not
> permitted me

The Counselors, we begin to understand, do not countenance
objections to their views. The alien's irrepressible mixed
feelings about the americans throw him into a violent mixed
diction as he ends up siding with the Counselors' stereotypes
of raw crude "earthlings":

> but for all their knowledge
> power and inventiveness not yet more than raw
> crude neophytes like earthlings everywhere

With the subsiding of his unresolved responses to the
Fourth of July, the alien wonders how his report on america
will strike The Counselors. Since he is, himself, delighted by

the ingenuity of his multiple disguises, he reminds himself *sotto voce* to induce approval in The Counselors by describing his stratagems. But even while reassuring himself that The Counselors will admire his powers, he still worries about their eventual estimation of his work. Hoping to curry favor, he describes his spy-costumes in a cascade of nouns and idioms learned, we feel, rather on the street than from the bland tapes of his language-lab):

> though I have easily passed for an american   in
> bankers grey afro and dashiki long hair and jeans
> hard hat yarmulke mini skirt   describe in some
> detail for the amusement of The Counselors and
> though my skill in mimicry is impeccable   as
> indeed The Counselors are aware   some thing
> eludes me   some constant amid the variables
> defies analysis and imitation   will I be judged
> incompetent

In his next, most analytical moment, the extraterrestrial rises to the philosophical diction natural to his culture — a discourse technologically supreme, wholly rational, but emotionally repressed. The minor role of america in the cosmic scheme of things ("an iota in our galaxy") is evident to him, but he is disturbed by its problematic existence as a conceptually insoluble entity, resistant — in its mobile lability of science and fantasy, logic, and imagination — to the analytic reason that is the pride of his civilization. He sighs in frustration:

> america   as much a problem in metaphysics as
> it is a nation earthly entity, an iota in our
> galaxy   an organism that changes even as i

        examine it   fact and fantasy never twice the
        same   so many variables

As the spy ponders the unintelligibility of america, its antagonism to all he has valued, he realizes that he is in physical danger from its natives: already his presence has been rumored in the newspapers. While the papers laugh at those "believing" in the existence of "humanoids," the "humanoids" in their spaceship laugh back at the scoffing newspapers. Quiet in his withdrawal from the company of his "crew," the alien reflects on all he has seen and heard: the gaudy Fourth of July parade, blonde miss teen-age america, the suspicious "earth-man" in the tavern, the street-riot between citizens and "sentinels," the awful decibels of both celebration and violence, the confluence in the streets of dashikis and yarmulkes. Lost in his memories, the alien, tensely frustrated, cannot define what the americans are: he knows only that the american personality confounds his own schooled, careful, sexless, logical self. He cannot, now, return unthinkingly to his own sterile planet, submit to The Counselors' rules, and censor his speech. Once home, he will ponder the "variegations" of his past journey — his adroit disguises of body, skin-color, gender, and manner of speech — but for all his wide-ranging observation, he will remain forever unable to solve the "quiddity" — the "thisness" — of this paradoxical population, this exuberant and savage rebel-tribe.

Hayden's science-fiction is doubly dystopian. His spacemen are like Swift's whinnying Houyhnhnms, inhuman, chilly, fastidious, rational; and their representative courier flinches at the americans' untidiness, their boasting, their costumed mimicry of the carnage of 1776, their cruelty, their childish "floats," their veneration of the "Goddess of Liberty" in the person of a teen-ager in a toga, their incoherent "metaphysics," their elusive essence.

Behind the agitated monologue of the visiting "humanoid" lies the implied story of his former life: he was born, he was schooled, he was reprimanded for any excess of act or emotion, he was indistinguishable from others of his tribe. Passionless, he needed no human relations (family, wife, children); he worshipped "technologists," and excelled in scientific observation, memory, and analysis. Posted to another planet to spy on the brash new tribe of "earthlings," he is disposed at first to dismiss their childish "civilization," but eventually, as he moves among them, he discovers in their "variegated" pigments and "various" behaviors much that he has lacked in his artificially rational former life. And what will his future be? He will be sadder, and wiser, forever alienated from his compliant fellow-citizens, unable to convey to them the extravagance of emotion and action, free from punitive supervision, that the americans, for all their faults, possess.

Hayden made room in his poem for his extraterrestrial's implied past and presumably alienated future to sharpen the contrast of the two cultures, the governed rational and the unbridled free. Both are insufficient, both are incomplete. The rational and disciplined one sees the unbridled one as ungovernable; the unbridled one would see the alien's author-itarian Counselors as intolerable. Neither culture is really admirable. The chief difference between them is that one is subjugated, the other free (in both virtue and vulgarity). The free culture has no stable government; its people are unruly, as likely to sponsor a riot as a parade. The governed culture has the dark stability of its euphemized "counseling" — coercive, repressive, severe, implacable.

Hayden invented from scratch the unusual sensibility and the "faulty" English of the alien, his innocence as to punctuation and spelling, his nervousness intermittently betrayed by his words' falling into pieces (not syllables), his complacent moral judgments, his intellectual scorn of the "earthlings" who have gotten to the moon but no further, his horror at the sheer noise of the american streets in parades and riots — all the while showing his opinions being put into question by that elusive "something" for which he has no words. It is, of course, freedom, both in creation and in destruction.

We can, if we choose, read this conflict of cultures as embodying on the one side technologically schooled and hierarchically socialized America and on the other side that supercilious America's view of African-American life. There is something to that reading, but not everything. Hayden repudiated the narration of victimhood as the chief resource of a minority writer, just as he repudiated despair at the racial division of his America. His "God-consciousness" (as he named it) led him to an unshakeable conviction of human brotherhood and enabled him ultimately to join his wife Erma's church, the Baha'i, which exists without a hierarchical structure and affirms belief in the unity of all humankind.

And yet Hayden had, by his own acknowledgment, periods of profound depression as well as periods of strenuous belief that relations between the races could not only improve but become harmonious. He incurred the wrath of the Black Power movement in the 1970s because of his conviction that the literature of organized protest movements tended toward propaganda, not art. Nor could he bring himself to refuse Emersonian symbolism in favor of literal statement.

Strangering

When an interviewer asked him why he wrote poetry, he said — disarmingly and wittily — because he liked it better than prose. He thought "confessional" poetry too naked to attain universality. He never stopped revising his poems in the direction of greater concision, greater symbolic power, and greater objectivity. Famous for his powerful sequences of African-American history — "Middle Passage," "John Brown"— he is justly remembered in most anthologies for the inexpressibly moving "Those Winter Sundays," an elegy for his laborer foster-father. "Sundays, too, my father got up early," it begins, with all the emphasis on the accented "too": — "got up early" as a kindness to the sleeping family in the cold house, "making banked fires blaze." "Nobody ever thanked him": that is the line of the poem that nobody can ever forget.

Once Hayden learned to read — by himself, at three — he read intensely and passionately in the major British and American poets. One can see him, over a lifetime, experimenting with nearly all poetic genres: nature lyrics, elegies, sequences, allegories, ballads. When he looked to African American predecessors, he saw some of them writing in dialect, others creating new folk ballads, still others choosing the high language of the canonical English lyric. He would learn from them, but equally from Whitman, Crane, and Auden (who taught Hayden at Michigan). Just as Elizabeth Bishop would not allow her poems to appear in single-gender anthologies because she took herself to be an American poet, not a "female poet," so Hayden always believed himself to be an American poet among other American poets. For him, the democracy of literature could not countenance partisan hostilities, nor could the brotherhood of human beings conceive of exclusions within the company of artists.

Born in Detroit in 1913 and named Asa Sheffley by his

birth-parents, the poet was given away, but not abandoned, by his mother when she moved to find work. He was raised (but never adopted) by a neighborhood family, the Haydens, and subsequently went by the name Robert Hayden. He came to feel that his foster-family meant well by him; his father did not obstruct his intellectual desires, and saved to help him through college, but it was a teacher, a librarian, and a social worker (assigned to the Haydens when they were on welfare), who saw something unusual in him and encouraged him. In his prose, he was candid about his group difficulties in school; with his thick glasses, his poor sight, and his love of poetry, he was called "nigger, Four-Eyes, sissy." In view of the violent racial divisions of American life, which he experienced from childhood with unavoidable pain, he thought that an artist had to cultivate a strict objectivity in social observation. He supported himself all his life by teaching. For twenty years he remained at Fisk (teaching fifteen hours a week, a taxing load for a conscientious teacher), and thereafter he closed his career at the University of Michigan. In 1976, the Bicentennial Year, he was appointed Consultant in Poetry to the Library of Congress (a congratulatory post now renamed, more accurately, Poet Laureate). The final triumph of Hayden's personal and impersonal objectivity was "[American Journal]," composed in 1976 as the Phi Beta Kappa poem for the University of Michigan and placed as the final work in his *Collected Poems*. You can hear Hayden read it in his quiet and musical voice on a tape he made for the Library of Congress in 1978, two years before he died, early, at 66, of cancer.

ROBERT ALTER

Lolita Now

After almost three-quarters of a century, how are we now to think about *Lolita*? It may well be the most commented on novel written in English in the past hundred years, alongside Joyce's *Ulysses*. In the case of *Ulysses*, the imperative for commentary is chiefly a consequence of the invitation to exegesis generated by that novel's dense network of allusions and the multiple complexities of its structure. In fact, Alfred Appel, Jr., in the introduction to his splendid *Annotated Lolita*, has observed certain affinities between *Lolita* and *Ulysses* in the centrality of parody for both novels, in their resourceful deployment of popular culture, and, of course in their shared elaborate mobilization of literary allusions: Nabokov, we should recall, was a great admirer of *Ulysses*, and *Lolita* has its own formal intricacies, which have been duly explicated by much apt criticism ever since its initial American publication in 1958.

Yet the more obvious reason why *Lolita* has elicited so much commentary through the years is the moral questions raised by its subject. The crudest notes of the discussion were first struck by readers who imagined that the author must be a pervert and that the novel he wrote was altogether a sordid thing. In more sophisticated guise, some conservative critics, such as Norman Podhoretz, have contended that *Lolita* may corrupt morals and must be approached with caution by right-thinking people. Inevitably, the novel has also been excoriated by the feminist Left. In her diffuse but influential article "Men Explain *Lolita* to me," Rebecca Solnit seems to classify *Lolita* (her meaning is a bit opaque) as one of the books that "are instructions as why women are dirt or hardly exist at all except as accessories."

Serious considerations of the novel have properly dismissed all such views, and, indeed, many of the earliest critics recognized it as a literary achievement of the first order of originality (but not Nabokov's erstwhile friend Edmund Wilson, who thought it regrettable). Indeed, powerful and persuasive arguments have been made for the moral character of the book, and these need not be repeated here.

What may be at issue for readers of *Lolita* in the twenty-first century is how to regard the book in an age when our culture has become so conscious of the sexual exploitation of children and of women in general, young or otherwise. This is, of course, a social problem that is alarmingly widespread and deserving of urgent reform, but it must be said that the public exposure of certain especially egregious cases has led much of the public to hair-trigger responses to any activity that is even obliquely related to such appalling exploitation. It is a sign of our confused and simplified and sanctimonious times that Dan Franklin, the editor-in-chief of the esteemed London publishing house Jonathan Cape, has declared that he would not publish *Lolita* if it were submitted to him now. His judgment stems from an acute nervousness about how thirty-year-olds on his company's acquisition team would respond if he proposed publication, as he himself has said.

Is the new awareness of sexual harassment likely to make it altogether uncomfortable to read the first-person narrative of a middle-aged male who repeatedly, extravagantly, and at times brutally commits carnal acts with a pubescent girl who is quite helpless to free herself from him? Novelists, of course, have not infrequently chosen to write books about deviant, criminal, or murderous characters — Humbert Humbert is all three — but the sexual exploitation of a child surely touches a raw nerve, especially now. (One highly intelligent reader, recently reading *Lolita* for the first time, told me that he could see it was a brilliant novel but found it difficult to stick with it because of the subject.)

I would like to suggest that the way Humbert's story is constructed anticipates this sort of discomfort, in a sense even aligning itself with the discomfort. Devoted as he was to the supreme importance of art, Nabokov had been concerned since his Russian novels with the phenomenon of the perverted artist, the person who uses a distorted version of the aesthetic shaping of reality to inflict suffering on others. Humbert Humbert is only his most extreme representation of such distortion. The perversion of the artistic impulse is a vital subject for Nabokov precisely because art matters so much to him.

The first thing that should be noted about the treatment of this subject in *Lolita* is that Humbert Humbert clearly regards himself as a monster, repeatedly emphasizing his own monstrosity. This goes along with the fact that he is insane, as he frankly admits, and that he has been several times institutionalized in asylums. Humbert's assertions of his own moral repulsiveness abound in the novel. "I am," he says of himself early in his story, as a boarder in the Haze home, "like one of those pale inflated spiders you see in old gardens. Sitting in the middle of a luminous web and giving jerks to this or that strand." With Lolita tantalizingly sitting in his lap on the Haze davenport, he invokes a familiar fairy tale that here will have no happy ending as he wriggles in order "to improve the secret system of tactile correspondence between beast and beauty — between my gagged, bursting beast and the beauty of her dimpled body in its innocent cotton frock." Humbert's framing of this allusion altogether reduces the man to his imperious sexual member. And as we shall see from other citations, he has a clear awareness that his absconding with Lolita is bound to have dire consequences for both.

When he finally consummates his lust for Lolita, he declares that it was she who seduced him, not an altogether improbable claim given her sexual precociousness, but she on her part says, fearing that he has torn her internally — though it is unclear whether she might be merely joking — that she ought to report him to the police for rape. At least in a moral sense as well as in the statutory one, this could be quite right. The year-long frenzy of sexual gratification with a sometimes reluctantly submissive, sometimes resistant, twelve-year-old has its particularly sordid moments beyond its intrinsic sordidness, as when Humbert insists on sex when Lolita is running a high fever or in his repeatedly bribing her

259

with magazines and treats to make herself available to his insatiable desire. Humbert's admission of all this repeated abuse culminates near the end of the novel in his often cited recognition, as he watches school children at play, that he has deprived Lolita of her childhood. But a summarizing assessment of what he has perpetrated in the throes of his obsession occurs earlier, as he and Lolita head back east in his car:

> We had been everywhere. We had really seen nothing.
> And I catch myself thinking today that our long journey
> had only defiled with a sinuous trail of slime the lovely,
> truthful, dreamy, enormous country that by then, in
> retrospect, was no more than a collection of dog-eared
> maps, ruined tour books, old tires, and her sobs in
> the night—every night, every night—the moment I
> feigned sleep.

Here the defiling of America and the defiling of Lolita are virtually interchangeable. This self-revelatory moment, coming at the end of a chapter, is very telling in two ways — first the invocation of slime, cognate with the earlier image of the spider, to indicate the repulsiveness of this sexual odyssey, and then, at the end of the little catalogue of the detritus of the journey, interwoven with it and constituting Humbert's first report of this wrenching fact, Lolita's sobbing through it all, night after night.

If *Lolita* were nothing but this, it would merely be a riveting and also unappetizing representation of a sexually obsessed madman. Yet what is enacted in the novel is more complicated and more interestingly ambiguous. In the afterword that Nabokov wrote to *Lolita* in 1956 to accompany the American publication of excerpts in *The Anchor Review*, he offers a curious origin for the idea of the novel. When he was laid up with illness in Paris in 1940, he came across a newspaper story about a caged ape in the Jardin des Plantes that had been given charcoal and paper and produced a sketch of the bars enclosing him in. (One thinks of Rilke's famous poem about the tiger, "Au Jardin des Plantes,": "It seemed to him there were a thousand bars / and behind those bars no world.") The ape inspired Nabokov to write a Russian story with a plot roughly like that of *Lolita*, but, unhappy with the piece, he destroyed it.

What does an ape in a cage drawing his prison have to do with *Lolita*? The obvious answer is that Humbert Humbert's predicament is of a man hopelessly imprisoned by his obsession. The narrative he produces is the representation of his prison, which is not an enclosure of vertical bars but rather an alluring and also vulnerable girl whom he has desperately fixed as the object of his desire. This transformation of a cage into a sexual obsession has a double effect: Lolita as its object is repeatedly celebrated in radiant prose as a thing of beauty, and the reader is led to perceive Humbert not only with horror but also with a qualified kind of sympathy, as a man hideously trapped in his own impulses that inflict grave harm on someone he comes to love and that in the end destroy him. It is relevant in this connection that the Russian story Nabokov discarded ended with the suicide of its perverted protagonist. The central paradox of *Lolita*, and one of the effects that makes it a great novel and not just the story of a psychopath, is that one simultaneously recoils from its narrator and is drawn into both the anguish and the lyric exuberance of his point of view.

261

Especially in regard to the second of these contradictory responses, the extraordinary style of the novel surely takes the book well beyond the fictional case-study of a madman. Nabokov himself characterized the book as his love affair with the English language, and there are few other novels since Joyce that deploy its resources with such pyrotechnic virtuosity. In the famous first paragraph, which is a spectacular prose poem, Humbert ends by saying, "You can always count on a murderer for a fancy prose style." Humbert, with his inventor standing firmly behind him, is wonderfully having it both ways: the extravagance of the musical prose might push to the brink of excess, and Humbert is perfectly aware of this, yet the prose is glorious and is surely a part of the reader's enjoyment of this troubling story. This is the narrative of a man repeatedly doing something morally ugly conveyed in language that is often quite beautiful. The contradiction between subject and style poses a certain moral dilemma for readers, who may well relish the novel and at the same time feel uneasy about the delight they take in it. Perhaps that double-take was part of Nabokov's intention.

For a characteristic instance of this tricky balancing act, let us return briefly to Humbert on the davenport in the Haze home with Lolita, who is evidently unaware of his sexual excitement, sitting in his lap. As he approaches climax, deliberately prolonging the pleasure, he says, in a phrase that shrewdly defines his relationship with the pre-pubescent girl, "Lolita had been safely solipsized." He continues in his habitual extravagant style:

> The implied sun pulsated in the supplied poplars; we were fantastically and divinely alone; I watched her, rosy, gold-dusted, beyond the veil of my controlled delight,

unaware of it, alien to it, and the sun was on her lips, and her lips were apparently still forming the words of the Carmen-barman ditty that no longer reached my consciousness. Everything was now ready. The nerves of pleasure had been laid bare....I was above the tribulations of ridicule, beyond the possibilities of retribution. In my self-made seraglio, I was a radiant and robust Turk, postponing the moment of actually enjoying the youngest and frailest of his slaves.

This entire scene is the most explicitly sexual moment in the novel — after this, Nabokov pointedly refrains from explicit representations of sex — but it is also something rather different. The murderer's fancy prose is exquisitely orchestrated in a virtually musical sense, the passage beginning with a spectacular set of alliterations that also incorporates a rhyme: "The implied sun pulsated in the supplied poplars." The sun is "implied" probably because Humbert, totally focused on Lolita and his pleasure, is not directly observing the sun and the "supplied" poplars on which it is shining, though he does notice the sunlight on her lips. Beyond that detail, Lolita's presence, radiant for Humbert, is evoked only in the brief phrase "rosy, gold-dusted" because Humbert is completely concentrated on his own sexual excitement.

The verbal pyrotechnics of the kind one sees here, which are abundantly deployed throughout the novel, are surely a source of delight for readers, perhaps even eliciting a certain sense of admiration for Humbert's "sensibility" or his inventiveness, though the acts he performs trigger moral revulsion. The novel's perverted protagonist is manifestly a man of high culture — and, at the same time, following the precedent established by Joyce, avidly attentive as well to

263

popular culture — and so this passage, like so many others in the book, spins a web of allusions in its very representation of sexual arousal. The invocation of Carmen, one of several in the novel, probably refers to Merimée's novella rather than to the opera based on it, as Alfred Appel, Jr. plausibly suggests, thus conjuring up from fiction a young and sexually alluring woman, here appearing in a silly ditty. Humbert as a Turk in his seraglio, depicted in still another alliterative chain ("In my self-made seraglio, I was a radiant and robust Turk") taps into an old cliché of Western culture in which the Orient is figured as a theater of exotic sexual license. Leopold Bloom plays more than once with this same Orientalist notion.

Again, I think that the articulation of Humbert's fantasy produces a double effect. A reader may enjoy the exuberance of his inventiveness, but surely what the fantasy reveals about his intentions is repugnant. What is especially telling is the phrase "enjoying the youngest and frailest of his slaves." Presumably, this compliant or helpless victim of the Turk Humbert's lasciviousness is almost or actually a child, and the fact that she is the "frailest" of the female slaves in the seraglio betrays his awareness of Lolita's vulnerability, an aspect of her that may well pique his twisted desire. What I have characterized as the balancing act of Nabokov's prose in this novel is abundantly evident here.

I would like to offer a final example of the odd allure created by Humbert's writing, a passage in which the sheer literariness of the writing is especially prominent. It is Humbert's first sighting of Lolita, peering at him over her dark glasses as she sunbathes on the patio. Her appearance will present to Humbert, or so he claims, the very image of Annabel Leigh, his first love met on the Riviera when both were still pre-teens, and then forever lost to him through an early death:

It was the same child—the same frail, honey-hued shoulders, the same silky supple bare back, the same chestnut head of hair. A polka-dotted black kerchief tied around her chest hid from my aging ape eyes, but not from the gaze of young memory, the juvenile breasts I had fondled one immortal day. And, as if I were the fairy-tale nurse of some little princess (lost, kidnapped, discovered in gypsy rags through which her nakedness smiled at the king and his hounds), I recognized the tiny dark-brown mole on her side. With awe and delight (the king crying for joy, the trumpets blaring, the nurse drunk) I saw again her lovely indrawn abdomen where my southbound mouth had briefly paused; and those puerile hips on which I had kissed the crenulated imprint left by the hem of her shorts—that last mad immortal day behind the "Roches Roses." The twenty-five years I had lived since then tapered to a palpitating point, and vanished.

The idea of a formative experience in early life imprinting itself so indelibly on the psyche that the person becomes its lifelong captive is, as quite a few commentators have noted, 265 Nabokov's mockery of the Freudian notion of the causation of sexual pathology by childhood trauma, a notion he famously despised. Given that it plays an altogether determinative role in Humbert's perversion, one must conclude that the "psychology" of the novel, based as it is on a parody of Freud, can scarcely be regarded as realistic.

It is, instead, a central instance in which playfulness is paramount in this representation of a sexual deviant, an unanticipated conjunction of manner and subject that may compel us to reconsider how to think about Humbert

Humbert. In one respect, he is a powerful fictional representation of a disturbed person that one can readily relate to troubling manifestations of this kind of disturbance in the real world; in another respect, he is a kind of pawn in a wild literary game. One should note that the caged ape in the Jardin des Plantes breaks through the surface here in Humbert's self-denigrating characterization of his own "aging ape eyes." He proceeds to embark on the fantasy of the little princess kidnapped by gypsies — the introduction of gypsies ties in with the allusions to Carmen, who is a gypsy — comically casting himself, a male figure to uncomfortable excess, as the nurse of the vanished infant.

The story of the kidnapped child rediscovered in adulthood through the recognition of a birthmark is very old, originating in the Greek romances of Late Antiquity and continuing to lead a literary life in the Early Modern period and beyond. Fielding, for example, employs it in *Joseph Andrews*, birthmark and all, with the kidnappers there identified as gypsies, a European fantasy about them in that era. Nabokov, then, is playing not only with Freud but also with the contrivance of an old tale told many times since the Greeks. What may properly be described as the highjinks of Humbert's consciousness, however tormented he often may be, is on display as he quickly switches roles from nurse to king, clearly the child's father, crying for joy over her discovery. The fact that the nurse is imagined to be drunk at this moment is a wildly extraneous and incongruous detail, Humbert indulging in a riot of the imagination as he recreates this old story for his self-explanatory purposes.

In regard to his function as a narrator of the novel, it should be kept in mind that Humbert speaks in two distinct and intertwined modes: his language reflects an obsessive and, indeed, deranged mind, as in the excessive doubled insistence on "immortal" in this passage; and it also deploys the extravagant resources of Nabokov, shrewd and witty observer and master stylist. One might note here the lovely precision of the adjective in "the crenulated imprint" and the wit of "my southbound mouth" to refer to the ultimate sexual destiny toward which the mouth is traveling. The two twelve-year-olds on the Riviera, it seems, were going a step beyond ordinary pre-adolescent fooling around. The wonderful concluding sentence goes on to strike a distinctively Nabokovian note. It is strongly reminiscent of at least a couple of sentences in *Speak Memory*, a book cast in its initial version not long before the composition of *Lolita*. The literary and, one could also say, stylistic recapture of the past was an urgent undertaking for Nabokov, splendidly achieved in *Speak Memory*, and in *Lolita* the intellectual joke of a "Freudian" childhood experience becomes also, at least at this moment, an emotionally fraught and joyous realization of the past returned in all its luminous presence.

This concert of surprising and vividly inventive effects in the passage, and elsewhere in the novel as well, leads me to propose an aspect of the readerly experience that one would certainly not expect in the narrative of a sexual abuser of young girls: for all the moral dubiety of the protagonist's story, *Lolita* is a pleasure to read, and anyone who denies this is likely to be suffering from terminal moralism or bad taste. In this important regard, we should consider the essential role of parody in this novel, because parody is also not something generally associated with the fictional portrayal of psychopaths.

Parody, of course, is pervasive in Nabokov's novels. What its presence necessarily implies is that we must see the novel not as a direct representation of reality — a word, we should keep in mind, that for Nabokov must always be wrapped in scare quotes — but rather as a response to the world outside literature entirely mediated by literature, which is to say, both the novelist's own literary contrivances and the variegated background of literary tradition on which he chooses to draw. As critics and scholars through the decades have abundantly shown, Nabokov constantly calls attention to the status of his fiction as literary artifice, executing what the Russian Formalists of the early twentieth century referred to as "laying bare the device." Yet the double edge of this procedure as he practices it may be a little hard to get a handle on. *Invitation to a Beheading* and *Bend Sinister* are ostentatiously self-reflexive novels, but they are also serious engagements with the horrors of totalitarianism, whose potential for the wholesale extirpation of humanity was all too evident during the years when they were composed. Much the same is true of the totalitarian state fantasized by Kinbote in *Pale Fire*. Nabokov's early novel *The Defense* abundantly calls attention to its own artifices, as we would expect, but it is also a wrenching representation of a genius trapped in the world of chess that is the vehicle of his genius. One could extend this Nabokovian catalogue of grave human predicaments, historical or personal, confronted through the medium of self-reflexive fiction.

In *Lolita*, then, we get the probing portrait of a sexual deviant who kidnaps a girl-child and inflicts great harm on her that is conveyed through a novel which reminds us of its status as an invented fiction and plays quite exuberantly with literary tradition. Parody, again, is ubiquitous. It begins on the first page of the novel with the quotation from Poe's

"Annabel Lee," a poem that lends the name Annabel Leigh to Humbert's first love. Is she, after all, a "real" character in a novel or a kind of personified citation, Humbert living out the role of the male speaker in Poe's poem? Allusions to Poe's poem are scattered through the novel. The "winged seraphs" of the poem flit across these pages. Here is one especially telling instance: "I should have known (by the signs made to me by something in Lolita — the real child or some haggard angel behind her back) that nothing but pain and horror would result from the expected rapture. Oh, winged gentlemen of the jury!"

The parodies and satiric references in the novel include Merimée, A. E. Housman, T.S. Eliot, Arthur Conan Doyle, Pierre de Ronsard, and many other writers. The elaborate development of Clare Quilty as Humbert's *doppelgänger* harks back to Dostoevsky's *The Double*, the work of a writer whom Nabokov despised, as well as to Poe's story "William William." Parody is also deployed generically, as in the old romance story of the kidnapped child discovered through a birthmark, or in the desperate, farcical physical battle between Quilty and Humbert, about which he himself observes, "elderly readers will surely recall at this point the obligatory scene in the Westerns of their childhood." All these allusions and parodic elements have a paradoxical effect. Humbert is an appallingly twisted figure repeatedly operating in a literary landscape evoked through his own rich background in culture high and low. In the climactic scene with Quilty, we do not cease to see him as a violently jealous lover seething with rage against the man who has stolen his beloved girl from him, but the scene, with its plethora of parodic literary and cinematic references, is also hilarious: fun and horror are interfused and unmediated. The aesthetic does not usurp the ethical, but the ethical is made to co-exist with the aesthetic, and in this way the reader is made to read complexly, and is never let off the hook.

Nabokov approaches two things with the utmost seriousness: the despicable act of sexually exploiting a child and the instrument of art through which the moral issue is represented. For all of the fun and games of his play with artifice, strong and moving emotions are expressed, as in the great moment near the end, when Humbert discovers the now pregnant Lolita with "her adult, rope-veined narrow hands and her goose-flesh white arms, and her shallow ears, and her unkempt armpits" (which earlier were called "pristine" when he watched her at tennis), and he can assert, "I loved her more than anything I had ever seen or imagined on earth, or hoped for anywhere else."

The defining dimension of art in *Lolita* must be kept in mind. Parody and the overlapping practice of allusion are essential to the adventure of the novel at the same time that they point again and again to its status as a work of literature. Allusion itself is intrinsic to the dynamic of most literature: you would scarcely think of writing a story or a novel or a sonnet or an epic if you had no familiarity with other such works, and allusion, through which you insert your own writing in the body of its predecessors, remaking them and often challenging them as you invoke them, is a recurrent method for the creation of new literature. Parody may be thought of as a special category of allusion, usually in a comic and critical vein. These twin processes in *Lolita* constitute an implicit affirmation of the artfulness of the novel, of the pervasive operation in it of literary art. That art is of course manifested in the spectacular prose that Nabokov creates

270

for his deranged narrator, at times deliberately over the top in keeping with his derangement but very often brilliantly original, witty, finely lyrical, and on occasion quite affecting. Here is a moment when Humbert introduces circus performance as a metaphor for art — the same trope will recur in *Ada* — that suggests how artistic skill can convey the plight of a pathetic and unseemly character, which is precisely what his author has done for him: "We all admire the spangled acrobat with classic grace meticulously walking his tight rope in the talcum light; but how much rarer art there is in the sagging rope expert wearing scareclothes and impersonating a grotesque drunk!"

Lolita is the most troubling and touching representation of a morally grotesque figure in the fiction of the last century. At the very end of his painful story, in his prison cell, his death imminent, Humbert affirms that he has used his fleeting time to make Lolita "live in the minds of later generations." He then goes on to proclaim these grand concluding lines: "I am thinking of aurochs and angels, the secret of durable pigments, prophetic sonnets, the refuge of art. And this is the only immortality you and I may share, my Lolita." The very last word of the novel, as Alfred Appel has observed, is the same as the first, affirming a kind of architectonic unity for the novel as a whole. The reference in "aurochs" to the cave paintings of early man and in "angels, the secret of durable pigments" to Renaissance art set this narrative in the grand tradition of art going all the way back to prehistory, much of it still enduring. There is a certain ambiguity as to who is speaking here at the end. Of course, it has to be Humbert, reflecting on what turns out to be in the end the truly beloved human subject of his story as he senses his own end approaching. Yet his voice merges with Nabokov's in the proclamation of the perdurable power of art.

Humbert Humbert is not Vladimir Nabokov: the point is worth emphasizing in our cultural circumstances. And the real identification of the novelist with his protagonist is not in regard to Humbert's perversion, as some readers of the book have misguidedly imagined, but in the celebration of art as a fixative of beauty and feeling, anguish and love — as a fixative of humanity. It is this, finally, that lifts *Lolita* above the currents of shifting attitudes toward sexual exploitation or toward sex itself. The novel is obviously not a case study in perversion, as the highly parodic foreword by the fictional psychologist John Ray, Jr. would have it. It is also something more than a riveting fictional portrait of a repellently disturbed person. A murderer may have a fancy prose style, but in this instance the prose style turns out to be both arresting and evocative, at moments sublime, leading us to experience through the moral murk of the narrator a great love story that seeks to join the company of the cave paintings of Lascaux and the sublime angels of Giotto and Raphael, and nothing less.

272

DARYL MICHAEL SCOTT

The Scandal of Thirteentherism

Amendment XIII
Section 1.
Neither slavery nor involuntary servitude, except as a
punishment for crime whereof the party shall have
been duly convicted, shall exist within the United States,
or any place subject to their jurisdiction.
Section 2.
Congress shall have power to enforce this article by
appropriate legislation.

In our age of roiling discontent, liberalism and its historical
achievements are under assault from all sides. For the past four
years, Donald Trump had little use for truth, science, progress,
mutual respect among races and identities — all the liberal
ideals embodied in the founding documents and embed-
ded in the history of American politics. Despite overseeing
the military that long ago defeated the Confederacy, Trump
nonetheless made the Lost Cause his own, becoming the
protector of Confederate monuments and place names, and
this support has gained him the appreciation of white nation-
alists and other "good people" like the ones who marched on

Charlottesville. Trump had little use for the colorblind state that liberals associate with the Party of Lincoln.

Even with Trump out of the Oval Office, Trumpism continues to be the perfect ideological provocation for those on the other side now questioning America's central political tradition. It sets the mood for their revisionism. At war with classical liberalism and "neo-liberalism" alike, the progressives are busy rewriting American history. They want a past that reflects their dim view of the American record and justifies certain policies to address racial grievances. American history, they now instruct, is dominated by topics that liberals allegedly marginalized, including settler colonialism, slavery, white supremacy, whiteness, and peoples of color. The editor of the eminent American Historical Review writes that he aims to "decolonize" American history. Ibrahim X. Kendi's book *Stamped from the Beginning* described racism as our very origins. Reducing four hundred years of black history to victimhood, the *New York Times'* 1619 Project echoed this sentiment. Racism explains slavery, which in turn explains the American Revolution and much else worth knowing about American history. Internal conflicts among whites — based on religion, ethnicity, or class — hardly explain anything, and there is certainly nothing exceptional about America.

Rather than claiming their own version of the liberal tradition articulated in the Declaration of Independence, the Reconstruction Amendments, the promise of the New Deal, and the Civil Rights Acts of the 1960s, the progressives play up the failures and the betrayals of previous generations of liberals, even as they are suspicious or grudging about the Biden victory. Unwittingly taking their cue from the Nation of Islam, they view American liberalism itself as a species of white supremacy, national in scope and operation: in their view, white supremacy is not an aberrant tradition rooted in the American South, as most twentieth century liberals saw it. They feel little solidarity with American liberals, except those they have dubbed radical and incorporated into what they call the "black radical tradition," especially Fredrick Douglass, Ida B. Wells, and Martin Luther King, Jr. Like some of the activists in the street, they would topple Jefferson, Lincoln, and Grant along with the Confederate generals. They see liberalism, past and present, as a huge obstacle to the remaking of America into what amounts to a fully integrated society with a social welfare state for all.

One of the pillars of American liberalism under assault is the Thirteenth Amendment. Many Americans now believe that slavery never ended — not despite but because of the amendment that fulfilled the promise of the Emancipation Proclamation. In the words of Bryan Stevenson, the head of the Equal Justice Initiative turned historian, slavery never ceased, it merely "evolved." In his thinking and that of other Thirteenthers, it was the great amendment of 1865 that led to the re-enslavement of black people and mass incarceration. The key to understanding its "evolution" is the exception clause in the amendment, which ended slavery and involuntary servitude "except as a punishment for crime." Under cover of those words, the Thirteenthers claim, ownership of slaves shifted from individuals to the state, even as the Thirteenth Amendment gave the American people, especially its newly freed people, the false impression that America had ended slavery once and for all. Some Thirteenthers do not simply believe that the amendment led to mass incarceration; they also hold that the loophole represented a diabolical scheme concocted by whites as a race. What all Thirteenthers

The Scandal of Thirteentherism

share is the belief that the loophole created a seamless history of black slavery from the seventeenth century until today.

When a person of Stevenson's commitment and stature gives such a dim appraisal of the efficacy of an amendment signed by Abraham Lincoln, attention must be paid. In his crusade to link mass incarceration to the Thirteenth Amendment, he is not alone. A wide array of historians, cultural studies scholars, activists, and artists have endorsed this view in full or in part, including Henry Louis Gates, Jr., Kimberlé Crenshaw, Khalil Muhammad, Alex Lichtenstein, Kanye West, and Ava DuVernay. Whatever chance this interpretation had for burning out on its own disappeared when DuVernay's documentary *13th* took the nation by storm in 2016. It is now taking root in the nation's schools: after watching DuVernay's film, my students believed that the convict lease system (about which more below) re-enslaved most blacks. They were shocked to learn that the percentage was much less than *one percent*.

An idea born in the 1960s has become a popular and pseudo-scholarly belief that many want to use as a basis for making public policy. Not many have gone as far as Kanye West, who— with all the erudition at his disposal — has called for the repeal of the Thirteenth Amendment. Most Thirteenthers aim for an amendment to close the loophole. Their objective is to put an end to mass incarceration, which is a fine objective. But the key to ending it, they suggest, lies in removing its supposed economic justification — black prison slavery.

Thirteentherism is best viewed as another episode in a long tradition of using history as a weapon in a political struggle. At times, the distinction between historical truth and propaganda gets lost. Yet in keeping with our era, bad history and worse social science have replaced truth as the intellectual underpin-

276

ning for a great deal of thinking about social change. Rather than making the incontrovertible case that mass incarceration as an inherent evil, they seek to hitch their cause to the moral opprobrium that already exists against chattel slavery. They have little use for differences and distinctions, and simply wish to call incarceration slavery. Never mind that Americans of African descent have always held historical truth as sacrosanct, believing that the dispelling of falsehoods is the proper foundation for black people's progress. Thirteentherism breaks with that black historical tradition of truth telling, hoping to end convict slavery and in the process misrepresenting some of the most momentous changes in American history.

The intellectual origins of Thirteentherism lie in the intellectual ferment of the 1960s. Prisoners commonly described themselves as slaves, whether on the prison plantations in the South or the workshops in other regions, since they all worked for little or nothing. It took an epiphany by Lee Wood, a prisoner in the California system, to link the Thirteenth Amendment to his condition. As part of a radical reading group, Wood read the amendment aloud to his comrades, and the loophole — "except as punishment for crime whereof the party shall have been duly convicted" — suddenly appeared to explain his plight. Few would do more to spread the idea. Once he had served his time, Wood dedicated himself to ending this "slavery," founding the Coalition Against Prison Slavery (CAPS). He became well known for spreading literature on the role of the Thirteenth Amendment, and with funding from the Quakers he published, along with his wife, a short volume tracing the history of prisoners as slaves.

Wood's idea of removing the loophole from the Thirteenth Amendment gained some traction in prison activist circles by the mid-1970s. He was not so much interested in ending imprisonment as he was against ending the exploitation of prisoner labor. Not only did CAPS receive funding from the Quakers, he also got the American Friends Service Committee to endorse his idea of removing the exception clause from the Constitution. From CAPS, the idea spread. In 1977, the New Afrikan Prisoners Association in Illinois petitioned the United Nations: "We protest the 13th amendment which legalizes slavery..." In 1980, William Coppola, a prisoner in Texas, cited the amendment as proof that slavery was alive and well in America. According to increasing numbers of prisoners, the Thirteenth Amendment had done them dirt. Not only did it not end slavery, it created more of it.

By the 1990s, the intellectual influence of prisoner advocacy spilled over into academic circles. Before joining the professoriate, Alex Lichtenstein worked on behalf of prisoners, then followed his interest into scholarship. He published a history of convict leasing, called *Twice the Work of Free Labor*. Notable mostly for its interpretation that the system contributed greatly to the industrialization of the South, the book promoted the Thirteenther view of the amendment to end slavery: "Ironically, this [convict lease] system emerged immediately on the heels of the passage of the Thirteenth Amendment to the Constitution, which intended to abolish bondage but permitted involuntary servitude solely as a punishment for crime." He named one chapter, "New South Slavery," and another, "Except as a Punishment for Crime."

Thirteentherism gained most of its academic visibility and activist credibility through the writing of Angela Davis, who embodies the continuity between the prison activism of

278

the 1960s and the modern prison abolition movement, which seeks to make prisons obsolete here and abroad. Her academic labors made cultural studies a central venue for the study of "the carceral state." Reminiscent of W. E. B. Du Bois, who laid the seed for whiteness studies with a passing comment about how whites benefited from black oppression, Davis wrote an essay on Fredrick Douglass' failure to oppose convict leasing and other forms of labor oppression. Of the amendment's clause, she wrote: "That exception would render penal servitude constitutional — from 1865 to the present day." As if this would have been impossible without the clause, she went on to say "That black human beings might continue to be enslaved under the auspices of southern systems of justice (and that this might set a precedent for imprisonment outside of the South) seems not to have occurred to Douglass and other abolitionist leaders." After her essay, the Thirteenth Amendment's loophole became intellectually important.

Wood, Lichtenstein, and Davis see a constitutional power in the Thirteenth Amendment to establish convict or prisoner slavery, yet they know that the various British colonies and American states had exercised legal authority to create systems of convict slavery. They often carry on as if the amendment was meant for blacks only — the original post-Civil War black code, if you will. But before and after the founding of the United States, convicts had been forced to labor against their will without recompense. During the colonial era, more than 50,000 whites convicts were given the most extreme Hobson's choice: an indenture (contract) to slave for a term of years in British North America or to be put to death for their crime. They were often sold to work for masters at the auction blocks where Africans were sold, and both types of slaves, convict and chattel, were known to run away together.

The American Revolution ended the importation of white convicts as slave labor, but the new sovereign states all put those deemed criminal, regardless of racial designation, to work without compensation in one form or another. In the new penitentiaries some worked directly under the supervision of the state, others worked at the prisons under the control of leases, and others still off site. By the end of the Civil War, the power of colonies and then states to inflict involuntary servitude or slavery for a term on whites and others as convicts had existed for over two hundred and fifty years — a period longer than the age of chattel slavery. Of those seeing a white conspiracy to re-enslave blacks as convicts, an obvious question needs to be asked: why would Congress need to create a special constitutional amendment for blacks to make convict slaves of them? They had done that very thing to whites for centuries. The exception clause merely recognized the existing police power of the states.

The history of white convict slavery notwithstanding, Thirteenthers often treat the amendment as a federal black code that applied uniquely to the freed people and blacks in general. Among many others, Lichtenstein and Davis suggest as much when they imply that something special could have been done in the language of the amendment to prevent the criminalization and re-enslavement of the freed people. In their account, the language as it stands empowered the Southern planters, and they point to a Southerner or two who read the amendment as a veritable black code for the treatment of freed people. For an alternative that could have made things different, Thirteenthers point to Senator Charles Sumner's attempt to offer a different version of the amendment that outlawed slavery and made no mention of crime and punishment. Many believe that his amendment without the exception clause would have changed history.

Yet Sumner simply wanted an amendment that clearly embodied the abolitionists' belief that blacks and whites would be free and equal under the law. Removing the exception clause would have ended chattel slavery, but it would have left convict slavery — for blacks and whites alike — in place. Criminalization and imprisonment go well with Sumner's desired wording of equality under the law. The difference of racism would have adversely impacted them at the hands of the states as it had plagued antebellum free blacks, North and South. Indeed, something more than an amendment touting equality under the law was needed.

The Republican-dominated Congress was interested in ending chattel slavery, nothing more, nothing less. They decided on the language that had been an effective chattel-slavery killer since 1787. The exception clause had become part of American federal law when Congress passed the Northwest Ordinance in 1787. Congress prohibited chattel slavery in the territories ceded to the federal government — except for those slaves found guilty of crimes, who could be subject to "involuntary servitude or slavery." Thomas Jefferson, who most likely drafted the provision, wanted to end the expansion of chattel slavery. Congress required the exception clause as part of every constitution submitted by territories to enter the union as a free state. Over time, Jefferson's proviso, as Sumner called it, ended chattel slavery wherever it was enshrined in a state constitution. It also made clear that Congress was not usurping a new state's police power to punish criminals in a manner consistent with the original thirteen states — some of which, as colonies, included enslavement.

Apparently few Republicans, including Sumner, understood that the exception clause allowed for a term of slavery for a conviction. The potential difference between Sumner's equality under the law proposal and the loophole version became clear immediately. In early 1866, the United States Army quashed the enforcement of a black code in Virginia that allowed freed people who did not sign a contract to be sold as a slave for a term. In November 1866, a judge in Anne Arundel County, Maryland, sentenced three black people to be sold for a term of service to local planters. The decision alarmed Sumner and other Republicans. The judge, in effect, was seeking to apply the old free person of color laws. The sentences were never carried out and the judge did not ultimately face prosecution. Yet Maryland was soon forced to remove its discriminatory laws. The loophole for any form of chattel slavery, even for a crime and even for a term, was closed. The Thirteenth Amendment was emphatically not a black code.

Without compromising the principle of equality under the law, the Republican-dominated Congress would have had to pass a version of the Thirteenth Amendment, or an additional one, that explicitly forbade convict slavery, not just chattel slavery. The new fundamental law would have done for whites what Thirteenthers wish it had done for blacks. It would have reduced the states' police power to decide the appropriate punishment and pushed the costs for prisons entirely on state taxpayers. In her impressive book *The Crisis of Imprisonment*, Rebecca McLennan laments the failure of the Framers to end prison labor. She points out the ubiquitous tensions within states to, on the one hand, bar unfree, unpaid prisoner labor from competition with free labor, and, on the other, meet the needs of taxpayers to defray the cost of a penal system.

A vote to end convict slavery in the Thirteenth Amendment likely would have divided Congress and ultimately the nation. Northern and borders states would probably have been unanimously opposed to an additional section to the Thirteenth Amendment that usurped state power and left them with an expense. Even the version that retained the state's power to use prisoners as involuntary or slave labor did not have universal support among Northern and border states; Delaware and Kentucky did not ratify until much later as it was. Texas and Mississippi held out. It was impossible to reach the necessary twenty-seven states to ratify the amendment without two of the rebellious states on board. With greater opposition from Northern and border states, a southern state movement to unite against the Thirteenth Amendment might have succeeded — but it was an unimaginable outcome. The political appetite to end convict labor, however it was defined, did not exist.

For the conspiracy theorists among the Thirteenthers, this insistence upon the limits of the politically possible will simply be received as further proof of an alliance between Northern and Southern whites. In their thinking the loophole is not happenstance, but a plan that allowed whites to catch and re-enslave black people. As early as 1977, the New Afrikan Prisoners Association in Illinois, in a petition to the United Nations against the Thirteenth Amendment. wrote, "It was never the intention of the rulers of the u.s. to 'abolish' slavery."

～と巛

The other elements of the Thirteenthers' re-enslavement plot are the black codes and the convict lease system. Most professional historians, including Thirteenthers such as Lichtenstein, know two things about the black codes that the amateurs ignore: first, that the aim of the black codes was to push blacks back onto the plantations, not into jails or prisons; and second, that the black codes lived and died before the rise of convict leasing as a system. The Civil Rights Act of 1866, various court decisions, and the Fourteenth Amendment eliminated them. In most states, the convict lease system started years after the black codes had been outlawed. Just as Southerners did not need a loophole to create the convict lease system, they did not need black codes to discriminate against black people and to convict them of crimes. In the Thirteenthers' narrative, the exception clause and the black codes are best understood as narrative devices to enhance the effect of their propaganda.

Although historians of convict leasing now argue that it served the industrializing New South, not the cotton, tobacco, or rice planters, Thirteenthers often cannot shake the image of their imaginary black codes being used to send the re-enslaved ex-slaves back to their former masters on the plantation. No less a figure than Henry Louis Gates, Jr. has produced a short video in which he argues that convict leasing and the black codes were part of a "labor system that took shape in the late nineteenth century [and] developed coercive means to ensure that cotton remained king." The convict lease system is the indispensable element in the Thirteenthers' narrative, and every effort is made to play up its size, its duration, and its profitability. They use percentages to show that the prison population shifted from white to black in a decade or so after the end of chattel slavery. And they emphasize the growth of the black prison population, how quickly it doubled.

In both cases, no effort is made to explain how a system largely closed to blacks in the antebellum years would show dramatic annual increases without much change in the size of the prison population. And little attention is paid to the size of the system throughout its duration. Instead the impression is given that re-enslavement captured a huge percentage of the black population. I repeat: the historical truth is that it captured less than one percent.

The focus on the late nineteenth century gives a false image of incarceration then and now. In Georgia, where we have the best numbers, about one third of one percent of the black population was imprisoned for most of the convict lease era. In 2017, by contrast, 1.4 percent of the black Georgia population was in state prisons. That is almost five times as many as in the age of mass incarceration. This tracks well with the nation as a whole in the era of mass incarceration, when at its peak, in 2006, 1.5 percent of the black population found itself in the prison system.

The small, brutish system of convict lease proved to be shorter in duration than the Thirteenthers suggest. They point out that Alabama's system existed until 1928, but rarely, if ever, do they note that it was an outlier. In the 1890s, Virginia, Tennessee, South Carolina, North Carolina, and Mississippi ended theirs. By 1913, only Florida and Alabama were engaged in leasing. DuVernay's film gives the impression that convict leasing and lynching caused the Great Migration out of the South, making blacks "refugees." Yet before the start of World War I convict leasing was already a moribund institution, barely a shadow of the monster it had been, and lynchings were in decline. Ironically, the white supremacist governments that brought the nation the illiberal institutions of state-mandated segregation and black disenfranchisement ended the system most associated with chattel slavery. Moreover, they put out of business the only profitable penal system in American history.

While trading on images of the Southern prison structure — convict leasing, the chain gangs, the prison plantations — Thirteenthers ignore the form of convict slavery that engulfed

285

most prisoners in America from emancipation forward. In the North and the West, the prisons predominated through most of the nineteenth and twentieth centuries, but in the Thirteenther narratives they simply do not appear, because the amendment is treated as a federal black code, enslaving only blacks, regardless of work life. In non-Southern prisons, leasing out prisons and prisoners stopped in the late nineteenth century, and production under prison control for state use became the system. With northern migration, blacks found their way into them. Undoubtedly, racism resulted in harsher treatment, but it did not Southernize the prison regimes as the Thirteenthers suggest. Convict leasing, road chain gangs , and prison plantations did not appear. Racism abounded, but it was hardly new in the West or the North.

Together the Northern and Western prisons dwarfed the Southern system in size and scale. Before the rise of mass incarceration, roughly a third of all black prisoners were serving time in them. By that time prisons were on the brink of rebellion, but the nature of prison life was different. Despite the inherent repression in all prison life, black convicts in the North and West found time, like their white counterparts, to pursue self-improvement. Malcolm X and many others like him became autodidacts with the assistance of prison libraries. Some received more formal education through vocational programs. If Northern and Western prisons produced white writers, they also produced black ones such as Chester Himes and Eldridge Cleaver. It was in federal prison that Angelo Herndon wrote his autobiography *Let Me Live*. To maximize the propaganda value of black men in conditions reminiscent of chattel slavery, the Thirteenther narrative ignores the growth of black incarceration outside the South, hinting that Southern ways moved north. Yet the rise of penitentiaries in

286

the South, along with the decline of the road-building chain gangs, suggests that the Southern penal system increasingly became more like the rest of the country.

Having used the black codes and convict leasing to create the impression that Thirteenth Amendment had subjected black people to massive, profitable, and brutal re-enslavement, Thirteenthers continue their discussion into the true age of mass incarceration, from the 1960s forward, as if nothing of substance had changed since 1865. Little thought is given to the inclusion of Hispanic bodies among the slaves, and white prisoners remain merely unfortunate by-products caught in the nets of a system that was designed to enslave blacks. The image presented is that of the state raking in profits from selling black labor to Fortune 500 corporations, consuming the fruits of black labor in prison industries and the various and sundry centuries-old plantations in the South. The truth is that most "convict slaves" are actually idle, and that the state and federal governments make revenues but never profits. All this seems wholly lost in the conversation.

And as serious scholars know, the origins of the expensive and unprofitable system of mass incarceration are to be located in the changes of the 1960s, not 1860s. Thirteenthers have little use for the works of scholars such as James Forman, Jr. and Elizabeth Hinton, who see mass incarceration arising largely from party politics and political choices made by politicians and communities, including African Americans. They do not take seriously scholars such as Ruthie Gilmore, who argues for examining the political economy — not narrow politics or the pursuit of revenue from prison labor — to explain the rise of mass incarceration. These are traditional scholarly debates, and so they lack a grand narrative of slavery or an explosive Jim Crow metaphor. They are not useful for propagandists.

The Scandal of Thirteentherism

Having penetrated the academy, popular culture, social media, and the classrooms, Thirteentherism has also become a basis for social activism and policymaking. Lee Wood's old CAPS agenda of ending prison slavery by removing the loophole from all American constitutions has been taken up by many. An increasing number of activists believe that by removing the "profit motive" from mass incarceration, locking up millions of people would lose its rationale.

Nationwide prison strikes have become almost annual occurrences. In 2016, the promotion and release of DuVernay's film overlapped neatly with a nationwide prison strike to end the abuse of prison labor. Originating in Alabama, the prisoners leading the strike invoked the role of the Thirteenth Amendment in making them slaves and protested against their being forced to work with little or no remuneration. The strike involved more than twenty thousand prisoners in twenty-four prisons. In 2018, coinciding with the fiftieth anniversary of the uprising at Attica, prisoners in seventeen states struck again and made ending prison slavery one of their ten demands. "The Thirteenth Amendment didn't abolish slavery," said the strike's spokeswoman, Amani Sawari. "It wrote slavery into the Constitution. There's a general knowledge that the Thirteenth Amendment abolished slavery, but if you read it, there's an exception clause in the abolishing of it. That's contradictory — that something would be abolished and there would be an exception to that."

Beyond the prison strikes of recent years, there has been ongoing pressure from activists to sever the purported link between constitutions, state and federal, and the use of convict slavery. Most of the calls from prison activists and reformers are for the country to "amend" the federal Constitution to end all forms of slavery. On August 19, 2017, for instance, the Millions for Prisoners March on Washington, DC proclaimed that "We DEMAND the 13th amendment ENSLAVEMENT CLAUSE of the United States Constitution be amended to abolish LEGALIZED slavery in America."

The activism on the ground had some impact on presidential politics in the recent election, but not much. Among the major candidates, only Bernie Sanders invoked the amendment. In making a case against the continuation of private prisons, he argued falsely and inexplicably that they had their origins in "chattel slavery." After the Civil War, he held, "prison privatization expanded rapidly when the 13th Amendment, which outlawed slavery but continued to permit unpaid penal labor, was ratified... Due to an extreme shortage of labor caused by the emancipation of slaves, former Confederate states exploited the legalization of penal labor by incarcerating newly freed black people." To his credit, Joe Biden, despite an unfavorable record on stoking the growth of mass incarceration while in Congress, did not pander or traffic in this nonsense. As he sought to reverse his record and come out for the reduction of incarceration rates, he did not invoke the Thirteenth Amendment in his policy statements.

At the state level, however, the situation has been different, and in the long run might bear fruit nationally. Given how deeply rooted the link between the Thirteenth Amendment and convict slavery has become in African American social thought, state-level politicians are responding to activists' calls to end the loophole. In various states, efforts are being made to remove the language. In Colorado, activists laboring under that assumption pressed for constitutional change and achieved the removal of the exception clause. In 2016, they succeeded in placing on the ballot "Amendment T," which, they believed, would have prohibited the state from using prisoners as labors without their consent. Despite a lack of opposition, the amendment failed by two percentage points because of its confusing language. Two years later a similar amendment passed, but a strange thing happened along the way — no one, not even its advocates, believed that the new amendment, despite its removal of the exception clause, would prohibit prisoners from being forced to work. By the time the bill was put before the people of Colorado, it became clear, as Vox reported, that the removal of the clause would not end virtually uncompensated labor. This was not a reform, it was a gesture; and too often reformist energy is squandered on gestural politics.

Even in the wake of Colorado's cosmetic change to its social contract, the movement to purify all state constitutions has not declined but rather increased. Policymakers and activists from a number of states (Utah, Colorado, Nebraska, South Carolina, New Jersey) have banned together recently to form "a national coalition fighting to abolish constitutional slavery and involuntary servitude in all forms." During the 2020 election, the red states of Utah and Nebraska revised their constitutions to eliminate the exception clauses with complete bipartisan support. These victories are largely symbolic because they seemed to interpret slavery as chattel slavery or as involuntary labor performed for private enterprises, not the state. Utah's Department of Correction will continue to require prisoners to perform work within the prison and to volunteer for other prison-labor opportunities, including with private industries. In Nebraska, State Senator Justin Wayne introduced a constitutional amendment to remove the exception clause in the state constitution. He assured voters that prisoners were paid a nominal amount for their labor. For many prison reform advocates, that nominal amount represented nothing less than convict slavery.

The only state initiative thus far that has had the potential to end convict slavery or any form of involuntary servitude is the one recommended by policymakers in New Jersey. (This initiative did not get on the ballot in the last election.) As one of the original thirteen colonies, the state's constitution never carried Jefferson's proviso that was imposed on territories brought into the union as anti-chattel slavery states. With convict slavery stretching back to its early colonial history, New Jersey would be breaking not with the Thirteenth Amendment but with its most deeply ingrained tradition.

Tying the abolition of convict slavery to the Thirteenth Amendment implies that the institution has shallow roots. Moved by the myth of Thirteenthism, however, lawmakers are adding rather than subtracting language to the constitution to uproot an ancient practice: "No person shall be held in slavery or involuntary servitude in this State, including as a penalty or a punishment for a crime." As the language on the ballot that will be presented to the voters of New Jersey explains, "This amendment would prohibit forcing an inmate to work as a penalty for a crime, even if they are paid. This amendment would not prohibit inmates from working voluntarily." And as Democrat Ronald Rice, one of the amendment's sponsors, put it, "We must set right the treatment of prisoners in our prison system and guarantee that no one is unwillingly forced to perform work, whether they are being compensated two dollars or not. Our justice system continues to tarnish our nations [sic] principles but this amendment would set New Jersey on the right path to finally ending indentured servitude in our state once and for all."

The Scandal of Thirteentherism

Only a new amendment to the Constitution of the United States could end convict slavery everywhere, and now, thanks to the bad history of the Thirteenther movement, such a legislative effort exists. With the support of the Congressional Black Caucus, the constitutional amendment introduced by then-Representative Cedric Richmond (who now works in the Biden White House) reads: "Neither slavery nor involuntary servitude may be imposed as a punishment for a crime." Here is the language that has been calling out to those opposed to convict slavery from the time of Jefferson's proviso. If it makes it out of the House, it will certainly die in the Republican Senate, though Senator Jeff Merkley of Oregon has expressed agreement with the Thirteenther argument. More than likely, the Thirteentherist amendment will become a perennial legislative offering, like the late Congressman John Conyers' reparations bill.

Born of the use of the Thirteenth as propaganda, the proposed Twenty-Eighth Amendment will ultimately rise or fall on its proponents' ability to win on the merits. Rather than trying to persuade Americans that mass incarceration is an inherent and expensive evil, which is an indisputable proposition, Thirteenthers have sought to trade on America's moral distaste for chattel slavery, pretending that convict slavery was its offspring. When the false association is stripped away, the proposed amendment will call for Congress and then three-fourths of the states to vote for millions of prisoners to shift from being mostly to completely idle with taxpayers footing the cost. It would not have won in 1865 and it is unlikely to do so now.

And there is a larger issue, a different integrity, at stake here. The Thirteenther use of history as propaganda to achieve a political end marks a break with the tradition of black history. From the antebellum period forward, black historians, professional and amateur, have believed that historical falsehoods justified black oppression and that the truth would therefore be an ally in the movement for racial justice and equality. By distorting the history of the Thirteenth Amendment and by denying one of black people's greatest triumphs in American history — the destruction of chattel slavery — this generation has sought to emancipate itself by diminishing its ancestors' prized accomplishment. It has also sought to free itself from culpability for a system that all Americans, including blacks, had a part in making. The legion of black intellectuals who have conflated convict labor and chattel slavery have reached the limits of false persuasion. History as propaganda works better to rationalize the status quo than to usher in change. Rejecting the historical meaning of the Thirteenth Amendment is not an avenue to progress.

ROSANNA WARREN

Theseus

A young king, swashbuckling, expensively schooled
in rhetoric and swordplay, with your gold-threaded tunic and
        plumed
helmet fitted over your patrician nose:
so you tossed bandits off cliffs and captured a bull—what do
        you know
about war? Labor is for peasants, labor pains
for women. But you waded among the suppurating dead
on the fields of Thebes and broke the pollution law
by washing corpses with your own royal hands.
"Which bodies are mine?" I thought, as Bill
Arrowsmith paced back and forth holding out his hands—
"With his own hands!' he kept saying. "Defiled!"
With his own hands he offered us glasses of dark red wine.
We perched along his couch, on his armchairs,
taking notes. We had not yet touched our dead.
Our labors were just beginning, mainly
in library stacks and the pages of dictionaries.
"Sophrosyne," Bill barked, "The virtue of moderation,"
with his round, sun-browned, wrinkled satyr's face
and black eyes flashing immoderately
just a few years before he toppled, alone
in his kitchen, his heart ceasing its labors and his corpse
becoming the labor of someone else's hands.

The Flood

—when angels fell out of the bookcase along with old
      newspapers, torn road maps from decades past, and a
         prize edition
of the *Très Riches Heures du Duc de Berry* : suddenly

the catalogue tumbled. The painting, the show, Peter Blume's
      Recollection of the Flood, the studio where I slept
as a child those nights when moonlight fingered

the looming canvases, the forest of easels, the jug of brushes
      like a spray
    of pussy willow boughs—all surged. In Peter's dream
the restorers stand on scaffolding to paint

the frescoed shapes between lines the flood has spared:
      and won't some massive wave of oil
and shit always storm a city's heart? Restore, restore—

there on the ghostly grid the angels dance
      holding hands in a two-dimensional ballet
of bliss, taking on substance with each cautious dab

to whirl with wings spread over the very rich hours
      of what we've lost. For they are sleeping
on the bench at the foot of the scaffold, the refugees—

the exhausted woman clutching her purse, a scrawny girl
        collapsed in her lap, the huddled, bony old man,
bald head in his hand. And everything they've saved

lies at their feet in a quilt bundle, or stuffed in a box
        tied with twine, or in that suitcase, desperately genteel.
Only the boy is awake. The artist stands

apart. Holds in his hands a sketch we cannot see.
        Blonde curls, like Peter's. Remembering, perhaps,
Cossacks, the flight from Russia, the ship, the Brooklyn

tenement where he learned to draw.
        A jug of brushes stands on the windowsill.
The angels keep twirling. I hear, beyond the door,

the growl of mountain streams all dragoning down.

"Dead Flowers"

If you hurt yourself before
someone else hurts you, is that
homeopathic? Watch me prick

>   poison into my skin, sign
>   my name in pain. Watch me miss
>   the appointment, cancel the call. Watch me

gulp smoke and receive a certificate
of enlightenment between
the smeared egg-yolk horizon to the west

>   and the bone-white eastern sky:
>   the emperor appoints
>   me to the Poetry Bureau and I

declare myself Queen of the Underground.
On the back road, the turkey vulture
plucked the guts from the squashed squirrel,

>   then flapped up to the dead
>   branch of the shagbark hickory
>   to examine us examining

the carcass. O sacerdotal bird
with your crimson scalp and glossy vestments, teach
us to translate the spasm, the cry, the dis-

integrating flesh, the regret.
What can be made of all this
grief. Over the butter-

yellow, humming, feather-grassed midday meadow
skim the shadows of vultures: ghostly, six-foot
wingspan, V, swiftest signature, turning death into speed.

Burning the Bed

Carefully you balanced the old mattress
against the box spring to create a teepee on that frozen
      December patch
behind the house, carefully

you stacked cardboard in the hollow and touched the match
to corners till flame crawled along the edges
in a rosy smudge before shooting

twenty-five feet into darkening air. Fire gilded each
looming, shadowed tree, gilded our faces as we stood with
      shovel and broom
to smack down sparks. So much

love going up in smoke. It stung
our eyes, our lungs. Pagodas, terraces, domes, boudoirs
flared, shivered, and crumpled

as the light caved in, privacies curled to ash-wisp, towers
toppled, where once we'd warmed each limb,
fired each nerve, ignited

each surprise. And now at dusk, our faces reddened in heat
so artfully lit, we needed all that past, I thought,
to face the night.

ALASTAIR MACAULAY

Balanchine's Plot

The great choreographers have all been more than dancemakers, none more so than George Balanchine. He was in truth one of the supreme dramatists of the theater, but he specialized in plotless ballets with no named characters or written scenarios, and so this aspect of his genius has gone largely unexamined. Instead, everyone accepts the notion — it has become the greatest platitude about him — that he was the most musical of choreographers — a notion that, for all his musical virtues, should be qualified in several respects. Even at this late date, there is much about Balanchine that we still need to understand. He belongs in the small august company of modern artists who shattered the distinction between abstraction and representation. His work renders such categories useless.

Balanchine's dance creations often eliminate ingredients that others regarded as the quintessence of theater. The performers of his works are verbally and vocally silent. Facial expressions and other surface aspects of acting are played down. In many of his works, costumes are reduced to an elegant minimum: leotards and tights, "practice clothes," often only in black and white; or simple monochrome dresses or skirts. In particular, he pared away layers of the social persona of his dancers, so that on his stage they become corporeal emblems of spirit. *Liebeslieder Walzer*, for example, his ballet from 1960, has two parts. In the first part, the four women wear ballgowns and heeled shoes; in the second, they dance on point and in Romantic tutus. "In the first act, it's the real people that are dancing," Balanchine told Bernard Taper. "In the second act, it's their souls."

Serenade, one of his supreme creations, made in 1934 to Tchaikovsky's Serenade for Strings, is a masterpiece for many reasons. No ballet is more rewatchable. (If you don't know it, there are at least two complete versions on YouTube.) Several of its configurations and sequences are among the most brilliantly constructed in all choreography. Pure dance is threaded through with threads of narrative, suggesting fate and chance, love and loss, death and transcendence. It consists almost as much of rapturous running as it does of formal ballet steps. Classicism meets romanticism meets modernism: it is all here. The opening image is justly celebrated, a latticed tableau of seventeen women who, in unison, enact a nine-point ritual like a religious ceremony. At its start, they are extending arms as if shielding their eyes from the light; at its end, their feet, legs, torsos and arms are turned out, open to the light like flowers in full bloom. This has often been interpreted as transforming them from women into dancers. Taking Balanchine's point about *Liebeslieder*, we might go further and say that the opening ritual of *Serenade* transforms them into souls.

Serenade also has an important place in history as the first work that Balanchine conceived and completed after moving to the United States of America. A serial reviser of his own work, he kept adjusting it for more than forty years. Only around 1950 did it begin to settle into the form we know now, with its women in dresses ending just above the ankle. (The nineteenth-century Romantic look of those dresses is now definitively a part of *Serenade*: it remains a shock to see photographs and film fragments from the ballet's first sixteen years, with the women's attire revealing knees and even whole thighs. Still, if you see the silent film clips of performances by Ballet Russes de Monte Carlo in 1940 and 1944, you can immediately and affectionately recognize most of their material as *Serenade*.) For more than fifty years, *Serenade* has been danced by non-Balanchine companies around the world; in the last decade alone, beloved by dancers and audiences, it has been performed from Hong Kong to Seattle, from Auckland to Salt Lake City.

Even so, for musical purists it is unsatisfactory. Tchaikovsky's Serenade for Strings, composed in 1880, was a score in which this notoriously self-critical composer took immediate and lasting pride: he conducted it many times, not only in Russia but in many other countries too. He made it in cyclical form: his opening movement, called Piece in the Form of a Sonatina, opens and closes with powerful series of descending *marcato* scales, while the final movement returns to descending scales with a jaunty Russian theme. Throughout

302

the work, the composer plays with musical effects as if he had the alchemist's stone — taking the weight off those descending scales by changes of orchestration in the first movement; reversing them in the climbing legato scales of the third movement, the Elegy; and returning at the end of the fourth movement to the work's opening scales, only to accelerate and show how closely they are related to the Russian theme. Tchaikovsky was deeply proud of his status as the most internationally successful Russian composer of all: by naming the final movement *Tema Russo* he reminds us that, if he had any extra-musical agenda in his Serenade for Strings, it was to win renown for the music of his nation.

Yet Balanchine made *Serenade* only to Tchaikovsky's first three movements. He was following the precedent of *Eros*, a ballet by Michel Fokine in 1916 which Balanchine had known in Russia, and which likewise omitted the final "Russian Theme." (Although Balanchine remarked at the end of his life that he had not much liked Fokine's ballet, he took several other ideas from it for *Serenade*.) A devotee of Tchaikovsky's music, he may have omitted the concluding Russian Theme in 1934 merely because his new American students did not yet have the speed and the brilliance that in his view the Russian Theme would require; later in the decade he sketched the Russian Theme with Annabelle Lyon, one of his original 1934 group, but was unable to stage it. He added the Russian Theme in 1940, by which time the youngest of his original students, Marie-Jeanne, had acquired the virtuosity he wanted to create its leading role. But not as a finale, as in the musical score: instead Balanchine inserted it between the second and third movements, thus erasing one of Tchaikovsky's most magical transitions, beginning the fourth movement with the same quiet high notes that ended the third.

How curious: Tchaikovsky ended his Serenade with a high-energy and dance-friendly finale, but Balanchine preferred to close his *Serenade* with the Elegy, which seldom sounds like dance music. His reason, I think, was dramatic: by ending his ballet with Tchaikovsky's elegiac penultimate movement, he found a way to conclude the work with a passage into the sublime. A number of Balanchine's ballets end with the leading character departing for a new world. This is one of them.

Balanchine's *Serenade* is quite as marvelous a work as Tchaikovsky's score. No, it is even more marvelous. Yet it is not a faithful rendition of Tchaikovsky's original. Instead the choreographer gave it its own enthralling musical existence. Balanchine took the liberty of revising this score — as he did with scores by several composers, but with none so much as Tchaikovsky — because he was impelled by a dramatic vision. If, as I say, *Serenade* is the most rewatchable ballet ever made, it is because, from first to last, the work is an exercise in theatrical drama. Its narrative is mysterious but undeniable. The work is an abundant kaleidoscope of changing patterns, images, encounters, communities; a tapestry of stories that movingly suggest fate, love, loss, death, transcendence, and the group's support for the individual. It is also an object-lesson in ambiguity and metamorphosis.

When Balanchine arrived in the United States in late 1933, at the invitation of Lincoln Kirstein, he was not particularly associated with pure-dance works. In Western Europe, between 1925 and 1933, he had staged Ravel's *L'Enfant et les Sortiléges*, Stravinsky's *Apollo*, Prokofiev's *Prodigal Son*, the Brecht-Weill *Seven Deadly Sins*, and other highly singular narratives. Once in New

York, he abounded in ideas for new ballets, many of which Kirstein reported in his diary. The projects of which he told Kirstein — sometimes he developed them for days or months — include versions of the myths of Diana and Actaeon, Medea, and Orpheus, an idea of his own named *The Kingdom Without a King*, a new production of *The Sleeping Beauty, Uncle Tom's Cabin* (Virgil Thomson was to compose the score), Brahms' *Variations and Fugue on a Theme by Handel*, Schumann's *Andante and Variations*, a ballet of waltzes starting with those of Joseph Lanner, and *The Master Dancers*, a Balanchine idea based upon the story of a dance competition. (Most of these ideas were never fulfilled, though some were probably inklings of dances that Balanchine choreographed much later.)

Kirstein's entry for May 6, 1935 gives us a vivid glimpse of the dramatically imaginative workings of Balanchine's mind in this note about a *Medea* ballet that never saw the light of day:

> Bal. thought of a new ending for Medea: Her dead
> body is executed by the troops: told me a story or
> idea for another pantomime : a court-room where the
> condemned is faced by a three headed judge. She is two
> in one like AnnaAnna: As evidence, objects like Haupt-
> mann's ladder are brought in — The whole crime is
> reconstructed. She is declared guilty, though innocent...
> Bal said it shd be like Dostoevski.

Anna-Anna had been the London title of *The Seven Deadly Sins*, in which the dancing Anna and the singing Anna express different aspects of the same person. Balanchine never lost this flair for radically reconceiving old radical stories. In that work and others, he was addressing different layers of being, in much the same way that D.H. Lawrence, when writing *The Rainbow*,

305

described to Edward Garnett about how it differed from his earlier *Sons and Lovers:*

> You mustn't look in my novel for the old stable *ego* — of the character. There is another *ego*, according to whose action the individual is unrecognizable, and passes through, as it were, allotropic states which it needs a deeper sense than any we've been used to exercise, to discover are states of the same single radically unchanged element. (Like as diamond and coal are the same pure single element of carbon. The ordinary novel would trace the history of the diamond — but I say 'Diamond, what! This is carbon.' And my diamond might be coal or soot, and my theme is carbon.)

The Balanchine ballets that seem to be reflections solely of their music — the specialty of the long American phase of his career, especially from 1940 onward — do not dispense with narrative. Not at all. They supply multiple narratives or fragmented versions of a single narrative. In one of his last masterpieces, *Robert Schumann's "Davidsbündlertänze,"* in 1980, four male-female couples express diverse aspects of Schumann and his relationship with Clara, his wife and muse. As in *Liebeslieder Walzer,* Balanchine introduced the women in heeled shoes but then brought them back onstage on point, as if setting their spirits free. The complication of having four Roberts and four Claras suggests the tragic splintering of the composer's tormented and echoing mind: not Anna-Anna but Robert-Robert-Robert-Robert alone with Clara-Clara-Clara-Clara. This is multiple personality syndrome at its most poetic.

There are ballets in which Balanchine moves from showing his dancers' bodies to showing their souls without employing any change of costume or footwear. The outer movements of *Stravinsky Violin Concerto*, from 1972, the Toccata and the Capriccio, are festive, with four leading dancers (two women, two men) each joined by a team of four supporting dancers. The mood is largely ebullient. But then Balanchine brings the concerto's two-part centerpiece, Aria I and Aria II, indoors, as it were, as if he were taking us into a marital bedroom for scenes of painfully raw, almost Strindbergian, intimacy. Different male-female couples dance each Aria, though Balanchine may have seen them as different facets of the same marriage.

The woman of Aria I is amazingly and assertively unorthodox, constantly changing shape, using the man's support to be even less conventional. In the most memorable image, she does bizarre acrobatics, bending back to place her hands on the floor and then turning herself inside-out and outside-in, fluently flipping through convex/concave/convex shapes in alternation. The duet is an unresolved struggle, not so far from the marital strife of *Who's Afraid of Virginia Woolf?* The woman of Aria II, much needier, is more subtly demanding. Stravinsky's music has a repeated chord that sounds like a sudden shriek. Here the woman strikes an X pose, balanced precariously on the points of both feet with legs and arms outstretched. She is both confrontational and insecure: it may be the most passive-aggressive moment in all Balanchine, as if the wife is demanding his support. As he goes to her, her knees buckle inwards; when he catches them before she crumbles further, it seems as if she has mastered the way to pull him back to her assistance. It works. He plays the protective husband that she needs him to be; she is the grateful wife. There are moments of touching harmony between them — one when he shows her a panorama view with his arm over her shoulder, another when he covers her eyes and gently pulls her head back. The tension between his control and her passivity is part of the scene's poignancy.

Serenade, too, tells multiple stories, or gives us dramatic situations that we are free to interpret in many ways. Balanchine's narrative skill is such that few observers follow this ballet without tracing some element of plot in it somewhere. This is a ballet about the many and the one: about how a series of individual women emerge from the larger ensemble, sometimes in smaller groups and occasionally with men, but recurrently supported by the corps. Over the years — as with no other ballet — Balanchine amused himself with the redistribution of roles: there may have been as many as nine soloists in the 1930s performances, but in the 1940s he gave most of the largest sequences to a single ballerina. (Perhaps he privately thought of it as one woman; in his late years he told Karin von Aroldingen that the work could be called *Ballerina.*) Yet there are moments when we see more women than one: there are tiny solo roles of great brevity, and in most productions all the women have been dressed identically. Again and again Balanchine makes us ask, Who is this? What is happening to her? At times the answer scarcely matters; at others it matters greatly.

After a string of quasi-narrative situations, the final Elegy has always seemed the most suggestive of plot. It is profoundly moving because of the story it seems to tell. At its start, one woman is lying on the floor as if abandoned, bereft, or even dead. A man is led to her by another, fate-like, woman, who keeps his eyes and chest covered with her hands until he reaches his destination. The woman on the floor is the first person he sees; he is the first person she sees. Balanchine presented the charged moment of their eyes meeting, with the man and woman framing each other's faces with their arms,

308

as a quotation from Canova's extraordinary sculpture *Psyche Awakened by Cupid's Kiss,* to which he drew the attention of some dancers. Although this Canova quotation was itself derived from Fokine's *Eros,* it must have gratified Balanchine that the three chief versions of the statue are to be found in the main museums of the three chief cities of his career: St Petersburg's Hermitage, Paris' Louvre, New York's Metropolitan Museum of Art.

What follows between the figures — we might also call them the principal characters — seems like love. But just as Diana of Wales once observed that "there were three of us in this marriage," so this love is shadowed by the constant presence of the female fate figure known in Balanchine circles as the Dark Angel. Other women pass through, one of them lingering for a while. (The dancer Colleen Neary told me that Balanchine once jokingly likened these three women to the man's wife, his mistress, and his lover. And added, "Story of my life!") An unhappy ending ensues. With startlingly swift force, the man lowers his "wife" to the floor. The Dark Angel stands aloof, averting her eyes from this tragic parting. She then returns as the agent of fate, beating her arms like mighty wings; once again she covers his eyes and chest with her hands; and she leads him offstage as if continuing the same diagonal paths by which they entered.

All this is a powerful re-telling of the myth of Orpheus and Eurydice — a myth to which Balanchine returned between 1930 and 1980, using music by Gluck, Offenbach, and Stravinsky, and to which he made many autobiographical connections. In the ancient myth, Orpheus, artist and husband, loses Eurydice when she is bitten by a snake. He is permitted to enter the realm of the dead — the Elysian Fields, the realm of the blessed — and to lead her back to life on condition he does not look at her until they both have reached the ground above. At the last moment, however, he looks back, and loses her forever. The Elegy in *Serenade* prolongs and suspends the bittersweet moment of their eyes' climactic meeting.

Unlike Balanchine's other treatments of the Orpheus story, this one leaves us with Eurydice, the dead Eurydice whom Orpheus has lost a second time. She is left by him on the floor exactly where she had been when he found her. When she rises, she parts her hands before her eyes, as if to ask if it were all a dream. Just at this point, in the confusion of her awakening, she is joined by a sisterhood: a small cortège of the women who have characterized the whole ballet. In grief, she embraces one of them — known as "the Mother" — before kneeling and opening her arms and head to the sky, in a gesture of utmost resignation and acceptance. As the ballet ends, she is carried off like a human icon, by three men, while her sisters and her "mother" flank her. She opens her arms and face to the skies in a backbend as the curtain falls, entering a new plane of existence. It takes several viewings before you realize that when she opens her arms and her head this way to the heavens, she is repeating what all seventeen women did in the ballet's opening sequence. One reading of *Serenade,* therefore, is that all of its dramatic narrative is set in the Elysian Fields. Those dancers we see at the beginning are ghosts consecrating themselves, as if saying their vows.

It is revealing that the eyewitness accounts of the first day's rehearsal of *Serenade* differ: not contradicting one another, but concentrating on different facets. Kirstein wrote in his diary:

Work started on our first ballet at an evening 'rehearsal class.' Balanchine said his brain was blank and bid me pray for him. He lined up all the girls and slowly commenced to compose, as he said — 'a hymn to ward off the sun.' He tried two dancers, first in bare feet, then in toe shoes. Gestures of arms and hands already seemed to indicate his special quality.

For Balanchine, looking back in the 1950s and 1960s, the compositional issue had been the fortuitous presence of seventeen women. Probably he knew anyway from the music that he wanted them to start with a slow arm ritual — but how do you take this unwieldy prime number, seventeen, and arrange it in space? His brilliantly geometric solution of this arithmetical problem was the diagonally latticed formation, a pair of two diamond shapes conjoined. These obviate the usual vertical lines of ballet corps patterns. Each woman commands space like a soloist, with genuine parity. Never mind the Elysian Fields of the dead: this pattern has often seemed like an image of American democracy (which may have seemed Elysian to Balanchine after his experience in Russia and Europe between 1918 and 1933).

And we have a third source for that rehearsal. Ruthanna Boris — one of those seventeen young women, who stayed in Balanchine's orbit for many years, dancing the foremost roles in *Serenade* for the Ballet Russe de Monte Carlo in 1944, and choreographing for New York City Ballet in 1951 — wrote an undated memoir in which she recalled that Balanchine — announcing that "we will make some steps!" — then spoke to the seventeen young women about his life in Russia ("it was revolution, bullets in street") and his move to Europe.

Balanchine's Plot

Little by little his talking became more and more like
a report — less conversational, more charged with
feelings of anger and distress: "In Germany there is an
awful man - terrible, awful man! He looks like me only he
has moustache - he is very bad man— he has moustache
— I do not have moustache — I am not bad man — I
am not awful man!"... It seemed to me he was tasting
his words and trying to get past them. To the best of
my memory no one knew what he was talking about.
We were adolescent and young ballet dancers, mostly
American, mostly aware of the dance world, unaware of
governmental affairs in the world beyond it....

Look again at that opening tableau: Balanchine choreographed
here as if he too had the alchemist's stone, transmogrifying the
Nazi salute in space until it became a quasi-religious vow.

The ritual that follows is similarly an exercise in metamorphosis, every staccato pause on the way taking the dancers
further away from politics and danger toward a great openness
to experience. In 1927, Paul Valéry had written, in *The Soul and
the Dance*, that dance was "the pure act of metamorphosis,"
and no ballet by Balanchine better illustrates the idea than
Serenade. The opening upper-body ritual has no logic in terms
of moment-by-moment meaning, but it shows us change in
action (and then leads to ballet's logic of turning out the limbs
and torso from the body's center). Balanchine was a practicing
Christian, and I like to think the start of *Serenade* comes close
to Paul's famous words in the first letter to the Corinthians:

Behold, I shew you a mystery. We shall not all sleep, but
we shall all be changed. In a moment, in the twinkling
of an eye, at the last trump: for the trumpet shall sound,

and the dead shall be raised incorruptible, and we shall
be changed. For this corruptible must put on incorrup-
tion, and this mortal *must* put on immortality, then shall
be brought to pass the saying that is written, Death is
swallowed up in victory.

Balanchine has started his ballet with what could easily be
an ending. But this dance prolegomenon abounds in thematic
material. Even after hundreds of viewings, we keep noticing
how myriad details of what follows — the bringing of a wrist
towards the forehead, the sideways pointing of foot and leg,
the arching back of the neck — were all introduced here, in
the beginning, as a prophesy of the ending.

He took pride in relating how he incorporated rehearsal
accidents into this ballet. One day, a girl fell over; he put
that into the ballet. Another day, another girl arrived late;
he put that in, too. The incidents began to look like a story.
Balanchine never worked quite that way again. What was it
about *Serenade* that made him so receptive to chance moments
of non-dance? Perhaps he could do so because he could see
how those two girls were images of Eurydice. He adjusted the
"girl who falls" so that she spins on the spot as if losing control
before collapsing to the floor, like Eurydice at the moment
of death; and in early performances (particularly in a film of
a Ballets Russes performance in 1940) he then presented her
supine body as if it was a corpse in its coffin. Likewise the
latecomer may simply be Eurydice taking her place among the
heavenly dance choir in Elysium. Who can tell now whether
these Orphic fancies are truly what Balanchine had in mind?

Certainly Balanchine had hidden imagery that he
seldom disclosed. His protégé John Clifford was surprised
when Balanchine, during a fierce argument about the fit of

313

movement to music, said that his choreography of the second movement in *Symphony in C*, the high-classical pure-dance that he created in 1947 to Bizet's score of that name, was "the dance of the moon... The grands jetés where she gets carried back and forth at one point are supposed to be the moon crossing the sky." This was not an image that Balanchine had ever given his dancers; but many readers of *I Remember Balanchine*, which contains the interview in which Clifford recounts this anecdote, have dutifully written of the moon crossing in the sky in that sequence. (I still don't see a moon in those lifts, though I enjoy watching both the moon and *Symphony in C*.)

Similarly, in 1979, Balanchine coached the dancer Jean-Pierre Frohlich in the first *pas de trois* of *Agon*, his master-piece of 1957. Performed in black and white leotards, tights, and T-shirts to a commissioned Stravinsky score, this work has often seemed a peak of pure-dance radical invention, infusing classicism with a new high-density and "plotless" modernity that moved dance far away from drama and role-playing. Yet Frohlich has recalled that Balanchine explained his role as "the court jester." For me, this made immediate sense: it did not change my understanding of the work as a whole, but it helped me to define one aspect of its character.

It matters to notice just how Balanchine tells his stories. The interesting thing about the young woman who falls to the floor in *Serenade* is not the way she falls but the entrance of the corps. Fifteen young women march in on point in five different rows, like radii towards her focal point. Yet they do not rush to console or to help her. In one of the strangest images in all dance theater, they coalesce around her in the shape of a Greek theater, whereupon they simply do staccato arm exercises. Has one dancer fallen? Then the dance will continue with the corps.

We can also interpret them as another facet of the Elysian sorority around Eurydice. Such a view, however, does not quite explain their formality and their impersonal behavior. *Serenade* may contain fragments of myths, but it is about a larger process than any myth: the constant subordination of the dancer to the dance. So what happens next? The fallen woman, the dead Eurydice, promptly picks herself up and dances the most difficult jumps in the ballet so far. She explodes in the air only to pounce precisely back down onto the music's beat.

As for the episode with the latecomer, what's dazzling is that her colleagues have all just resumed the ballet's opening tableau. Sixteen of them stand again just as they did in the beginning, yet they look quite different now: their statuesque immobility is in total contrast to the quietly informal way in which she, the missing seventeenth, traces her way through their ranks. ("Drama is contrast," said Merce Cunningham.) Just as she takes her place to join them in the ballet's opening ritual, Balanchine hurls two other masterstrokes. The other sixteen dancers softly turn into profile, beginning slowly to depart, as if leaving her to her destiny. And a man enters, walking toward her with the same inevitability with which they are walking away. Again Balanchine is the master of geometry: the man's path is a straight diagonal, the corps' path is a straight horizontal, but both his advent and their exit are focused on her, this innocent latecomer who sees none of them. Even if you do not imagine Orpheus coming to rescue Eurydice from the realm of the dead, you cannot miss how mysteriously fateful this strange scene is. Balanchine fits it perfectly to the final bars of the Sonatina, so that we reach the music's end in complete suspense.

Another of the strangest features of *Serenade* is that it abounds in echoes. The "mother" at the end of the Elegy enters

315

from the same corner and along the same diagonal as another woman did in the Sonatina. Five women in the Sonatina dance in a chain that prepares us for five different women who form a chain at the start of the Russian Theme. The man who enters along the long diagonal at the end of the Sonatina prepares us for the other man who enters at the start of the Elegy (Orpheus I and II). The woman who falls in the Sonatina is echoed by one — added in 1940 — who tumbles more spectacularly at the end of the Russian Theme. The mysterious kingdom of *Serenade* is a land of second chances. And so too, for Balanchine, was America. A serious case of tuberculosis in 1932-1933 had rendered him unable to work for a year. Lincoln Kirstein, after inviting him to America in 1933, kept hearing from Balanchine's ballet friends that he had a poor life expectancy. Balanchine, left with only one functioning lung, later told a friend, "You now, I am really dead man." But he lived in his new-found-land for almost fifty years, prodigiously prolific until a few months before his death.

316

Balanchine liked to envisage himself meeting his composers in the next life. When he died, I wrote an elegiac essay in which I gleefully imagined the scene with all of them waiting by the elevator door to greet him as he arrived and gushing appreciatively about the fabulous things that he had made from their scores. Yet prolonged acquaintance with his ballets now makes me imagine a different scenario. Gluck: "Okay, that's a beautiful *pas de deux* he made to the Blessed Spirit music in my *Orphée et Eurydice*, but surely he could have seen that I meant it as the middle section of a da capo structure! It has to be A-B-A, but he cuts the return to A." Tchaikovsky, who has quite a list of complaints, begins: "When I wrote my Third Symphony, I took a deliberate risk by giving it five movements. But he cut out the first movement in his *Diamonds* and made it just another four-movement symphony! Also I never wanted the Siloti edition of my second piano concerto — it tidies up all the irregularities in which I was changing concerto form! His *Serenade* I will forgive; it's not my Serenade, but, yes, it is just as beautiful, I can see that now. But why re-order my *Mozartiana*? And why all that tinkering to my *Nutcracker*? A genius, yes, but an impossible one." And so on.

Among all the dead composers impatiently awaiting Balanchine in paradise, I long most to overhear Stravinsky. "George and I were good friends for over forty years - and yet, the very year after my death, he makes all those ballets to my concert music as if I were writing plays about men and women! He uses my music for plots! And my blood boils about what he did to the *Divertimento* from *Le Baiser de la fée*. He cuts some of it, he interpolates another bit from elsewhere in *Baiser*, it's really quite fraudulent. All right, what he created was quite beautiful — and it is so amazingly dramatic — no way is this a divertimento!" The composer's aggrieved ghost would be right. Balanchine's *"Baiser" Divertimento* is a misnomer. It is too profound for that name.

Stravinsky composed the complete ballet *La Baiser de la fée* in 1928. It is his re-telling of Hans Christian Andersen's story *The Ice Maiden* as if the protagonist were Tchaikovsky, whose music is employed throughout in a modernist and neo-Romantic collage. The story chillingly illustrates Graham Greene's point that "there is a splinter of ice in the heart of a writer." The ballet's hero is singled out in infancy by the Fairy, who distinguishes him from other mortals by planting a kiss on his brow: a vision of the muse at her most heartless.

317

He becomes engaged to a girl, but the Fairy, often disguised but sometimes revealing herself with terrifying clarity, keeps parting them. The ballet ends with him helplessly following the Fairy into her icy realm while his fiancée is left alone in desolation.

Balanchine first staged this complete *Baiser* in New York in 1937, at the Metropolitan Opera. For some fifteen years, he kept it in repertory of the successive companies to which he was attached (the American Ballet, Ballets Russes de Monte Carlo, New York City Ballet) until, in the early 1950s, he finally dropped it. But Stravinsky had arranged a concert suite of the ballet's music, *Divertimento from Le Baiser de la fée*, in 1934, and Balanchine turned to it in 1972, as he created a flood of new ballets in celebration of Stravinsky (who had died the year before). Oddly for a Stravinsky Festival, Balanchine made major structural changes to this score. (Just to call it *Suite from "Le baiser de la fée* would have been more accurate.)

In particular, as the dance scholar Stephanie Jordan first noted in 2003, he introduced, from elsewhere in the complete ballet, a dance for which he created the most poetically dramatic male solo of his career. The music depicts how the Fairy's irresistible spell begins to infect the hero. The 1972 solo, beginning with great elegance and formal charm, is an accumulating soliloquy, in which the hero's conflicting energies and self-contradictory aspirations pour forth with uncanny seamlessness. With no histrionics, he seems both inspired and tormented, changing speed and direction in one dance paradox after another. He pivots on his own axis as if keeling over; he jumps forward while arching back; he punctuates a briskly advancing diagonal with sudden slow turns that gesture upwards and away; he softly circuits the stage with jumps that arrive in slowly searching gestures. It is

318

a completely classical statement within a classical *pas de deux*, and yet it turns the drama around: it tells us that this hero is no longer the fiancé he was.

In 1974, Balanchine tinkered some more with this already remarkable non-divertimento *Divertimento*. He now added music from the ballet's finale, in which Stravinsky makes a heartbreaking arrangement of Tchaikovsky's famous song "None But the Lonely Heart." Now, however, Balanchine omitted the Fairy that Stravinsky had signified in this music. The only two leading characters in his drama are the hero and his fiancée, who, though trying to embrace, are repeatedly interrupted by an impersonal line of women corps dancers. Yet this cruel interruption makes less impact than the way the man and the woman now part, evidently forever, as if accepting separation as destiny. They retreat on separate paths that depict them both as figures of tragic isolation. Both walk with their torsos backward, unable to see where they are going. Slowly they zigzag their ways into ever greater distance from each other, without resistance. Man and woman are sundered, the ballet suggests, not by an external figure of fate but by their own internal impulses, which are just as inexorable. It's as if, in *A Doll's House*, Nora and Helmer had agreed to end their marriage without anyone slamming the door at the end. This ballet begins as a divertimento but ends as a tragic psychodrama; and the progression from plotlessness to plot, from the delight of form to the heartbreak of alienation, proceeds in an unbroken sequence.

To praise Balanchine as the most musical of dancemakers is to persist in a cliché that misunderstands the full magnitude of his achievement. There are technical aspects of music — melody and harmony, in particular — of which his contemporary Frederick Ashton sometimes found more in the same scores than Balanchine did. Yet this does not make Ashton, an artist dear to me, the greater artist. It is better to see Balanchine as an incomparable exponent of Director's Theater. His musicality was of a far more interventionist kind than has generally been admitted. He was not just the grateful servant of his scores; he imposed his own vision on his music, which was often an intensely dramatic vision, a vision of humans in the fullness of their relations, and where necessary he tweaked his scores to fulfill it. In the vast majority of his ballets, music and dance work in brilliant counterpoint, different voices that combine to dig deep into our imaginations and our nervous systems. Ear and eye collaborate closely and uncannily in a genre of dance theater that, even now, takes us where we had not been before.

DAVID GREENBERG

Naming Names

Fiorello La Guardia was a great mayor of New York — he even has an airport named after him — but he made some boneheaded errors. Some years after the Sixth Avenue El in Manhattan was razed, La Guardia and the city council decided to rehabilitate the neighborhoods around the thorough-fare, which had become run down from hosting the elevated train. And so, in October 1945, they officially rebranded Sixth Avenue as Avenue of the Americas.

City planners must have found the cosmopoli-tan-sounding name exciting. New York City was emerging as the global capital, on the cusp of the American Century:

home to the new United Nations and soaring International Style skyscrapers, a hub of commerce, a dynamo of artistic creativity. But this act of renaming by fiat, against the grain of public opinion, failed spectacularly. A survey ten years later found that, by a margin of 8 to 1, New Yorkers still called the street Sixth Avenue. "You tell someone anything but 'Sixth Avenue,'" a salesman explained to the *New York Times*, "and he'll get lost." Generations of visitors have noticed signs that still say "Avenue of the Americas" and wondered fleetingly about its genesis and meaning, but for anyone to say it out loud today would clearly mark him as a rube.

Names change for many reasons. While designing Washington, DC in the late eighteenth century, Pierre L'Enfant renamed the local Goose Creek after Rome's Tiber River. It was a bid for grandeur that earned him mainly ridicule. After Franklin Roosevelt was elected president, Interior Secretary Harold Ickes saw fit to cleanse federal public works of association with the most unpopular man in America, making the Hoover Dam into the Boulder Dam. With independence in 1965, Rhodesia ditched its hated eponym to become Zimbabwe, and its capital, Salisbury, became Harare. When it was conquered by the Viet Cong in 1975, Saigon was reintroduced as Ho Chi Minh City, however propagandistic the appellation still sounds. On Christmas Eve, 1963, Idlewild Airport became JFK. In 2000, Beaver College, tired of the jokes, chose to call itself Arcadia. (*Et in Beaver ego.*) Even old New York was once New Amsterdam.

Like the misbegotten Avenue of the Americas moniker, though, new names do not always stick. Who but a travel agent calls National Airport "Reagan"? Where besides its website is the New York Public Library known as "the Schwartzman Building"? In 2017, the Tappan Zee Bridge formally became the Mario M. Cuomo Bridge, thanks to its namesake's son, but everyone still calls it the Tappan Zee. (Few knew that for the thirteen years prior it had been named for former New York governor Malcolm Wilson; in fact, few knew that someone called Malcolm Wilson had been governor.) Everyone also still calls the Robert F. Kennedy Bridge the Triborough and the Ed Koch Bridge the Queensborough.

Political events prompt changes, too. When in 1917 German aggression forced the United States into World War I, atlases were summarily revised. Potsdam, Missouri became Pershing. Brandenburg, Texas, became Old Glory. Berlin, Georgia became Lens — but after the war, with the rush to rehabilitate Germany, it reverted to Berlin. (During the next world war this Berlin declined to change its name again, though 250 miles to the northwest Berlin, Alabama rechristened itself Sardis.) In 1924, the Bolsheviks saddled splendid St. Petersburg with the chilling sobriquet Leningrad — "after the man who brought us seventy years of misery," as tour-bus guides tell their passengers. Only with Communism's demise could city residents reclaim their old appellation.

The revision — and re-revision — of place names is thus a common enterprise. But how and why those in control choose to re-label streets, cities, schools, parks, bridges, airports, dams, and other institutions has always been a strange, unsystematic process — subject to changing social norms, political fashions, historical revisionism, interest-group pressure, the prerogatives of power, consistent inconsistency, and human folly. The current craze for a new public nomenclature, in other words, is far from the straightforward morality play it is often made out to be. How we think about it and how we go about it deserve more deliberation than those questions have received.

323

Today's nomenclature battles mostly turn on a specific set of questions: about race and the historical treatment of non-white peoples. Every day, in the United States and abroad, new demands arise to scrub places, institutions, and events of the designations of men and women who were once considered heroes but whose complicity (real or alleged) in racist thoughts or deeds is now said to make them unworthy of civic recognition. Not only confederate generals, upholders of slavery, and European imperialists are having their time in the barrel. So too are figures with complex and even admirable legacies, as diverse as Christopher Columbus and George Washington, Andrew Jackson and Woodrow Wilson, Junipero Serra and Charles Darwin, David Hume and Margaret Sanger — even, although it sounds like parody, Mohandas K. Gandhi.

What has led us to set so many august and estimable figures, along with the more flagrantly reprehensible ones, on the chopping block? It helps to look at the criteria being invoked for effacement. To be sure, advocates of renaming seldom set forth clear, careful, and consistent sets of principles at all. Typically, the arguments are ad hoc, each one anchored in some statement, belief, political stance, or action of the indicted individual, the wrongness of which is presumed to be self-evident. But occasionally over the years, governmental committees, university panels, or other bodies have gamely tried to articulate some criteria. Their language is telling.

One body that recently made plain its standards for naming was a Washington, D.C. mayoral "working group" with the ungainly label "DCFACES." (An ungainly name is an inauspicious quality in a body seeking to retitle streets and buildings.) That acronym stands for the equally ungainly "District of

324

Columbia Facilities and Commemorative Expressions." In the summer of 2020, DCFACES released a report declaring that any historical figure would be "disqualified" from adorning a public building or space in Washington, DC if he or she had participated in "slavery, systemic racism, mistreatment of, or actions that suppressed equality for, persons of color, women and LGBTQ communities." These rules resulted, among other absurdities, in a call to re-label Washington's Franklin School (which now serves as a museum) because Benjamin Franklin, though a magnificent patriot, politician, democrat, diplomat, writer, thinker, inventor, publisher, and abolitionist, also owned two slaves, whom he eventually freed.

Here is how the report's executive summary presents the rules:

IMPERATIVES

Commemoration on a District of Columbia asset is a high honor reserved for esteemed persons with a legacy that merits recognition. The DCFACES Working Group assessed the legacy of District namesakes, with consideration to the following factors:

1. Participation in slavery — did research and evidence find a history of enslaving other humans or otherwise supporting the institution of slavery.
2. Involvement in systemic racism — did research and evidence find the namesake serving as an author of policy, legislation or actions that suppressed persons color and women.
3. Support for oppression — did research and evidence find the namesake endorsed and participated in the oppression of persons of color and/or women.
4. Involvement in supremacist agenda — did research and

evidence suggest that the namesake was a member of any supremacist organization.

Violation of District human rights laws — did research and evidence find the namesake committed a violation of the DC Human Right Act, in whole or part, including discrimination against protected traits such as age, religion, sexual orientation, gender identity, and natural origin.

Several difficulties with this formulation are immediately apparent. For starters, the list is at once too broad and too narrow. It is too broad because phrases such as "support for oppression" are so vague and subjective that they could implicate any number of actions that might be defensible or explicable. It is also too broad because it implies that a single violation is altogether disqualifying, so that someone like Hugo Black or Robert Byrd (both of whom joined the Ku Klux Klan as young men, only to repudiate their actions and go on to distinguished careers) can never be honored.

At the same time, the lens is also too narrow. Its single-minded focus on sins relating to race and sex (and, in one instance, other "protected traits") in no way begins to capture the rich assortment of human depravity. A robber baron who was untainted by racist bias but subjected his workers to harsh labor would seem to pass muster in the capital. So would a Supreme Court justice with a clean record on race who curtailed freedom of speech and due process. Dishonesty, duplicity, and cowardice are nowhere mentioned as disqualifying. Neither are lawlessness, corruption, cruelty, greed, contempt for democracy, any of the seven deadly sins, or, indeed, scores of other disreputable traits any of us might easily list.

The Washington mayoral working group was not the first body to set down naming rules focused on racism and other forms of identity-based discrimination. In fact, committees have propounded such frameworks for a long time. In 2016, the University of Oregon, in considering the fate of two buildings, adopted seven criteria that largely dealt with offenses "against an individual or group based on race, gender, religion, immigration status, sexual identity, or political affiliation." (The Oregon list, to its drafters' credit, also contained some nuance, adding the phrase "taking into consideration the mores of the era in which he or she lived" and making room for "redemptive action" that the individual might have engaged in.) In 1997, the New Orleans school board proscribed naming schools after "former slave owners or others who did not respect equal opportunity for all." Few objected when this policy was invoked to exchange the name of P.T. Beauregard on a junior high school for that of Thurgood Marshall. More controversial, though, was the elimination of George Washington's name from an elementary school, no matter how worthy his replacement appeared to be. (He was Charles Richard Drew, a black surgeon who helped end the army's practice of segregating blood by race.) So the battles now being waged in city councils and university senates, though intensified by the recent racial ferment, long predate the latest protests or even the Black Lives Matter movement of 2014.

Like so many skirmishes in our culture wars, these go back to the 1960s. That era's historic campaigns for racial and sexual equality; the widespread criticisms of government policy, starting but not ending with the Vietnam War; the deepening skepticism toward political, military, and religious authority; the blurring of boundaries between public and private; the exposure of criminality in high places; the demise of artistic standards of excellence — all these elements conspired to render quaint, if not untenable, old forms of patriotism and hero worship. Debunking thrived. Not just in the counterculture, but also in the academy, there took hold what the historian Paul M. Kennedy called "anti-nationalistic" sentiment: arguments (or mere assumptions expressed via attitude and tone) that treated the nation's past and previous generations' values and beliefs with disapproval, disdain, or even a conviction, as Kennedy wrote, that they "should be discarded from … national life." Growing up in the 1970s and after, Generations X, Y, and Z were never taught to passively revere the Founding Fathers or to celebrate uncritically the American experiment. On the contrary, we were steeped in dissidence, iconoclasm, suspicion, and wisecracks. At its best, this new adversarial sensibility instilled a healthy distrust of official propaganda and independence of mind. At its worst, it fostered cynicism and birthed a propaganda of its own.

The thorniest questions of the 1960s stemmed from the challenge, thrown down by the civil rights movement, for America to live up to its rhetoric of equality. "Get in and stay in the streets of every city, every village, and hamlet of this nation," the 23-year-old John Lewis said at the March on Washington in 1963, "until true freedom comes, until the revolution of 1776 is complete." With uneven resolve, Americans devoted to human equality have striven to meet the challenge. And this effort has included, crucially, rethinking the past. To highlight and learn about our nation's history of racial exclusion and discrimination is among the noblest goals we can have in our public discourse, because it is the intellectual and cultural condition of justice: we will not be able to achieve equality without understanding the deep roots of inequality in our society.

By the 1990s American society had become an irreversibly multicultural one. WASP values, assumptions, priorities, and interpretations of the past could no longer dominate. "We Are All Multiculturalists Now," declared the title of a somewhat unexpected book by Nathan Glazer in 1996. But with that watershed, Glazer noted, it became necessary to pose a new set of queries (which Americans had indeed been asking for some time): "What monuments are we to raise (or raze), what holidays are we to celebrate, how are we to name our schools and our streets?"

Probably no group of historical actors has been subject to as much contentious debate as the secessionists who founded the Confederate States of America. Yet by the third decade of the twenty-first century, there was not much of a debate left about their virtues. Arguments for their valor already seem hopelessly antiquated. Partial defenses of Robert E. Lee, of the sort that David Brooks earnestly mounted in the *New York Times* just five years ago, now induce cringes. ("As a family man, he was surprisingly relaxed and affectionate... He loved having his kids jump into bed with him and tickle his feet.") Were the *Times* to publish a piece like Brooks' in the current environment, the whole masthead would be frog-marched out of the building under armed guard.

The public, or some of it, has now learned that Southerners imposed most of their Lost Cause nomenclature, iconography, and narratives not in innocent tribute to gallant soldiers, but as part of a rearguard racist project of forging and upholding Jim Crow. This new awareness — along with the political agitation of the last decade — has altered how many Americans think about a military base honoring Braxton Bragg or a park memorializing Nathan Bedford Forrest. The Lincoln scholar

Harold Holzer confessed last year that statues and place names which "I long regarded as quaint were in fact installed to validate white supremacy, celebrate traitors to democracy, and remind black and brown people to stay 'in their place.'" It became increasingly incongruous, if not bizarre, to see in a redoubt of suburban liberalism such as Arlington, Virginia, a boulevard evoking the Confederacy's leading general.

Still, as the protests in Charlottesville in 2017 showed, Lee retains his champions. Plying his demagoguery that August, Donald Trump — at the same press conference at which he defended the Charlottesville firebrands — warned that if Lee were to be scrubbed from public commemoration, George Washington ("a slave owner") and Thomas Jefferson ("a major slave owner") would be next. "You have to ask yourself, where does it stop?" To this slippery-slope argument, many have given a sensible and convincing answer: Lee, Jefferson Davis, Stonewall Jackson, and the others were traitors to their country; Washington, Jefferson, and the founders were not. Removing the former from streets and schools while retaining the latter admits no contradiction. As far back as 1988, Wilbur Zelinsky, in his fascinating history *Nation into State,* remarked that "as the military commander of an anti-statist cause, there is no logical place for Lee in the national pantheon alongside Washington, Franklin, and others of their ilk," explaining that Lee entered the pantheon (or stood just outside its gates) only "as an archetypal martyr — the steadfast, chivalrous, sorrowful, compassionate leader of a losing cause."

Yet the distinction between traitors and patriots, while perfectly valid so far as it goes, does not answer the big questions. It does not address, for example, whether every last venue commemorating a Confederate must be taken down. Yes, let us lose the Confederate flags and Confederate statuary,

330

and change the place names that keep alive the Lost Cause. But would it be acceptable to keep a handful, for considered reasons? Doing so would show that we know that our history includes the bad along with the good, as all human history does; and it would remind us that our predecessors at times were not able to tell the bad from the good. It would remind us that our country was once riven to the core by a struggle over evil and inculcate sympathy for the difficulty, and the cost, of the struggle. It might also deflate a presentist arrogance that tempts us to think that our current-day appraisals of the past, fired off in the heat of a fight, are unerring and for the ages.

The distinction between traitors and patriots also fails to address the larger and more humane question of whether there is a way, notwithstanding the hateful cause for which the Confederates fought, to extend some dignity to their descendants who renounce the ideology of the Old South but wish to honor forbears who died by gun or blade. In the right context, and without minimizing those forbears' attachment to an evil institution, this goal should, I think, be achievable. At the Gettysburg battlefield, monuments to Southern regiments stand arrayed opposite those to Northern troops, but in no way does a walk through the austere, beautiful environs suggest an exculpation or a whitewash. To erase any possible doubt, a professionally designed and intelligently curated museum nearby spells out the war's history, including the centrality of slavery, in cold detail.

And the distinction between traitors and loyalists is insufficient for yet another reason, too: it speaks only to the period of the Civil War. Outright traitors are a small, discrete subset of those who have come under fire in the recent controversies; the nomenclature wars span much wider terrain. Identifying secession as grounds for censure is fine, but it provides no

331

limiting principle to help us think through, in other circumstances, whose names should and should not remain. It says nothing about Theodore Roosevelt, Winston Churchill, John Muir, Kit Carson, Louis Aggasiz, Henry Kissinger, Voltaire, or anyone else.

Most regrettably, the distinction does not persuade everyone. In addition to the Lost Cause devotees, some on the left likewise deny the distinction. We saw New Orleans retitle George Washington Elementary School back in 1997. When Trump cited Washington in his press conference in 2017, he was unknowingly describing something that had already happened. Could it be that he recalled the campaign at the University of Missouri in 2015 to defenestrate Jefferson, whom students, apparently knowing little about his quasi-marriage to Sally Hemings, excoriated as a "rapist"? Even if Trump was ignorant of these precedents, as seems probable, he must have felt some vindication when protesters in 2020 targeted Abraham Lincoln, Ulysses S. Grant, Frederick Douglass (!), and other assorted foes of slavery. Trump and these leftwing activists agree that the current renaming rage should not "stop" with traitors to the Union. They share a fanatical logic.

Few participants in the nomenclature wars have reckoned seriously with this slippery-slope problem. The Yale University officials who renamed Calhoun College because its eponym flew the banner of race slavery were well aware that Elihu Yale earned his fortune at a powerful British trading company that trafficked in African slaves. But Yale remains Yale, for now. Similar contradictions abound. Are we to make a hierarchy of hypocrisies? If Woodrow Wilson's name is to be stripped from Princeton University's policy school because he advanced segregation in the federal bureaucracy, by what logic should that of Franklin Roosevelt, who presided over the wartime

Japanese internment, remain on American schools? If the geneticist James Watson's name is scratched from his research institution's graduate program because he believed that racial IQ differences are genetic, why should that of Henry Ford — America's most influential anti-Semite, who published the *Protocols of the Elders of Zion* in his *Dearborn Independent* — remain on the Ford Motor Company or the Ford Foundation? In what moral universe is Andrew Jackson's name erased from the Democratic Party's "Jefferson-Jackson" dinners, but Donald Trump's remains on a big blue sign near the 79th Street off-ramp on the West Side Highway? How can the District of Columbia go after Benjamin Franklin and Francis Scott Key but not Ronald Reagan, whose name adorns the "international trade center" downtown? It is not a close contest as to who made life worse for the city's black residents.

The problem with the contemporary raft of name alterations is not that historical or commemorative judgments, once made, cannot be revised. Change happens. It may have been silly for the Obama administration to rechristen Mt. McKinley "Denali," but it was not Stalinist. The real problem (or one problem, at any rate) is that no rhyme or reason underwrites today's renaming program. Like the social media campaigns to punish random innocents who haphazardly stumble into an unmarked political minefield, the campaign of renaming follows no considered set of principles. It simply targets whoever wanders into its sights.

If we wish to impose some coherence on the Great Renaming Project, a good first step would be to create a process of education and deliberation. Our debates about history generally unfold in a climate of abysmal ignorance. How much is really known about the men and women whose historical standing is now being challenged? What matters most about their legacies? Were they creatures of their age or was their error perfectly evident even in their own time? What harm is perpetuated by the presence of their name on a street sign or archway? The answers are rarely straightforward.

In many public debates, the participants know little about what the men and women under scrutiny did. In April 2016, a Princeton undergraduate and stringer for the *New York Times* wrote incorrectly in the paper of record that Woodrow Wilson "admired" the Ku Klux Klan. The next day the paper ran a letter correcting the error, noting, among other facts, that in his *History of the American People* Wilson called the Klan "lawless," "reckless" and "malicious"; but just two weeks later another stringer, one year out of Yale, parroted the same mistake. That even Ivy-educated youngsters got things so wrong should not be surprising. The undergraduates I teach tend to know about Andrew Jackson's role in Indian Removal, and that he owned slaves. But most know little of his role in expanding American democracy beyond the elite circles of its early days. Millions of young people read in Howard Zinn's *A People's History of the United States* about the horrors that Columbus inflicted on the Arawaks of the Caribbean. But Zinn was rebutting the heroic narratives of historians like Samuel Eliot Morison, whose Columbus biography won a Pulitzer Prize in 1943. How many students read Morison anymore? How many have a basis for understanding why so many places in North America bear Columbus' imprint in the first place? Were all those places consecrated to genocidal conquest? Without efforts to educate the young — and the public in general — about the full nature of these contested

334

figures, the good and the bad, the inexorable complexities of human thought and action, these debates will devolve into a simplistic crossfire of talking points.

On occasion, mayors, university presidents, and other officials have recognized that a process of education and deliberation is necessary before arriving at a verdict on a controversial topic. In 2015, Princeton University came under renewed pressure to address the racism of Woodrow Wilson, who was not only America's twenty-eighth president but a Princeton graduate, professor, and, eventually, a transformational president of the college. At issue was whether to take his name off the university's policy school, a residential dorm, and other campus institutions (professorships, scholarships, book awards, etc.). Desiring a process that was democratic and deliberative, the president of the university, Christopher Eisgruber, convened a committee. Multiracial and multigenerational in composition, it included members of the board of trustees, Wilson experts, higher education leaders, and social-justice advocates. It solicited the views of students, faculty, staff, and alumni. Historians wrote long, thoughtful, well-researched letters weighing the merits of the case. Some 635 community members submitted comments through a dedicated website (only a minority of whom favored eliminating Wilson's name).

The committee weighed the evidence, which includes the record not just of Wilson's deplorable racism but also his undeniable achievements. Although many students today know little about Wilson besides the racism — which, we must be clear, went beyond private prejudice and led him to support Cabinet secretaries Albert Burleson and William McAdoo in segregating their departments — he was for a century considered one of America's very best presidents. Wilbur Zelinsky, in his meticulous study, called Wilson "one of four presidents since Lincoln whom some would consider national heroes" (the others being the Roosevelts and John F. Kennedy). Wilson could claim in his day to have enacted more significant progressive legislation than any president before him; since then, only Franklin Roosevelt and Lyndon Johnson have surpassed him. Wilson also built upon Theodore Roosevelt's vision of a strong presidency to turn the White House into the seat of activism, the engine of social reform, that it has been ever since. Nor was Wilson successful just domestically. He was a historic foreign-policy president, too, and a winner of the Nobel Peace Prize. After exhausting all bids for peace with Germany, he reluctantly led America into World War I, which proved decisive in defeating Teutonic militarism, and he pointed the way toward a more democratic and peaceful international order — though, crippled by a stroke and his own arrogance, he tragically failed to persuade the Senate to join the League of Nations, leaving that body all too ineffectual in the critical decades ahead.

The Princeton committee's fair-minded report was adopted by the Board of Trustees in April 2016. It recommended keeping Wilson's name on the buildings. But Eisgruber and the board of trustees simultaneously promised that campus plaques and markings would henceforth provide frank accounts of Wilson's career and beliefs, including his racism. More important, the university would, it said, take bold steps in other aspects of campus life to address the underlying grievance: that many black Princetonians do not feel they are treated as equal members of the campus community. And there the matter rested, until 2020. Following the Memorial Day killing of George Floyd by a Minneapolis policeman, protests erupted nationwide calling for police reform and other forms of racial justice — including, once again, the reconsideration of names. This time Eisgruber launched no deliberative process, appointed no diverse committee, solicited no external input, convened no searching conversation. He simply declared that the Board of Trustees had "reconsidered" its verdict of a few years before. His high-handed decree, more than the ultimate decision, violated the principles on which a university ought to run. For Eisgruber, it also gave rise to some new headaches: in what can only be seen as an epic troll, Trump's Department of Education opened an investigation into whether Princeton's confession of rampant racism meant it had been lying in the past when it denied engaging in racial discrimination.

Curiously, at the same time as Princeton banished Wilson, Yale University also performed a banishment — this one with regard to John C. Calhoun, whose name graced one of its residential colleges. But there were crucial differences between the two cases. Although Calhoun has been recognized as a statesman, grouped with Henry Clay and Daniel Webster as the "Great Triumvirate" of senators who held the nation together in the fractious antebellum years, he is a far less admirable figure than Wilson. He made his reputation as a prominent defender of slavery and a theorist of the nullification doctrine that elevated states rights over federal authority — a doctrine that later provided a rationale for Southern secession. But beyond the huge political differences between Wilson and Calhoun are the differences in the processes that Princeton and Yale pursued. Princeton jettisoned a deliberative decision to implement an autocratic one. Yale did something like the reverse.

Following the Charleston massacre of 2015, the president of Yale, Peter Salovey, told his campus that Yale would grapple with its own racist past, including its posture toward Calhoun.

337

Then, the following spring, he declared that after much reflection on his part — but no formal, community-wide decision-making process — Calhoun would remain. Salovey contended, not implausibly, that it was valuable to retain "this salient reminder of the stain of slavery and our participation in it." To get rid of Calhoun's name would be to take the easy way out. At the same time, Salovey also announced (in a ham-handed effort to balance the decision with one he expected students and faculty would like) that one of Yale's two new residential colleges would be named for Pauli Murray, a brilliant, influential, underappreciated midcentury civil rights lawyer who was black and, for good measure, a lesbian.

Students and faculty rebelled. Salovey backtracked. He now organized a committee, chaired by law and history professor John Fabian Witt, to tackle the naming question systematically. Wisely, however, Salovey charged the committee only with developing principles for renaming; the specific verdict on Calhoun would come later, decided by still another committee, after the principles were set. To some, the whole business seemed like a sham: it was unlikely that after vowing to take up a question a second time he would affirm the same result. Still, the exercise of formulating principles—in the tradition of a storied Yale committee that the great historian C. Vann Woodward led in the 1970s to inscribe principles for free speech on campus — was worthy, and Salovey populated the Witt committee with faculty experts on history, race, and commemoration. Even more than the Princeton report, the Witt Committee's final document was judicious and well-reasoned. When, in 2017, Yale finally dropped Calhoun's name from the residential college, no one could accuse the university of having done so rashly.

Deliberation by committee, with democratic input, may be necessary to ensure an informed outcome on a controversial subject, but as the example of DCFACES shows, it is not always sufficient. Setting forth good principles is also essential. One mistake that the Washington group made was in asking whom to *dis*qualify from recognition, rather than who might qualify. Historians know that the categories of heroism and villainy are of limited value. Everyone is "problematic." And as Bryan Stevenson likes to say, each of us is more than the worst thing we have ever done.

Thus if we begin with the premise that certain views or deeds are simply disqualifying, we have trouble grasping the foolishness of targeting Gandhi (for his anti-black racism), Albert Schweitzer (for his racist and colonialist views), or Martin Luther King, Jr. (for his philandering and plagiarism). In any case, how can we insist that racism automatically denies a historical actor a place in the pantheon when the new reigning assumption — the new gospel — is that everyone is (at least) a little bit racist? We all have prejudices and blind spots; we all succumb to stereotyping and "implicit bias." By this logic, we are all disqualified, and there is no one left to bestow a name on the local library.

A more fruitful approach is the one the Witt Committee of Yale chose: by asking what are the "principal legacies" of the person under consideration, the "lasting effects that cause a namesake to be remembered." We honor Wilson for his presidential leadership and vision of international peace. He is recognized not for his racism but in spite of it. We honor Margaret Sanger as an advocate of reproductive and sexual freedom, not for her support of eugenics but in spite of it. Churchill was above all a defender of freedom against fascism, and the context in which he earned his renown matters. Of the recent efforts to blackball him, one Twitter wag remarked, "If you think Churchill was a racist, wait until you hear about the other guy." Not everything a person does or says is of equal significance, and people with ugly opinions can do great things, not least because they may also hold noble opinions.

Principal legacies can evolve. They undergo revision as people or groups who once had little say in forging any scholarly or public consensus participate in determining those legacies. It may well be that by now Andrew Jackson is known as much for the Trail of Tears as for expanding democracy, and perhaps that is appropriate. Arthur M. Schlesinger, Jr., made no mention of Indian Removal in his classic *The Age of Jackson* in 1945, but by 1989 he had come to agree that the omission — common to Jackson scholars of the 1940s — was "shameful," if all too common among his peers at the time. But as the Witt Committee noted, our understandings of someone's legacies "do not change on any single person's or group's whim; altering the interpretation of a historical figure is not something that can be done easily." For all that Americans have learned about Thomas Jefferson's racial views and his slaveholding in recent decades, his principal legacies — among them writing the Declaration of Independence, articulating enduring principles of rights and freedom, steering a young country through intense political conflict as president — remain unassailable. We will have to learn to live with all of him.

The Witt Committee also asked whether the criticisms made of a historical figure were widely shared in his or her own time — or if they are a latter-day imposition of our own values. The difference is not trivial. As late as 2012, when Barack Obama finally endorsed gay marriage, most Democrats still opposed the practice. But norms and attitudes evolved. Today most Democrats think gay marriage unremarkable, and the Supreme Court has deemed it a constitutional right. It might be fair to condemn someone who in 2020 seeks to overturn the court's decision, but it would be perverse to label everyone who had been skeptical of gay marriage ten years ago a homophobe or a bigot. Historians must judge people by the values, standards, and prevailing opinions of their times, not our own. No doubt we, too, will one day wish to be judged that way. Yet the pervasive impulse these days to moralize, to turn analytical questions into moral ones, has also made us all into parochial inquisitors.

It is also worth asking what harm is truly caused by retaining someone's name, especially if the person's sins are obscure or incidental to his reputation. Many buildings and streets commemorate people who are largely forgotten, making it hard to claim that their passing presence in our lives does damage. A federal court forbade Alabama's Judge Roy Moore from placing a giant marble Ten Command-ments in the state judicial building, but the phrase "In God We Trust" is allowed on coins because in that context it is consid-ered anodyne and secular — wallpaper or background noise — without meaningful religious content. By analogy, the preponderance of place names hardly evoke any associations at all. They are decorations, mere words. The State University of New York at Buffalo removed Millard Fillmore's name from a campus hall because Fillmore signed the Fugitive Slave Act. But it is doubtful that Fillmore's surname on the edifice had ever caused much offense, for the simple reason that almost no one knows anything about Millard Fillmore.

Then, too, as Peter Salovey initially suggested about Calhoun, a person's name can sometimes be a useful and educational reminder of a shameful time or practice in our past. In 2016, Harvard Law School convened a committee to reconsider its seal, which depicted three sheaves of wheat and came from the family crest of Isaac Royall, a Massachusetts slaveowner and early benefactor of the school. While the committee voted to retire the seal, historian and law professor Annette Gordon-Reed and one law student dissented, arguing that keeping the seal would serve "to keep alive the memory of the people whose labor gave Isaac Royall the resources to purchase the land whose sale helped found Harvard Law School." Historical memory is always a mixed bag — if, that is, we wish to remember as much as we can about how we came to be who we are. Sometimes, a concern for history is precisely what warns us not to hide inconvenient or unpleasant pieces of the past.

Often context can serve the purposes of promoting antiracism or other noble principles better than erasure. Museums and other forms of public history are experiencing a golden age. Historic sites that once lacked any significant information for tourists are being redesigned to satisfy the hungriest scholar. Plaques, panels, touch-screen information banks, and other displays can educate visitors about the faults and failings — as well as the virtues — of the men and women whose names appears on their buildings and streets. Addition — more information, more explanation, more context — may teach us more than subtraction. But even here, there are limits. A recent show at the National Gallery of Degas' opera and ballet pictures did not mention that he was a virulent anti-Semite. Should we care? If the museum had "contextualized" the tutus with a wall caption about Captain Dreyfus, the information would not have been false, but it would have been irrelevant, and in its setting quite strange. We don't need asterisks everywhere.

Above all, renaming should be carried out in a spirit of humility. The coming and going of names over the decades might inspire in some a Jacobin presumptuousness about how easy it is to remake the world. But what it should more properly induce is a *frisson* of uncertainty about how correct and authoritative our newly dispensed verdicts about the past truly are. "We readily spot the outgrown motives and circumstances that shaped past historians' views," writes the geographer David Lowenthal; "we remain blind to present conditions that only our successors will be able to detect and correct." Public debates and deliberation about how to name our institutions, how to evaluate historical figures, and how to commemorate the past are an essential part of any democratic nation's intellectual life and political evolution. Our understandings of our history must be refreshed from time to time with challenges — frequently rooted in deeply held political passions — to widely held and hardened beliefs. There are always more standpoints than the ones we already possess. Yet passions are an unreliable guide in deriving historical understanding or arriving at lasting moral judgments. In light of the amply demonstrated human capacity for overreach and error, there is wisdom in treading lightly. Bias is everywhere, even in the enemies of bias. Nobody is pure.

CELESTE MARCUS

The Student

He acts it as life before he apprehends it as truth.

RALPH WALDO EMERSON

Entering an unfamiliar classroom for the first time, met by a cacophony of greetings, shuffles, and the flutter of unsettled nerves, a student experiences a particular strain of vertigo — a a kind of thrownness. Unbalanced, she glances about, wondering if her fresh peers are already friends, if they know or care more about the subject than she does, if the professor will command attention or beg for it. She wonders also about the subject — how it will stretch or resist or entice her; and what personal qualities, as well as intellectual qualities, she ought to bring to her studenthood. She must wait for an internal order to develop, and for the nerves to slow gently into a new rhythm.

The experience catapults her from the grooves of ordinary life. She has the sensation of a swift transit.

That is what learning is meant to do. The developments that will occur in that homely but exotic room over those few months ought to confuse, not confirm, her. Each time she enters the classroom she must again try to recapture the vertigo and recover the instability — to distance herself from herself. She cannot learn, or learn well, if she conceives of that place and those hours as a sphere in which to calcify who she already is. Alienation is essential to study. The classroom is a community of the alienated. Genuine learning demands courage and adventure. The room must be a realm apart, a space with a strange energy and a different gravity — a foreign country, populated by real and imagined strangers. Discomfort is its air.

The comfort of one's own couch, then, is a bad place to set up school. And so the question is begged: Is remote learning possible? Is the setting of study a matter of indifference to the activity of study? The question was relevant before Covid19 bleakly introduced the age of Zoom. In the United States over the past fifteen years, enrollment in online courses has more than quadrupled. This trend, the success of which was meteoric, was a response to the equally monumental and endlessly mounting cost of college for the average student. In America, higher education now costs students thirteen times what it did forty years ago, and that price has swelled while state funding for public universities has decreased. As tuition has risen, returns on investment have dropped. The pioneers of MOOCs — "mass open online courses," for those born too late to remember the old country in which they required introduction — explained that this disconnection is due to the uselessness of traditional curricula for the contemporary

345

workforce and the "revolution in work." All this reading and writing, all this training in thought — all this humanistic exploration — seemed impractical, and practicality has increasingly become the standard of judgement. If not for a job, then for what? And so they developed cheaper, skills-based models. Those models are online, a "convenience" which proclaims that the classroom, like the libraries cluttering university campuses, is redundant, and even archaic.

For years now, Coursera has offered a fully online master's degree from the University of Pennsylvania in computer and information technology for one-third of the cost of the on-campus version. MIT boasts a supply chain management degree which begins with an online segment on edX (a global non-profit founded in 2012 by Harvard and MIT). Similarly, Arizona State University's Global Freshman Academy kicks off with a virtual first year. In both the Arizona State and MIT programs students complete the initial leg of their degree online and then are invited to apply for the on-campus portion at a fraction of its usual price. edX, like most similar platforms, considers education the process through which students are armed with tools to earn money. From its website: "[we are] transforming traditional education, removing the barriers of cost, location and access.... [our students are] learners at every state, whether entering the job market, changing fields, seeking a promotion or exploring new interests." It tells us "edX is where you go to learn." A professionalized application of the term, to be sure; but because of the overwhelming success and reach of these platforms, they have largely successfully redefined "learning" and "education."

Anant Agarwal, the founder of edX, called 2012 "the year of disruption" for higher education. Disruption indeed, and on what a scale! In its first year, edX had 370,000 students. Coursera, founded in January of 2012, reached over 1.7 million students within just a few months, and in the same stretch of time formed partnerships with thirty-three of the most elite institutions in higher education, including Princeton, Brown, Columbia, and Duke. Often when people talk about education now, they mean education as edX defines it. And when they talk about it in the years of the pandemic, they may be referring to the only pedagogical means possible. Imagine life in lockdown without the internet! And yet one must ask, in this field as in many other fields of contemporary life, at what price convenience?

~⁓⁓~

Of course, a certain kind of learning can be done online. Knowledge comes in many types and has many purposes and brings many satisfactions, and many people will find that better jobs and better lives will result from the acquisition of what can be obtained digitally. These are not trivial considerations. But the technological expansion of educational resources may also come with a significant cost. The critique of the digitalization of life is not Luddism. It is the only responsible way to reap the benefits of digitalization, and it is an intellectual duty now that there is no going back. It would be foolish not to utilize the new technological opportunities, except when we utilize them foolishly. So what, exactly, can a screen capture and transmit, and what can it not capture and transmit? If we are serious about the supreme value of education for the individual and society, we must not passively acquiesce in every online excitement and remain worshippers in the church of "disruption." It sounds almost silly to say, and yet many realms of contemporary life often ignore this truth: there are significant things that numbers cannot measure.

One way to evaluate the new technology is by the old purpose. If the new technology cannot serve the old purpose, and if we continue to believe in the old purpose, then the new technology must be judged by its limits. Learning has a long history, at all its levels. We know a lot about it. And by the standard of what we know about it, we have reason to ask whether digital learning is, strictly speaking, learning at all. Perhaps, owing to the constraints it imposes upon the student and the teacher, it is something else entirely: perhaps it is merely training, the communication of useful information, which may be structurally similar to learning, but which has the opposite mental and spiritual effect.

That there is a difference between learning and training, between meanings and skills, has been noticed before, in a variety of traditions and eras. Here is an ancient example. The distinction is alluded to in the opening chapter of *Pirkei Avot*, or *Ethics of the Fathers*, a tractate of the Jewish legal text known as the Mishna. This particular tractate has no laws; it is an anthology of rabbinical wisdoms. Here it is twice stated *"aseh lecha rav,"* or "make for yourself a teacher" — in the sixth article of the first chapter, "make for yourself a teacher, acquire for yourself a friend, and give every person the benefit of the doubt"; and again, ten articles later, "make for yourself a teacher, and avoid confusion, and do not become accustomed to estimating tithes." That the imperative appears twice indicates — I am reasoning here in the old Talmudic way — that each instance must refer to a different type of authority.

In both cases the word *"rav"* is used. This is the traditional term for the figure to whom one turns for legal rulings, and also for the teacher with whom one studies. The same person can serve both functions and traverse the distance between the two roles. Less arcanely, think of a professor who offers expert insight to a journalist before meeting with a student about her doctoral thesis: she could have been discussing the same subject in both places, but her tonal shift, and the change in the scholarly level of her intervention, would be considerable. In both roles she wields authority, but while speaking to the journalist her authority is meant to be the final word, whereas with her student it ought to stimulate curiosity and conversation.

The *rav* who is discussed in the latter dictum has the sort · of authority that obliterates doubt. This figure gives rulings, and dispositive answers to practical questions, and the listener take note and acts accordingly. The students of this *rav* are not provoked, they are steadied. They have heard the stabilizing certainties of an expert — no thought is required of them, just trust and a willingness to follow instructions. This authority is different in kind from the first sort of *rav*, the one mentioned just before the "friend" and just after an article that treats of relations between wives and husbands. Extrapolating from this sequence — husband-wife; student-teacher; friend-friend — the rabbis establish that, after family, this sort of teacher-student relationship is the most intimate form of companionship, more intimate even than friendship.

In both these articles the same unexpected verb is used: one must *make* a teacher. There are, predictably, centuries of argument in the Jewish tradition over exactly what this making means. Teachers are not found, they are made; and not only are they made, but they are made together with people other than themselves — by their students. Note that "make" is immediately distinguished from "acquire" ("make for yourself a teacher, acquire for yourself a friend"). "Acquire" intimates

349

that a friend comes readymade, as it were — prepared for friendship. Both partners decide independently to commence the friendship. But a teacher cannot be a teacher unless he (the *Mishna* assumed that all students and teachers were male) is made into one by a student. This is a more radical and obscure observation than that one becomes a teacher only through teaching, by means of practice. It is well known that no textbook or· graduate study can inculcate the peculiar sensitivities that a teacher must develop: that only the work of teaching does that. But the Mishna makes a stranger and more stringent demand upon the teacher: he owes his status to a collaboration. His pedagogical certification derives from a personal relationship with the individual who comes to him for knowledge. Closeness and trust, intimacy and vulnerability: these are the terms of teacher-making.

These conditions are not optional but obligatory, as it is also established from the article that it is a duty that the student make a teacher. One must not simply wait for a teacher to turn up, and one must not try to learn alone. Maimonides, whose reading of the ancient injunction is echoed by subsequent commentators, strikingly declared that the student must secure a teacher even if the teacher is not intellectually superior to the student. Not your equal or your better; just your interlocutor. This is an extraordinary refutation of our commonplace assumptions about pedagogical qualifications. This ideal of study is not hierarchical, it is dialogical. (The Jewish tradition has plenty of hierarchical reverence for teachers in other places.) Dialogical study is always superior to solitary study. In a significant sense, solitary study is oxymoronic.

If a teacher does not have to be smarter than his student, then cleverness and even erudition are not the most important quality in the setting of study, or in the classroom.

What matters most, it seems, is that it be a human encounter, an exchange of intellectual electricity. Maimonides' notion has humbling implications for both teachers and students. Clearly, it humanizes the teacher, whom we may otherwise be tempted to cast as an infallible sage. In this scenario of study, the teacher, too, is vulnerable. And it also reminds the young and the bright that precocity is beside the point: in the classroom, obtaining knowledge and understanding not yet acquired is the overriding objective. One must not come to class eager to glitter. A student who is mesmerized by her own rhythms and insights will not grasp the subject and enter its new world, which is what study is. Better to be empty and attentive than clever and ahead. Learning is travel. "When you travel," Elizabeth Hardwick observed, "your first discovery is that you do not exist."

All of which is to say that education, I mean of the deepest questions and themes, is first and foremost an *experience*.

~⬱⬱

The difference between the first *aseh lecha rav* and the second is the difference between training, which transmits a practical skill, and learning. Skills make one useful; they provide the security of a straightforward purpose. The goal of training is problem-solving; and since life is full of solvable problems, two cheers for training. But not all of our problems are of the solvable, or easily solvable, or obviously and familiarly solvable, kind. Problems of meaning do not have technical or replicable solutions. Learning, therefore, is the opposite of training. It is a different sort of preparation for a different sort of difficulty. Learning acclimates students to the looming awareness that life is not governed by simple laws clearly stated. It is messy,

351

murky, essentially contested, often mysterious. In the realm of meaning, neatness is not natural. (Though there have been philosophers who have thought otherwise.)

It is certainly possible for trainees to train in the spirit of study — for example, through the rigors and drudgeries of a legal education a law student can be stimulated by the philosophical implications of her casebooks. It is also possible for disciples to study in the spirit of a trainee: to master the weeds and memorize the footnotes. This is Casaubonism, or humanism degraded, robbed of its soul — in sum, humanism minus doubt. True study does not obliterate doubt. The longer one spends inside a new world, the more acutely one recognizes that there are facets of it that can never be wholly penetrated. And the deeper into the world one goes, the more exasperating and incontrovertible that truth becomes. Moreover, the eventual comparison of another world with our own is itself one of the classical sources of doubt. Authority in a field does not confer certainty, as the greatest scholars know.

It is impossible to become comfortable in an alien world without a guide — it is impossible to learn without a teacher. Even Emerson, the learner par excellence, whose enchanted mind thrived in unbalanced confusion and ecstatic chaos, had teachers whom he imitated, revered, differed with, and finally abandoned — but only after having been transformed. Emerson, to be sure, was a genius — but again, a teacher does not have to be smarter than her students. She simply has to have knowledge that they do not have, and a willingness to deliberate together. The distance between what a teacher knows and what a student knows will always be considerably smaller than the distance between what a teacher knows and what it is possible to know. No matter how many books and manuscripts and archives a scholar discovers and masters, there will always be secrets unknown, always someone who knows something the expert does not (even if this other person knows less than she does). And so the amount of information she has mastered will never be as essential to a learner as the attitude she has towards what is strange. It is the development of this attitude, an acquired openness, that all learners have in common.

The objective of study is not self-expression. A genuine student must quiet her own rhythm in order to focus intensely on the rhythms of an alien system — another person, another religion, another civilization — they all have their own rhythm. Still, quieting one's own is not the same as forgetting it. A student is not a blank slate, she brings her experiences with her to the classroom; it is after all her own mind, her own self, that she is cultivating by means of study. But she does not hold them at the forefront of her mind while she works. She must never find herself more interesting than what she studies. If she captivates herself, she is captive to herself. She is self-shackled. Instead she must strain to allow her subject to set the pace of study. If she is to understand thoughts that are not her own and lives that are not her own, the question that she must ask is how they are different from her, not how they are the same.

The exploration of what is alien is not always exciting. In some stages of study it will almost certainly be tedious. Everything worth understanding demands discipline. There will be drills: *amo, amas, amat, amamus, amatis, amant*, flashcards, charts, red pens. These drills are not stimulating, but serious intellectual stimulation is impossible without them. They are the humanist's training — training-for-learning, training that is only preparatory, that makes the student fit for the transit to a different and non-utilitarian plane. Drills are not learning,

353

the way stretching is not running, but try running without stretching.

The result of this training for learning is a ready mind, a mind primed for and open to the unfamiliar and the alien. These monotonous exercises are the scaffolding that will hold and support the new universe into which the student ventures. Openness is finally the greatest quality of the learner. A student who is constantly comparing an alien grammar to the grammar to which she is accustomed will never experience the tingly mental reorganization particular to thinking in and about a new vocabulary. This openness is a peculiar kind of emptiness: it is rigorous emptiness, well-equipped and well-appointed, a tensed readiness to be filled in. It withholds judgment only so as to judge more correctly later, which is especially necessary when studying ideas or figures for which the student lacks natural sympathy. After all, the only negative evaluation that has intellectual integrity is an evaluation made after an intimate understanding has been developed — in the way, for example, that Isaiah Berlin for decades dedicated himself to the study of his intellectual opposites.

Why is this capacity useful? The question is often asked. It is a reasonable question, insofar as people deserve to be given reasons for humanistic exertions, but it is also a crass question, because it makes utility paramount. Answers have been given to the question on its own grounds: that the study of art, history, and philosophy can make the difference between brilliant lawyers, politicians, and doctors and ordinary ones, because the more professionals know about human existence, the wiser they will be when their professional activities may require a gloss of wisdom. All this is true and familiar: these are the apologias that adorn the welcome catalogs of liberal arts departments. These practical rationales for humanistic study are further proof of the infiltration and triumph of edX's flattened "education." The defense of learning in the terms of training, the justification of the humanities in economic and vocational terms: this is the hemlock that the humanities (and the arts more generally, starved for funds) now serve and swallow. Recall the English majors now flourishing at McKinsey. No, learning for its own sake is the only justification that treats the subject on its own terms — and so learning for its own sake is the only sake there is. In that spirit we may gladly acknowledge the social and personal "utility" of humanistic pursuits, as it is presented by writers and historians and philosophers, since it will inevitably inform and enrich the lives of students and teachers. Anyway, spiritually speaking, the enrichment of human life *is* useful.

The obsession with outcomes is hard to resist in an outcomes-based culture. It may penetrate the most impractical of pursuits. In her admirable book *Lost in Thought*, Zena Hitz, a tutor at St. John's College, bears witness to one iteration of this phenomenon: "[as a professor] my focus shifted — without my noticing — to the outcomes of my work rather than the work itself. I had lost much of the ability to think freely and openly on a topic, concerned lest I lose my hard-won position in the academic social hierarchy." Her lament brings to mind Nietzsche's strictures about the professionalization of philosophy. "It is probable," he wrote in 1874 in *On the Use and Abuse of History for Life* "that [a professionalized philosopher] will attain cleverness, but he will never attain wisdom. He compromises, calculates, and accommodates himself to the facts." He conducts research in order to publish, which he does in order to maintain a reputation for publishing, which he does in order to keep his job. The wonder and the vertigo disappear from his work.

Pardon the unreconstructed idealism, but there are higher reasons.

"What do you think about translation?"

She asked me that question a few months after we met. In that time I had developed a familiarity with the cadence of her thoughts, so different from mine, gentle and complicated, and always swaying, studying, interpreting. This ruminative cadence was the first thing I noticed about her. I knew she would introduce me to a new rhythm, a different pace of thought. My pace unnerved her: it was too fast and forward, she got spooked. *Slow down, slow down.* It was difficult for me to slow down. I wanted to learn it from her. Too early, and incessantly, I would ask her the questions that occupied me because I wanted to hear them played back at her tempo. It would transform them, make them strange, open them up. Even the words we both use we do not use in the same way. She has cultivated her own relationships with language.

"What do you mean?"

(It was an act of generosity that she answered me instead of concluding that I wouldn't be able to understand her, and then withdrawing from me. That is a particularly bitter kind of rejection. Once, years ago, a man pulled back from me and muttered, "No, no, I shouldn't have tried to tell you." I remember where I was standing when he said that.)

"I mean — well, if you're in love with someone and he's asked you to explain a thought that you've had, or a fear or anxiety or any example of the many sorts of things that are specific to you, but you know he can't understand it because it's the kind of thought he wouldn't have or even have imagined was possible (not because he's stupid or self-centered, but because it just isn't within his framework) you have to translate it for him. Is that bad? If he can't understand it, does that mean he can't understand *me*? That he can't really love me if translation is necessary? ..... I suppose it's all a question of degree." (It was so characteristic that she added that last thought, a signature suffix.)

Her trust reminds me of an exchange I had with a writer who asked me whether her use of esoteric language, of arcane foreign words, in an essay that she had written made it incomprehensible to uninitiated readers. I reread it and responded: Many of the terms you used felt foreign, like the language of an alien tradition or an exotic religion. *I like that feeling.* For the duration of your essay I could develop an acquaintance with the rhythms of the tradition of which you are an emissary. It is the rhythm that would have been lost in translation. You were right to be uncompromising about a taste of the original. Since you didn't define those words, which would have ruptured or mangled their melody, their verbal music remained intact, even if I couldn't explain in my own language exactly what you were saying. If someone who has never danced asks you what the sensation of dancing is like, the best you can do is show them. I trusted that you would compose your essay in such a way that it would eventually allow me to understand your meaning, and I was grateful that you trusted me to savor what I did not yet understand. You worry about uninitiated readers, but your essay is their initiation, and initiation is education.

But books are not people. Isn't reading a form of remote learning, too? Isn't a page somewhat like a screen — a blank surface for language to occupy?

Emerson was a radical reader. Ravenously he sucked the souls of writers out of their books. His great biographer Robert Richardson marveled that "it sometimes seems as though no book published from 1820 until his death evaded his attention completely." On its face, Emerson's bookishness is odd given that he worshiped activity and had contempt for "meek young men grow[ing] up in libraries." But Emerson's reading was charged, active. It offered entry to a symposium out of time. Reading works of genius, he wrote, one "converses with truths that have always been spoken in the world and becomes conscious of a closer sympathy with Zeno and Arrian, than with persons in the house." A relentless thirst for the nectar of intellectual companionship informs Emerson's writing. This is what permitted him to read the way he read. He was able to coax what he sought from the pages of a book because of the enthusiasm (his holy word) that charged his entire approach to living. Wrestling with intellectual and spiritual possibilities in conversation with others was a familiar exercise for Emerson. He took this method, this experience, this dialogical energy, to his books, which he believed were as sure a portal as a classroom.

Yet he never mistook a book for a person, or recommended reading as an adequate substitute for teaching, lecturing, conversing — for the experiential dimension of study. ("Books are for the scholar's idle times. When he can read God directly, the hour is too precious to be wasted in other men's transcripts of their readings.") But if a book is an example of remote humanistic study, what are we to say of digital remoteness? The text or the image is there on the screen, and so is the tiny apparition of the talking teacher, hovering above it. Ideas in some form may certainly be imparted. But is this the full transit to another world that constitutes the fulfillment of humanistic education? Isn't it rather the case that the screen leaves one where one began? That it is a buffer, a fancy buffer between the student and the world?

A screen is too familiar to propel a student from her deepest grooves, particularly for a student who has never left her couch. On a screen everything, no matter how vividly presented, is flattened and made less real, and all the realms are compressed and equalized into a comfortable, closable haze. Most importantly, all the Zooming in the world has not established the screen as anything but a simulacrum of human interaction, a dim facsimile of pedagogical experience. One is no more than a partial student when one has no more than a partial teacher, or no teacher at all. Zooming is a stopgap measure that leaves one longing for actual presence, which is the condition of actual learning. It is a lot better than nothing, but nothing must never be the standard.

LEON WIESELTIER

Some Possible Grounds for Hope

I don't see how we get out of this. There is nothing truer that can be said of this time. It is a perverse measure of its truth that we have been inundated with books and bromides that purport to show the opposite, that have hit upon the way out, the solutions, or better, the solution, the formulas for the miracle, all the how's and all the why's. How can so many people understand so much and so immediately, when so many of our torments are so unfamiliar? Isn't anybody stunned into silence anymore?

So many words, so many numbers, so many "frames." They are fortifying, I guess, and we certainly need strength. Let everyone come forward in the dark with their light. But I don't see how we get out of this, not yet.

The empty streets of the covid nights are so candid in their desolation. They are thronged with the people who are not there. They provide a peculiar serenity, in which one can be alone with one's fear, and take it for a walk.

Philosophers since Seneca have known that fear and hope are twins. They are alternative ways of interpreting the opacity of the future.

If hope were rational, it would be redundant. Hope picks up where reason leaves off, like changing guides at the frontier. Hope is the best we can do with uncertainty. It is an image of happiness that cannot quite be dismissed as an illusion. If it cannot be proven, neither can it be disproven. Its enchantment lies in its cognitive limitation. It comes to an end with knowledge.

One of the characteristic errors of the American debate is to mistake the homiletical for the analytical — preaching for teaching. The objective of moral and social thought is not uplift. And as every religious person knows, castigation, too, can be experienced as uplift. It warms the heart to be told that we are all sinners, doesn't it? Drop a coin in the charity box on the way out, you miserable excuse for finitude, and recover your contentment. It was never really damaged anyway. Of course this high-level complacency is abundantly found among the secular as well. They, too, like a warm sensation of their

Some Possible Grounds for Hope

own shortcomings, as long as you do not overdo it. They, too, are lifted up by the sound of sermons, as in the editorial "must": "We must restore trust." Yes, we must!

For many years I travelled around the country, like an itinerant preacher, chastising American Jews for their ignorance of Hebrew, which is their language even if they cannot speak it. I was received cordially almost everywhere I went. But I became suspicious of this cordiality: after all, I had come to discomfit them. And on the occasions when I did discomfit them — as when, after one of those lectures, a woman came up to me and testily said, "Sir, that was a wonderful presentation, but I did not feel affirmed!" — I smiled politely and triumphantly. (Actually, what I said to the woman was this: "Madam, I did not come all this way to affirm you.") But those occasions were rare. The futility of my efforts was owed to the tragi-comic fact that feeling bad makes some people feel good. Criticism assures them of their meaningfulness, which is really all they seek.

"I don't see how we get out of this." Thank you for your honesty. It is not nearly as disagreeable as our circumstances.

If hope and history ever rhyme, in accordance with the poet's wishes, it will be a soft rhyme, a weak rhyme, a half-rhyme.

I don't see how we get out of this. The country is poisoned. There is contempt everywhere; contempt and certainty. There are also wonderful people doing wonderful things for the weak and the needy and the scorned — a national plenitude of local kindnesses; but all these practices of solidarity have not yet altered the character of our politics and our culture, or banished our furies. Not just yet. The rampaging passions — otherwise known as populism — have not yet exhausted themselves. Perhaps it is just a matter of patience, except that patience is in ideological disrepute and was long ago retired by our technology.

The greater the suffering, the greater the dream of redemption. An apocalyptic is a man in extreme pain. He can imagine only an extreme cure. He is not concerned that he may cause pain to end pain. He hurts *that* much. But must the magnitude of the cure always be commensurate with the magnitude of the pain? What if there are cases in which the only genuine relief is gradual relief? This is insulting to the sufferer, who expects that his view of his suffering to be definitive. Yet our compassion, our love, does not require that we agree with him. A person in pain knows only one thing, but he will be saved with the help of people who know more things. For example: a person in pain hates time, which is abolished by the immediacy of his torments. He lives (to borrow Robert Lowell's piercing word) momently. A person in pain experiences time as an eternity. (In this way he resembles a person in ecstasy.) But time may be his ally, insofar as it is the only condition of his healing. Recovering from pain is a way of returning from eternity to time. Or, more practically, of taking concrete and steady and reasoned steps.

Of course there are sufferers who do not have time on their side. When we discover this about physical ills, we call it tragedy. But we have no right to invoke tragedy about social ills. The tragic sense connotes a certain helplessness about circumstances, or more precisely, about other people's circumstances. It promotes resignation. But whereas it may be legitimate for me to resign myself to my troubles, it is not legitimate for me to resign myself to your troubles. I can surrender myself, but I cannot surrender you.

To approach injustice from the standpoint of tragedy has the effect of relaxing the will and shrinking the sense of agency, and even of usurping ethics with aesthetics. How do you fight tragedy?

Was slavery tragic? In retrospect, yes. But in its time, no. In its time it was odious and disgusting and abominable. In its time it demanded resistance and abolition. Only evils of the past are tragic. The evils amid which we live are challenges -- occasions of responsibility. Tragedy is precisely what we are charged to preempt.

Was the catastrophe in Syria tragic? Only because nobody stopped it.

"Interventionism" is now a dirty word. But it signifies more than a controversy — well, I wish it were still a controversy — about foreign affairs. Who ever did the right thing without intervening? Ethical action is always an intrusion, a refusal to leave a situation as one found it. Morality is a theory of meddling. What is intervention if not the Biblical injunction not to stand idly before the spilled blood of another? I do not recall any mention of costs and benefits in the verse. A government, of course, needs more than the Bible, more than high principle, to guide its actions. But does power exist only for the perpetration of evil? What about the costs and benefits of doing nothing? Or shall we acquiesce in the deformities of the world, except when there is money to be made?

"But it's complicated": the streets of the capital, the corridors of power that masquerade as the corridors of powerlessness when it suits them, echo with those allegedly extenuating words. It is always smart to say that a problem is complicated. As if it is the duty of government to pursue justice only when it is not complicated.

Tragedy, remember, is designed, in its most influential definition, to excite "pity and fear" so as to bring about "the proper purgation" of those emotions. It is a performance that exercises certain feelings so as to annul them. Never mind that those feelings may be put to good use outside the theater. Tragedy is an entertainment.

Catharsis is the enemy of action. It leaves one spent and sated. It is the orgasm of conscience. I wondered about the relation of catharsis to politics as I joined the protests at Black Lives Matter Plaza. I was not worried about "performativity," since the public expression of opposition is an essential element of opposition. I was worried about the problem of spiritual stamina, about the durability of the energy in the streets, about the overestimation of excitement, about the preference for the adventure of protest over its pedantic translation into policy. The politics of the streets can make do with catharsis. We will see.

Concrete and steady and reasoned steps taken patiently and resolutely over time for the purpose of mitigating and eliminating the sufferings of others: in a word, liberalism.

The most widespread cliché of our time is "polarization." Everyone laments it, and many scholars and commentators regard it as the most dire of our ills. It has provided work for a generation of social scientists. That we are living in an age of spectacular social division is undeniable, and the excesses of this discord are sometimes lunatic and criminal. But a little intellectual pressure needs to be put on this obsession with our lack of harmony. Is it worse than covid, or discrimination, or poverty? Of course not. There are those who argue that it will be impossible to address those monumental wounds in our society unless we overcome polarization. Barack Obama squandered the first two years of his presidency, when he had a majority in both houses of Congress, on lyrical exhortations to bipartisanship. But there is nothing freakish, or surprising, or unAmerican, about partisanship, even extreme partisanship. It is the stuff of which politics is made. But then one must take politics seriously — more, one must think highly of politics, and even revere it, and recognize that its ruthlessness is not inconsistent with its nobility; which is to say, one must come to value power.

The words "value" and "power" look strange together, don't they? The juxtaposition certainly makes many liberals uncomfortable. They have been mildly embarrassed about power for many decades, probably since Vietnam. But if you are not serious about power you are not serious about change.

If despair is born of powerlessness, then power is a reason for hope. It sounds harsh and unlovely, but there is no other way to protect human dignity and its political home, which is democracy.

Political ideas are not poems. They do not exist to deepen our grasp of reality. Their objective is to modify reality. For this reason, political thinkers may be held accountable for the consequences of their thoughts. Anyone who lacks the stomach for consequences should stick with poetry. (For the purpose of a rich life, however, it beats politics.)

When the mad and beautiful Phil Ochs was asked for his verdict on the 1960s, he replied: "They won the war, but we had the best songs."

Polarization is one of the effects of partisanship and partisanship is one of the effects of human association.

To acknowledge reality without becoming complicit in it. To correct the world without destroying it. Those were the accomplishments of James Madison. His genius, and it was nothing less, was for being an optimist and a pessimist, an idealist and a realist, at the same time. He got the balance right, while the globe is littered with the ruins of political experiments that got it wrong. The equilibrium was revolutionary, especially on the question of the place of conflict in human affairs.

A revolution of equilibrium: the American innovation.

A reading from *The Federalist Papers*, 10. Please rise.
> The latent causes of faction are thus sown in the nature of man; and we see them everywhere brought into different degrees of activity, according to the different circumstances of civil society. A zeal for different opinions concerning religion, concerning government, and many other points, as well of speculation as of practice; an attachment to different leaders ambitiously contending for pre-eminence and power; or to persons of other descriptions whose fortunes have been inter-

Some Possible Grounds for Hope

esting to the human passions, have, in turn, divided mankind into parties, inflamed them with mutual animosity, and rendered them much more disposed to vex and oppress each other than to co-operate for their common good. So strong is this propensity of mankind to fall into mutual animosities, that where no substantial occasion presents itself, the most frivolous and fanciful distinctions have been sufficient to kindle their unfriendly passions and excite their most violent conflicts. But the most common and durable source of factions has been the various and unequal distribution of property. Those who hold and those who are without property have ever formed distinct interests in society. The regulation of these various and interfering interests forms the principal task of modern legislation, and involves the spirit of party and faction in the necessary and ordinary operations of the government.
Here endeth the reading.

So be of good cheer: it was always nasty. To borrow the famous phrase of Madison's successor in the formulation of the American philosophy, the better angels of our nature are not the only angels of our nature. The American system was constructed on the assumption that conflict is ineradicable. The foretold conflicts concern both principles and interests, and the expectation is that they will be brutal. "The causes of faction cannot be removed," is Madison's conclusion. Out of this dourness he designed a democracy.

It should be added that the conflicts that constitute a permanent feature of society are not — as we, in our psychologizing habits, often prefer to think of them — misunderstandings.

Liberties

There is no clarification, no revision of language, that will make them vanish. A misunderstanding is an apparent conflict, a temporary conflict. It can be resolved with some exploration and some patience, and an apology. But a contradiction between worldviews cannot be resolved; it can only be respected, and then managed. And if the opinions are sincerely and thoughtfully held, neither side has anything to apologize for.

Error is a form of innocence. There are many worse things in life than being wrong. (This is the courtesy that Americans seem no longer able to extend to each other.)

Respect is more valuable, and more arduous, than reconciliation.

The alternative to "polarization" is not consensus. *There will be no consensus.* Madison already warned against "giving to every citizen the same opinions, the same passions, and the same interests." In the American tradition there is no fantasy of unanimity. Social agreement is not our eschaton. The American hypothesis is that consensus is not necessary for cooperation, that social agreement is not necessary for social peace.

369

The horror of uniformity is the democratic idea itself.

In his painstaking attempt to describe an "overlapping consensus" for a democratic system that must accept "the fact of pluralism," John Rawls admitted that "we do not, of course assume that an overlapping consensus is always possible, given the doctrines currently existing in any democratic society." It is a bleak moment in his heroically optimistic enterprise. I think it passes too swiftly. He was a philosopher and he insisted upon a philosophical conception of justice, and for this reason he dismissed what he called a "mere *modus vivendi*." He accused Madison (and Hobbes and Locke and Hume and Kant) of philosophical failure by contenting himself with the ideal of compromise between interests. Rawls thought that such a purely improvisational system is too fragile. Indeed it is; but it may be the finest we can do — one fragile compromise after another fragile compromise until the end of time. The problem is not only that we are not a nation of philosophers; it is also that in a pluralist society there is nothing "mere" about a *modus vivendi*. Madison should not be treated as the first transaction-alist. It is dangerous to delegitimate compromise philosophically. Indeed, many unphilosophical activities hide philosophical principles and teach philosophical lessons. There are worse failures than theorylessness.

I am always a little shocked, and pleasantly so, by the Founders' ease about interests. They were unembarrassed by human partiality. And from the grubby they rose to the sublime.

The United States Constitution is the greatest tribute to, and the greatest rebuke of, Hobbes.

A philosophy and a system of government that proposes to accept the collisions of society and leave the cacophony alone is a prescription for tough-mindedness. Or more accurately, tough-mindedness in the cause of the tender mercies. We are called upon to be not only sensitive but also effective.

Too many worriers about "polarization" are so sentimental, so nostalgic, so exquisite in their sensitivity to the injuries of democratic combat, so anxious that taking a side might be a human failure. Yet an open society is a rough society. Polemic is one of the central methods of persuasion. "Deliberative democracy" is not the work of professors, even if it is the invention of professors.

We are a society that makes a cult out of honesty and then wants to be protected from it.

In an open society, inoffensiveness may be a delinquency of citizenship.

Democracy is wasted on the timorous. The emboldening of ordinary men and women is its very purpose.

A reading from *The Social Contract,* Book I. Please remain seated. Properly understood, all of these clauses [of the social contract] come down to a single one, namely, the total alienation of each associate, with all his rights, to the whole community...Instantly, in place of the private person of each contracting party, this act of association produces a moral and collective body, composed of as many members as there are voices in the assembly, which receives from this same act its unity, its common *self*, its life, and its will...For if the opposition of private interests made the establishment of societies necessary, it is the agreement of these same interests that made it possible....Either the will is general or it is not, It is the will of the people as a body, or of only a part...There is often a great difference between the will of all and the general will. The latter considers only the common interest; the former considers private interest, and is only a sum of private wills...In order for the general will to be

371

well expressed, it is therefore important that there be no partial society in the State.....

Rousseau adds a footnote: "In order for a will to be general, it is not always necessary for it to be unanimous, but it is necessary that all votes be counted." Not always! There is here a dream of social and political seamlessness, which is achieved by the dissolution of the individual in the community, the collectivity, the state. It was appropriate that the animadversion about unanimity, the mild concession to the stubbornness of difference, be a footnote, because in the holistic ethos of Rousseau's state it really is just a footnote. These passages, and the notorious remark, also in Book I, that "whoever refuses to obey the general will shall be constrained to do so by the entire body, which means only that he will be forced to be free," provoked a renowned historian to describe Rousseau's ideal as "totalitarian democracy."

He aspires to a perfect union, but we aspire to a "more perfect union." The difference between democracy and totalitarianism is the difference between the belief in perfectibility and the belief in perfection. (I do not concur that Rousseau was a totalitarian, exactly; but his democracy repels me. I am an American.) He holds that the individual must "alienate" his rights, but we hold that the individual's rights are "inalienable." If you wish to understand the philosophical and political excruciations that France has endured in the wake of the murder of Samuel Paty, may his memory be a blessing, you could do worse than begin with the distinction between these notions of alienation and alienability.

There they do not wish to recognize difference. Here we wish to recognize nothing else. Or so it sometimes seems.

Is a nation a community? The communitarians among us would like to think so. It is certainly the case that a sub-national idea of community would leave us a state of states, a community of communities, a bubble of bubbles, a collection of monocultures paradoxically justified by multiculturalism. This would amount to a degradation of the pluralist promise, according to which we can live together *and* apart. In order to cohere as a nation, we must extend ourselves beyond our particularities, beyond our cloisterings. A homogeneous nation has no need of universalism, but a heterogeneous nation is proof of its beauty.

Of course there is no such thing as a homogeneous nation. It was one of the necessary fictions of nationalism, and minorities have been paying dearly for it ever since. There is always someone unlike ourselves within our borders, and even if there were only one such person, he or she would still be the test of our decency. (And he or she may think it is me.)

Perhaps a nation should not be a community. Perhaps it is enough that it is a nation.

In 1813, in a case in New York called *People v. Philips*, which considered the question of whether a Catholic priest could be forced to provide information that was obtained in the confessional, a lawyer named William Sampson told this to the court: "Every citizen here is in his own country. To the protestant it is a protestant country; to the catholic, a catholic country; and the jew, if he pleases, may establish in it his New Jerusalem." An epochal declaration, a genuine liberation from the Old World. But what he described is both a blessing and a curse. It is pluralism carried to the limits of psychosis For even if we are all of those countries, we are not any of those countries. We are a whole that does not devour its parts, but we are still a whole.

Who in his right mind would wish to live only among his own? Give me goyim, please! Traditions wither in isolation. Only the infirm of identity seek more of themselves.

It is the stupendous irony of a multiethnic society that it exposes the limitations of particularism.

In 1966, the brilliant Jewish historian Gerson D. Cohen gave a commencement address at the Hebrew Teachers College in Boston that he called, with a hint of wickedness, "The Blessing of Assimilation in Jewish History." Reading it now, when a soft kind of separatism is enjoying a new prestige, is exhilarating. "A frank appraisal of the periods in which Judaism flourished will indicate that not only did a certain amount of assimilation and acculturation not impede Jewish continuity and creativity, but that in a profound sense, this assimilation and acculturation was a stimulus to original thinking and expression, a source of renewed vitality." Our borders give us our shape, but their porousness contributes to our substance. A border is not a wall, it is the opposite of a wall, and the confusion of a border with a wall is a prescription for social and cultural disaster.

In the name of authenticity, people imprison themselves. And when they do so, these loyal sons and daughters, they usually insult their ancestors, who were less afraid of influences.

The recent history of American society can be told as a story about the vicissitudes of the idea of integration.

Differences are not discrepancies, except from the haughty standpoint of somebody else's norm. They do not have to be brought into line. But we are not wanting in arguments for difference. Everybody screams their difference, which makes them all so tediously alike.

Permeability ought to be a source of pride in mature individuals and mature societies.

A possible ground for hope: the individual. In a country in which people are masterfully manipulated by disinformation and demagoguery, in an electorate that increasingly consists of mobs and herds and gangs, in a society in which citizens are encouraged to seek intellectual strength in numbers, it is past time to remind ourselves of the dignities and the powers of the ordinary man and woman, of the autonomy of adults, of the ability of individuals to think for themselves and rise above the pernicious nonsense that their individuation is what ails them.

The religious extol the uniqueness of souls, the secular extol the uniqueness of selves. In this way they issue the elevating challenge that their integralist currents, religious and secular, retract.

You cannot take your country back until you take your mind back.

I used to like bowling alone. Not always, but sometimes. Anyway, there is nothing like company to make you feel lonely. Loneliness is a social emotion.

Individualism is a far larger dispensation than egotism, which is not to be confused with it. Egotism is a debasement of individualism, in the way that selfishness is a debasement of selfhood. The problem of individual self-love is as nothing compared to the problem of collective self-love.

The moral superiority of the community to the individual seems dubious to me. Belonging does not insulate anybody from transgression. Worse, there are depredations that we commit together than we would not commit alone. The haters among us, the killers among us, they may be members and they may be loners. They may speak for themselves and they may speak for their group. And communities may be kind or cruel. It's a wash. The human heart is busy everywhere.

In Hebrew, the root for "hope" is the same root for "gather together," as in "Let the waters under the heaven be gathered together to one place." As the authoritative concordance notes, *sperare* and *congregatio*. I have often pondered this mysterious etymology. It suggests that hope is premised upon the end of a dispersal. But what has been dispersed that must be brought together — the community or the individual? If it is the former, if united we stand and divided we fall, then hope is to be found in the reconstitution of community. If it is the latter, then the dispersed self is what bars the way to hope, and the reconstitution of the self will confer the sought-after encouragement. I am reminded of a work of clinical psychology that appeared in the 1960s called *The Psychology of Hope,* which concluded with a chapter on "the therapy of hope." In his account of what he calls "a therapeutic *tour de force*," the author describes a clinician who "explicitly and deliberately employed communication of his high expectations of patients as a therapeutic procedure."

The critics of individualism, the whole army of them, propound a doctrine of demoralization. They have no faith in the actual person, or worse, they detest her. This is uncharitable, and also inaccurate about human capabilities. Given the irreversible fact of individuation, it can be spiritually damaging.

There is another option: that divided we stand. Madison's motto!

The Covid-19 virus came along to illustrate what genuine isolation is. Monads in masks now yearn nostalgically for their allegedly atomized life before the pestilence. They miss all the communal meetings and social minglings that were said to have been lost. Except of course the political ones, which have all thrown epidemiological caution to the winds.

In a period of national emergency, and the Trump years were such a period, the ubiquity of politics, its penetration into the deepest recesses of life, its saturation of experience, is understandable. If you believe that your cause or your country is in peril, you will become a sentry and a soldier. There is integrity to such an intensity of commitment, though the question of whether your analysis is correct, whether reality warrants your panic and your politicization, is an important one. But liberals and conservatives both used to believe, as an axiom of both their worldviews, in the limits of politics, in fair weather or foul. Then foul weather arrived and their wisdom collapsed.

Instead of decrying "polarization" and dreaming of the disappearance of division, we might turn our attention to the overpoliticization of human existence in America. There is no longer any domain of life from which politics is barred. People who deplore the destruction of privacy by Silicon Valley acquiesce in the destruction of privacy by politics. Perhaps the one prepared them for the other, and softened them up for the tyranny of publicity and the public. People who engage in politics for the defense of dignity acquiesce in the destruction of dignity that attends the destruction of privacy.

The first casualty of our overpoliticization was our culture, just about all of it. Art is now politics by other means, full stop. What fools we are to rob ourselves of what we do not have enough of, and for the sake of what we have too much of.

"All art is political," says Lin-Manuel Miranda. Bullshit.

The most chilling instance of our overpoliticization, of course, is the ideological repudiation of science. When told by the government that their lives were in danger, millions of Americans said only, don't tread on me. There is no longer any Archimedean point outside these political self-definitions.

As for the progressive bedroom, and the infiltration of intimacy by political standards for sexual behavior: make love, not history.

What would a post-"polarized" America look like? I have a visionary inkling. It would consist of men and women who are not only who they vote for and not only who they agree with. They would hold political convictions and defend them, but they would be known also, and mainly, by other beliefs. They would accept the political dissonance but make themselves a little deaf to it, out of respect and for the sake of comity. They would have friends whose views they despise. They would not look forward to family gatherings as an occasion for gladiatorial combat about the issues of the day. They would give up their erotic relationship to anger, and to rectitude. They would renounce their appetites for last battles and last judgements. They would refuse to let even their own extremely correct views interfere with the fullness of living. They would march, and then they would come home. They would mobilize, and then repair to those realms in which mobilization is beside the point. They would not display their politics as proof of their goodness, because they would take note of the good people on the other side. (There are sides, of course, where no goodness can be found, but they are not many.) They would forgive.

Joy in the struggle for justice: outside the contested epiphanies of mysticism, is there a more astonishing spiritual accomplishment? It is joy in the face of misery, after all; joy amid injustice, but deployed against it. When I watch films of the civil rights movement of the 1960s, I am always dumbfounded by the joy, which somehow never got in the way of strategy. What powers of soul!

In ancient Greece there was a sect of philosophers known as the *Elpistikoi*: the Hope-ists, or in another translation, the Hopefulists. We know nothing about them. They are mentioned only once, in Plutarch, in a discussion about "whether the sea or the land affords better food." According to a certain Symmachus, "they believe that what is most essential to life is hoping, on the grounds that when hope is not present to make it pleasant, then life is unbearable." Or in another translation: "in the absence of hope and without its seasoning life is unendurable." Seasoning, indeed: Symmachus compares hope to salt. This is a utilitarian case for hope, which is undeniable, because in the absence of any verification we cling to hope entirely for its effects. But it is also more: for the hopefulist, life was not bearable or unbearable, but unbearable or pleasant. The hopefulist does not wish only to make it through the night. He wants a pleasant morning, too, and pleasant days.

Is hope a pleasure? I suppose it depends on what one fears. There may be terrors that hope cannot dispel. Or does hope rise to match them in scale? Hopelessness, in any event, appears when ignorance has passed. Ignorance is the soil of hope, which may be a chapter of its own in the legend about ignorance and bliss.

Not so, say the economists, whose subject is now the whole of life. Hope, they say, is an assessment of probabilities. But the more the probabilities are known, the less need there is for hope. If the probabilities could be entirely known, we would all be enlightened and hopeless. I am not sure I like the sound of that. But hope is not an assessment. It is a prayer — perhaps the only prayer that the godless, too, can pray.

380 Symmachus, lying in the Ionian sun, picking at salted delicacies, voluptuously hoping.

And back here, in the winter wastes, two possible grounds of hope: a new vaccine and a new president. We are not yet getting to the end.

381

CONTRIBUTORS

ANTHONY JULIUS is a lawyer in the United Kingdom, and the author, among other books, of *Transgressions: The Offences of Art.*

NICHOLAS LEMANN is a professor at Columbia University Graduate School of Journalism and the author of *Transaction Man: The Rise of the Deal and the Decline of the American Dream.*

ALFRED BRENDEL, the pianist, is the author most recently of *The Lady from Arezzo: My Musical Life and Other Matters.*

PAUL BERMAN is the author of *Power and the Idealists*, among other books.

JORIE GRAHAM's *Runaway*, her fifteenth volume of poetry, was published last fall.

FOUAD AJAMI, the author of many books about the Arab world, died in 2014. "The Story of Dalal" is taken from his unpublished memoir *When Magic Ends.*

JACK GOLDSMITH teaches law at Harvard University. His most recent book is *In Hoffa's Shadow: A Stepfather, a Disappearance in Detroit, and My Search for the Truth.*

EDWARD LUTTWAK has written many books on strategy, including *The Rise of China vs. The Logic of Strategy.*

ROBERTO CALASSO is the publisher of Adelphi Edizioni in Milan and the author most recently of *The Celestial Hunter*. This essay was translated by Richard Dixon.

ISHION HUTCHINSON's *House of Lords and Commons*, a volume of poems, was published in 2016. He teaches at Cornell University.

WALTER SCHEIDEL is professor of Classics and History at Stanford and the author of *The Great Leveler: Violence and the History of Inequality from the Stone Age to the Twenty-First Century*.

HELEN VENDLER is the author of *Our Secret Discipline: Yeats and Lyric Form* and *The Ocean, the Bird, and the Scholar: Essays on Poets and Poetry*.

ROBERT ALTER is professor of Hebrew and Comparative Literature at the University of California at Berkeley. His new book, *Nabokov and the Real World: Between Appreciation and Defense*, will appear this spring.

DARYL MICHAEL SCOTT is professor of History at Howard University.

ROSANNA WARREN is an American poet and the author most recently of *Max Jacob: A Life in Art and Letters*.

ALASTAIR MACAULAY is a critic and historian of the performing arts who was the chief dance critic of the *New York Times* and the chief theater critic of *The Financial Times*. Lincoln Kirstein's hand-written diaries, quoted in this essay, are kept in the New York Public Library for the Performing Arts and are cited here by permission of his literary executor, Nicholas Jenkins.

DAVID GREENBERG is a historian at Rutgers University. He is writing a biography of John Lewis.

CELESTE MARCUS is the managing editor of Liberties.

LEON WIESELTIER is the editor of Liberties.

383

Liberties — A Journal of Culture and Politics is available by annual subscription and by individual purchase from bookstores and online booksellers.

Annual subscriptions, which offer a discount from the individual cover price, can be ordered from libertiesjournal.com. Gift subscriptions are also available.

In addition to the regular subscription discount price, special discounts are available for: active military; faculty, students, and education administrators; government employees; and, those working in the not-for-profit sector at libertiesjournal.com.

Liberties — A Journal of Culture and Politics is distributed to booksellers in the United States by Publishers Group West; in Canada by Publishers Group Canada; and, internationally by Ingram Publisher Services International.

Liberties, a Journal of Culture and Politics, is published quarterly in Fall, Winter, Spring, and Summer by Liberties Journal Foundation.

ISBN 978-1-7357187-1-2
ISSN 2692-3904

384

Printed in Canada.

The insignia that appears throughout *Liberties* is derived from details in Botticelli's drawings for Dante's *Divine Comedy*, which were executed between 1480 and 1495.